Buddhist Law

Buddhist Law

I.N. Singh

PRASHANT PUBLISHING HOUSE
DELHI-110094

Published by :
Prashant Publishing House
C-34, 28 Foota Road, Gali-3,
West Karwal Nagar, Delhi-110094
Phone : 011-22963970, Mob. : 9810396373
e-mail.: prashantpublishinghouse@gmail.com

Buddhist Law
Reserved
First Published 2017

ISBN 978-93-80565-80-4

PRINTED IN INDIA
Published by Mr. R.K. Jha M/s Prashant Publishing House and Published at H.S. Offset House Press, Delhi.

Contents

Preface

Buddhism is a religion to about 300 million people around the world. The word comes from 'budhi', 'to awaken'. It has its origins about 2,500 years ago when Siddhartha Gotama, known as the Buddha, was himself awakened (enlightened) at the age of 35.

The first truth is that life is suffering i.e., life includes pain, getting old, disease, and ultimately death. We also endure psychological suffering like loneliness frustration, fear, embarrassment, disappointment and anger. This is an irrefutable fact that cannot be denied. It is realistic rather than pessimistic because pessimism is expecting things to be bad. Instead, Buddhism explains how suffering can be avoided and how we can be truly happy.

Karma is the law that every cause has an effect, i.e., our actions have results. This simple law explains a number of things: inequality in the world, why some are born handicapped and some gifted, why some live only a short life. Karma underlines the importance of all individuals being responsible for their past and present actions. How can we test the karmic effect of our actions? The answer is summed up by looking at (1) the intention behind the action, (2) effects of the action on oneself, and (3) the effects on others.

Karma is the law of moral causation. The theory of Karma is a fundamental doctrine in Buddhism. This belief was prevalent in India before the advent of the Buddha. Nevertheless, it was the Buddha who explained and formulated this doctrine in the complete form in which we have it today.

Buddhism teaches that wisdom should be developed with compassion. At one extreme, you could be a goodhearted fool and at the other extreme, you could attain knowledge without any emotion. Buddhism uses the middle path to develop both. The highest wisdom is seeing that in reality, all phenomena are incomplete, impermanent and do no constitute a fixed entity. True wisdom is not simply believing what we are told but instead experiencing and understanding truth and reality. Wisdom requires an open, objective, unbigoted mind. The Buddhist path requires courage, patience, flexibility and intelligence.

Nirvana is the "blowing out" of existence. It is an eternal state of being where karma and the life cycle stop.It is a place where desire and individual consciousness ends.Buddha described it as "a condition, where there is neither earth nor water, neither air nor light, neither limitless space, nor limitless time, neither any kind of being, neither ideation nor non-ideation, neither this world nor that world. There is neither arising nor passing-away, nor dying, neither caused nor effect, neither change nor standstill."

This book will be an essential resource for all students and teachers in Buddhist studies, law and religion, and comparative law.

—I.N. Singh

1

Ten Paramitas

The Ten Paramitas are the ten perfections of the heart to cultivate in one's practice of the Dhamma.

The Ten Perfections

1. Generosity (dana)
2. Moral conduct (sila)
3. Renunciation (nekkhamma)
4. Wisdom (paññâ)
5. Energy (viriya)
6. Patience (khanti)
7. Truthfulness (sacca)
8. Determination (adhitthana)
9. Loving-kindness (metta)
10. Equanimity (upekkha)

GENEROSITY

The Paramitas—*ultimately*—are actions which are free from the crimp of duality – actions which arise spontaneously from the non-dual state. They are the actions of the bodhisattva—*the awakened-mind warrior*—who has gone beyond the confines of referentiality, and who dwells within the meaning of *ocean* and its *ornamental waves*. In Tibetan the word which equates to 'bodhisattva' is 'changchub sempa' *(byang chub sems dPa)*. Changchub sempa has a specific meaning which differs from the Sanskrit word, which means 'one who has Bodhi' or 'one who has awakened-mind' or 'one who has the compassionate

Mind of enlightenment'. The Tibetan spelling should be 'byang chub sems pa' – but we find instead that it is 'byang chub sems dPa'. 'dPa' is a contraction of the word 'dPa bo' which means 'warrior' rather than 'pa' which means 'person'. Changchub sempa therefore means *awakened-mind warrior.*

The first of these examples of appropriate spontaneity is generosity *(jinpa – sByin pa – dana paramita).*

The awakened-mind warriors delight in unbounded wealth because their appreciation is unlimited. Appreciation generates generosity which knows no limits. It is unobstructed by the self-referencing territorialism which generates manipulative pusillanimity. Awakened-mind warriors need no territory. Their refuge is the security of insecurity. Their refuge is the territory of intrinsic space, which is self-validating without the requirement of reference points. Objects, circumstances, and people—as subjects of appreciation—are not required to be fixed or frozen by awakened-mind warriors. Objects, circumstances, and people are not employed for self-validation – and are therefore free to move. It is their natural reflex to move in the direction where they facilitate the greatest pleasure and satisfaction.

The Vajrayana view of wealth is grounded in the understanding that one owns everything that enters one's sense fields. We own whatever we appreciate, to the extent that we appreciate it and for the duration that we appreciate it. We do not require personal ownership in order to own. Our ownership does not restrict the ownership of others, because our ownership is simply that of appreciative faculties.

This non-possessive, non-controlling absence of tenure is called 'vajra greed' or 'non-dual greed' – greed on behalf of others. Greed on behalf of all beings is both the maximum possible avarice, and the ultimate expansion of generosity.

Vajra greed is non-dual acquisitiveness – everything goes where it needs to go, with respect to where and by whom it will be most appreciated.

If my interest is in appreciation, then if *you* want something more than *me*—in terms of your capacity to appreciate it—then that is where it should naturally go. To focus on someone else's greater appreciation is a far more profound experience of avarice for me than if I sought sole possession. Generosity—in this view—is that sense of connection, the sense of energy in relation to other people and their infinitely varied circumstances.

For those practitioners who have *capacity*, generosity is the non-referential acknowledgement of a superior position – a self-existent position of profound responsibility.

It is an interesting perceptual phenomenon, that adults are regarded as equal – regardless of their capacity, and regardless of their level of interpersonal responsibility. People are patently not equal with regard to many variables. When we say 'people are not equal', we are not saying 'people are not intrinsically equal'. People are all equal as beginninglessly enlightened beings – but in terms of their capacities, they are unequal. In terms of generosity, those with greater capacity—in whatever area—should naturally wish to help those who lack capacity.

We often assume that because someone is an adult, that they have our level of responsibility. If they do not, then we judge them according to that criterion as being deliberately culpable of lack of responsibility. *Compassion as generosity* is not feasible with such a view. If everyone is equally responsible for their acts, then we are impelled to judge them accordingly. We assume that they know what they are doing on the basis that we would appear to know what we are doing.

This view has nothing to do with shoring up self-esteem – but everything to do with bearing responsibility. As an awakened-mind warrior, one takes responsibility for being 'the one who has to forgive'. As an awakened-mind warrior, one takes responsibility for being 'the one who makes the first move towards better relationships.' As an awakened-mind warrior, one takes responsibility for being 'the one who does not become angry in the face of those who are locked in neurotic patterns'.

A mother forgives the child who drops his dinner on the floor. She acknowledges her child's incapacities. Her generosity provides instantaneous forgiveness. Her generosity provides opportunities for her child to acquire greater motor skills.

In this way the awakened-mind warrior develops infinite generous capacity to act for the benefit of everyone and everything, everywhere.

DISCIPLINE

Discipline *(tshul khrims / shila paramita / ethics or morality),* according to Dzogchen, can also be spoken of as energy – naturally arising energy or spontaneous energy. Non-duality incites the flow of spontaneous compassionate activity in precise relation to circumstances. Each situation—with all its complicated facets—guides the activity of pure appropriateness.

Pure discipline—in the Tantric sense—is the ecstatic embrace of the *Lama's vision of ourselves*. Pure discipline is based on our devotion to the Lama, rather than the self-determined and wilful adoption of a rigid code of conduct.

The process of referentiality saps the energy of naturally present compassionate activity. This is why discipline needs to be applied – in terms of adhering to a pattern of guidance given by the Lama. This is then a skilfully evoked pattern which approximates to compassionate activity for the disciple concerned.

The purpose of discipline is to overcome the compulsive nature of our habit patterns. For this to succeed we need to become transparent to ourselves. As practitioners we need to dwell in a limpid pool of *self-awareness*.

Discipline is necessary because of our *primary ambivalence* concerning practice and its result – realisation. Our primary ambivalence is that we *wish for* realisation at the same time as *wishing against* it.

Acknowledging this fact needs to underpin our lives as practitioners. There can be no progress unless we spend considerable time watching the play of this fact unfolding: day-by-day, week-by-week, and year-by-year. There are endless opportunities to watch.

We might love to think of ourselves as ceaselessly working for the benefit of everyone and everything, everywhere – but there are other things for which we might work more assiduously, such as our need to referentially establish ourselves in terms of solidity, comfort, distinction, continuity, and definition. These needs pervade our lives and pervert the sparkling through of our beginninglessly enlightened nature. We are extremely dishonest about realisation. We want it but not now: we need a few more minutes in bed; we need to vent our spleen; we need to retreat into the form of boredom at tonight's dinner plan – all rather than sit in the discomfort of non-conceptuality.

What we really want is to get as close as possible to realisation... and then sit back and admire our accomplishment.

Watching this *push and pull* – toward and away from the rules which we have applied to ourselves, is a primary practice of living the view. It induces an energetic sensation with which we must sit until it dissolves – this, is the acute claustrophobia of being a practitioner. It is a magnification of what occurs in formal practice, because it is applied in our everyday lives and is therefore endless. When it reaches uncomfortable intensity, hilarity and relaxation are often the only way to encourage the sense of spaciousness. To cling to that intensity is merely to add another layer of referentiality.

Discipline is like a band-aid for the injury of duality. However, band-aids have their limitations. They lose adhesion and fall off as we lapse in our application. 'Spiritual' band-aids become dirty when we judge others according to the discipline we have adopted. They become dirty because our discipline exists in order to temper our personal styles of playing with the primary ambivalence of wanting and not wanting realisation. 'Band-aid discipline' is no substitute for the real skin of realisation, but it has to suffice until such time as we can change.

We are immensely attracted to manipulating our lives in terms of discipline as another excuse to play with form in order to avoid emptiness. 'Spiritualised earth element neurotics' love nothing more than to impose strict sets of rules on themselves *(and others)* until they become crippled by such self-imposed bondage. When this crippling point is reached, we binge on whatever it is we were attempting to avoid.

This is the *game* where we divide ourselves into two people: the good and the bad – both of which are ugly, and far more entertaining than our tedious selves. This is the trap of 'discipline as reference point'. Without the guidance of the Lama, we will need to watch ourselves falling into this trap – possibly over and over again, before it wears itself out.

PATIENCE

Ngak'chang Rinpoche was once travelling by car to a retreat with our disciple Naljorma Jig'mèd. They became embroiled in a lengthy traffic jam and she commented, I've never known anyone with such patience. To which Ngak'chang Rinpoche replied, Why do you say that? I think of myself as extremely impatient. Naljorma Jig'mèd responded, But you don't seem to be in any anxiety about being late.

Rinpoche laughed at that point and pointed out, Well, I'm not impatient when there is nothing I can do to change a situation. If I thought we could get out of this jam by cutting across a field, then maybe you might witness impatience on my part.

Vajra-impatience is a paramita of the buddhakarma of destruction – but dualistic impatience is desperation – a frenetic kicking against limitations imposed by situations in which we feel insecure, fearful, out of touch, anxious, or lost.

Impatience is a means of seeking to control the momentum and direction at which circumstances unfold. The extent of impatience is commensurate with the degree to which reality refuses to cooperate with our dualistic derangement.

Patience—on the other hand—does not mean abdicating responsibility for attempting to move a circumstance or a person in a compassionately preferable direction. From the view of Vajrayana, patience or Zopa *(bZod pa – kshanti paramita)* does not mean acceptance, forbearance, and suffering. According to Vajrayana, patience involves *intelligent open-minded striving,* in which the situation is propelled at its optimal velocity –

neither forcing it, nor failing in the attempt to facilitate movement. Both apathy and coercion are the result of referentiality with regard to the pace at which visible success is apparent. Patience looks different according to circumstances.

Patience does not mean that Lamas would not push a person to achieve – if they knew that failure to encourage, coax, or cajole would mean stagnation in the student.

Any form of teaching or learning exposes our degree of *intelligent open-minded endeavour* with regard to *that for which we strive*. This process becomes visible if we take the example of teaching a child to play a musical instrument. To force the pace of the child's learning can often result in a spectacular backfire, in which those involved in the situation lose all impetus to continue. If, however, we were not to encourage practice, the child would never develop the degree of self-discipline required to practise daily, and to achieve the results which provide continued motivation.

The practice of shi-nè involves the renunciation of attachment to form as a reference point. Through shi-nè we learn that we cannot force thought. We need to be completely *purposelessly welcoming*. Whatever thought arises simply moves in its own way. Any approach involving force results either in hilarity or frustration. One needs a sense of humour about one's condition. One catches oneself trying to force meditation – repeatedly. All we can do, however, is watch ourselves in the process of *trying*, until *trying* wears itself out with trying in the open space of awareness. This is patience in terms of shi-nè – as we speak of it from the point of view of the Four Naljors of Dzogchen sem-dé.

Patience is required in terms of learning anything: shi-nè, horse riding, thangka painting, or marksmanship with a .500 Linebaugh. If you have found the right Lama, patience requires the implementation of their instructions. The Lama's instructions need to be followed exactly, rather than according to our own ideas – either in terms of our supposed meagre limitations, or in terms of our inflated sense of ourselves as perfectly qualified.

The only factor which alters the nature of our pace – is practice. Genuine practice is imbued with *intelligent open-minded striving*. The Lama provides the fount of knowledge from which we can glean the practices in which we could most effectively engage.

Practice is energetic; so if we disengage from the lugubrious slough of apathy and concomitantly open-mindedly persevere, the vectoral velocity of our energy becomes suffused with the brilliant nature of our non-dual unfolding.

DILIGENCE

Diligence—tsöndrü *(brTson 'grus – virya paramita)* was described by Chögyam Trungpa Rinpoche as energy. It could also be described as the quality of delight, of cheerful commitment or of joyful involvement.

Diligence is present when we relinquish resistance or when we refrain from obstructing situations. Outside the sphere of diligence there is always something we hold in reserve in order to maintain a solid, permanent, separate, continuous and defined project which is insulated from the intentionality of the Lama. We want to work with the Lama, but somehow we find ourselves incapable of the utter trust required to dispense with ancillary self-protective strategies and self-defensive manœuvres.

Diligence is the free energy we make available to the Lama and to ourselves in terms of carrying out the advice of the Lama. This is the energy which allows us to respond to circumstances appropriately.

This lack of resistance means that a quality of our energy manifests brilliantly in our activity. Vectoral movement towards the goal becomes an effortless effort – we plough through the waves of circumstances like a ship with 'three sheets to the wind'. Without the free energy of tsöndrü we have yet to weigh anchor and leave the anal retentive harbour of rationalisation.

Confidence in the Lama allows tsöndrü to manifest as fearlessness with regard to the open sea. With tsöndrü we can face waves that swell higher than the t'gallants, and therefore situations move towards successful conclusions with self-governed impulsion. We do not have to stand outside the situation keeping a running commentary on our relative position, and therefore no time is wasted.

The energy of tsöndrü ensures that we do not miss the swell of opportunities as they arise in the ocean of our life circumstances. Tsöndrü is the joyous energy of complete involvement, rather than the timid parsimonious feeling of obligation. Joyful involvement is beyond self-referencing – and therefore we fail to seek refuge in tiredness or boredom in respect of situations which are beyond our conceptual control.

Boredom with practice circumstances arises when the Lama's advice fails to give us a greater sense of solidity, permanence, distinction, continuity and definition.

When we find it difficult to change from one activity to another at the Lama's suggestion, there is usually some self-cherishing notion of 'having a better idea' with respect to 'me and the ongoing me project'. I could breed surreptitious ploys in order to convince the Lama that perhaps I should be engaged in another more valuable task than the one he or she has devised.

Without tsöndrü it takes time to settle into what we are engaged upon at the behest of the Lama, and to feel that something is moving – but with tsöndrü we move immediately and are immediately fulfilled.

Tsöndrü is the sense of joyful involvement which is continuously present. It is not a question of merely getting into things or settling down to something – tsöndrü is the self-arising energy which becomes available through devotion. With devotion, tsöndrü is effortlessly instantaneous.

SAMTEN

Samten *(bSam gTan – dhyana paramita – meditative stability, concentration)* is defined as Tsé gÇig Nyon-mong 'méd *(rTse gCig nyon mongs med)* meditative stability or stable attention bereft of conflictive emotions – the absence of referentiality.

Where referentiality is abandoned, conflictive emotions—such as territorialism, aggression, addiction, paranoia, and depression—spontaneously manifest as generosity, clarity, compassionate activity, self-accomplished activity, and pervasive intelligence.

The disconcerting human situations which arise for us all, fail to disquiet a person who has experience of samten. This is due to the fact that a person with experience of samten is not unavoidably impelled to act in a self-referencing manner. Experience of samten provides the stability to act appropriately and to be steadfast, rather than suffering the government of habitual patterns and their concomitant manipulative self-serving strategies.

In the everyday world, a practitioner with experience of samten prioritises practice over their compulsive patterning. This does not mean that the person is not afflicted by conflictive emotions – but simply is not ridden by them. This allows such a person to make emotionally fraught decisions without the pain to self and others which is caused by vacillation and tortuous indecision. Lacking experience of samten, one lacks the ability to live the view with integrity – particularly under duress. One becomes a fair weather practitioner – one who lacks consonance with Dharma, when Dharma would be most valuable. Lacking the ability to be consonant with Dharma under duress forces the bit firmly into one's mouth and places the reins in the hands of the dementedly despotic monkey of the conflictive emotions. The monkey has the whip and spurs which we have provided through our lack of experience of samten – and we are ridden with a brutality commensurate with the intensity of our neurotic neediness.

A practitioner with experience of samten has the capacity to be courageously honourable and forthright. This is evidenced by their ability to keep their word, to live a reliable existence, and to evolve a cheerful disposition in the face of difficulty. A practitioner lacking experience of samten thus exhibits moodiness, temperamental disposition, addictive tendencies, and interpersonally inexplicable behaviour.

A practitioner with experience of samten is a rider rather than one who is ridden. A reflection of samten is to be found in the rider's ability to maintain their seat through difficult circumstances. Whatever the circumstantial movement: bucking, shying, bolting, jumping, rearing, working trot, or collected canter – the rider of samten has a body of experience which absorbs the movement without disturbance to the security of his or her seat. The rider displays a co-operative movement in relation to the movement of circumstances – and the nature of that cooperation is Dharma.

To develop meditative stability requires an actual reliance both on the view and on the advice of the Lama. Meditative stability is only achieved through effort. It requires many hours in the saddle of the view. It requires many hours in the arena of meditative practice. It requires riding the trail of real vajra relationship with the Lama – rather than malingering in the slough of slovenly armchair equestrianism.

Life as a practitioner who rides rather than being ridden, can be excruciatingly uncomfortable. Some practitioners fall off and decide it is preferable to be ridden – in order to be closer to the warmth of the sand and the dung of the riding arena floor. To be a rider is to undermine reference points, and to ride cannot fail to elicit the fact of the level of our competence: insubstantiality, fear, isolation, vulnerability, and self-protective ignorance. It is in our worst moments that we need to rely on our hours in the saddle of samten, in order to manifest the reality of the view and our relationship with the Lama.

At moments of difficulty, those without experience of samten adopt a fœtal position in the saddle – abdicating responsibility and expecting the Lama to rescue them. They cherish hopes that the Lama will co-operate with their neuroses, rather than overriding their dualistic rationale. Others will try to hide at the back of the riding arena, rather than face the challenge of abandoning their cherished yet useless methods of indulgence in repeated failure. The authentic practitioner, however, will ensure that their experience of samten is sufficient to proceed with courage and stability in devotion.

KNOWLEDGE

Shérab *(shes rab – prajnaparamita)* means intelligence or insight. Chögyam Trungpa Rinpoche called it: '... the all – seeing eye, the opposite of the ego's watching itself doing everything.'

Shérab is complete insight into the referential patterns of the participants playing in every situation. The highest intelligence is to know the process of referentiality for *what it is*.

Practitioners develop shérab as they develop their practice. This process emerges through immersion in the relationship with the Lama, and the Lama's teaching. Under these conditions of commitment and devotion – there is no choice regarding the development of shérab – flashes of insight simply begin to occur. You find out and understand who you are. You discover the stylistics of the patterns by which your perception is conditioned. You discover the texture and fabric of your concept consciousness, your projections, and your relationship with your world.

This only occurs when we apply the teachings to ourselves and when we agree to accept a degree of discomfort, horror, hilarity, regret – and a great many other tones in the mind.

Shérab manifests at the point at which experiences of nyi'mèd percolate through the structure of the Tantric ngöndro *(sNgon 'gro)*. This is the point at which the preliminaries are no longer preliminaries and one begins to see that one could practise in this way for the rest of one's life.

Shérab exists in two forms. There is the shérab of *knowing* and the shérab of *seeing*. The shérab of *knowing* deals with the emotions – it cuts through self-referencing and its resultant emotions. The shérab of *seeing* is the transcendence of primitive preconceptions of the world, seeing situations as they actually are without our own projections. It allows for the possibility of pure appropriateness when dealing with situations.

Shérab is regarded as the two-edged sword that cuts the bondage of the confusion of self-referencing. The sword is two-edged – because it can cut in any direction – which is the manner of spontaneous appropriate activity.

To develop shérab is to become a vajra politician – aware of surrounding circumstances, yet aware of creating our version of those circumstances.

Vajra politicians do not submit to their perception of what is happening – they are slightly suspicious of their versions of reality and yet know that their versions are nonetheless connected with reality. Shérab enables vajra politicians to see around conditioned perceptual corners.

Shérab is immediate non-conceptual insight, yet—at the same time—it provides the basic inspiration for intelligent study. There is a natural desire to clarify and articulate the teachings and a curiosity to read and hear of how others have expressed their insight into mind and the nature of Mind. At the same time it is necessary to maintain continuing discipline of meditational training. In this way concepts are never 'merely concepts' – and one's approach remains fresh and alive.

Shérab, or discriminating awareness, is the state of clarity in which one is able to distinguish different states of mind; we are no longer excited or depressed by particular states of mind. States of mind are the ornaments of one's awareness. Shérab—or intellect—is intuitive, yet intellectually precise. The working of shérab is such that when we pay proper attention to persons or situations, they automatically give us answers or understanding. The quality of intelligence is all-pervasive but at the same time it is precisely to the point. It is sharp, accurate, and direct. It has the qualities of the water element.

The purpose of shérab is to cut through intelligence when it changes into intellectual speculation or when it obscures itself with philosophical beliefs. Intellectual speculation is reinforced endlessly by beliefs and dogmas – either: theological, moral, ethical, culturally empirical, or societally pragmatic. Intellectualism such as this should be destroyed on the spot. It is extremely damaging because it bases itself on shoring up self-image. Intellectualism such as this is entirely self-referencing and gives rise to bulimic informational vomiting which poses as conversation. Information regurgitated for its own sake eliminates the possibility of spontaneous communication and the appropriateness of linguistic play. It is often the case that the intellectualism becomes the two-edged sword of indiscriminate aggression.

Is he a man of information?

All his statements seem correct.

(from the film '*Emma*', adapted from the book by Jane Austen.) This quotation is a short description of shérab, and is based on the irony of the situation.

The man in question was Mr Frank Churchill, at one time the darling of Highbury society, but later exposed as a schmuck – a liar who toys with the emotions of others in a callous manner for his own ends. We have met people with enormous funds of informational knowledge but who seem singular most unpleasant affronts to decent society. Informational knowledge for its own sake must never to be mistaken for shérab.

Where information is deified, there is resistance to the Lama. The Lama is the root of the two aspects of wisdom, shérab and yeshé *(ye shes – jnana – primordial wisdom)*and therefore the student who takes refuge in information loses his or her refuge in Dharma and becomes little more than an esoteric philatelist. Such esoteric philatelists are so deeply mired in their referential patterns that they remain untouched both by the relationship with the Lama and by the teachings.

The fabrication of dualism causes us all to exhibit some form of spiritual materialism – but the practice is to hold the knowledge of this fact in one's heart so that one can recognise it and observe what unfolds. Awareness of our motivation must pervade practice. If we fail to acknowledge that our motivation is mixed—and mistake intellectualism for Dharma—then we will sink ever further into the swamp of duality and shérab will remain beyond our experience.

METHOD

Thab *(—method – thabs – skilful means, compassionate activity)*—is the way of unconditioned appropriate responsiveness to nowness. Method is the response to space. Because pure perception is not based on referentiality – phenomena are perceived as display, and unconditioned appropriate responses naturally unfold.

Riders must apply appropriate responses in relation to the condition of their horses. Eventually this must transcend concept as the riders' responses need to occur more rapidly than would be possible through conceptually instigated manœuvres. Perception and response need to be a non-dual dance on the floor of the equestrian arena.

The héruka *(khrags mThung – traktung – blood drinker)* is the energy of skilful means, powerful method, who creatively drinks the heart blood of duality. The héruka is the active aspect of knowledge, which is spontaneous and searingly precise in every situation. The primæval héruka is exemplified by Tamdrin *(rTa mGrin – Hayagriva)*, the wrathful yidam whose head is surmounted by that of a horse. The horse's head is a symbol of the subjugation of Rudra *(ru dra)* – 'nihilistic freedom' or 'absolute spiritual sociopathology'. For Rudra to be subjugated it has to be humiliated in the utmost violent manner – nothing less suffices. If Rudra is given even the most infinitesimal hope of preserving its 'dignity', it will merely re-emerge. Neither Hitler nor Stalin would have responded to Rogerian therapy. Rudra is exploded from the inside out. Everything is simultaneously exposed. The pig of wisdom and the horse of method enter Rudra via his anal passage. The pig explodes through Rudra's torso and the horse explodes through the crown of Rudra's head. Wisdom and Method enter in the most objectionable manner because they are not afraid of what needs to be accomplished. Success is heralded by the shattering cry of the horse's neigh which announces the death of narcissism.

It is impossible to predict how method will appear as it arises in response to circumstance, so methods can never be prescribed. The four Buddhakarmas are an example of how methods differ. They take the form of pacification, enrichment, magnetisation, and destruction. The account of the subjugation of Rudra is an example of the Buddhakarma of destruction.

Compassionate activity is direct – it is not necessarily comfortable. There may be no warm soggy smiles after the event. There is no guarantee of safety – even though our indestructible non-dual nature is our ultimate guarantee. Compassionate activity may appear unconventional – it does not accommodate nonsense, placate pomposity, or mollify our 'inner child'. It reveals situations *as they are*. It deals with situations *as they are*. It might be painful to be dealt with in such a way and by such an energy. Compassionate activity tears away the reference points behind which we hide.

From the point of view of referentiality *(our means of dualistically comforting ourselves)* compassion is blunt and somewhat ruthless. It demolishes the walls of our limiting patterns, in order that we may step outside to taste our colourful inspiring world. In stepping outside we become more than we were – we become practitioners.

Method involves heroism. If one is not subject to referentiality then one feels invincible – there is nothing whatsoever to lose as one is completely convinced of one's aloneness. This allows one to act appropriately without hesitation or inhibition.

The symbol for method is the full moon which shines in the night sky. The moon does not discriminate between the individuals on whom it sheds light. It simply shines. The moon does not observe itself shining. The moon does not seek congratulations or rewards for the gift of its light, it simply shines – gloriously.

Method *(thabs)* covers a vast range of meaning—a range as vast as 'that which arises from emptiness'—and to manifest the paramita of method one needs to be sensitive to the precise needs of every individual circumstance. We could review a few terms which contain the words *thabs* in order to gain some feeling for what is meant by method.

sKye gNas 'dams ba'i thabs – method for choosing the place of birth; bsKur thabs – method of conferring; bsKul thabs – method exhortation; khyim thabs – a synonym for 'husband'; khrid 'chad thabs – method of instruction; mKhar thabs – a fortress, turret, or stately home; gang 'dul thabs mKhas – skilful method of taming whoever needs to be tamed; gang 'dod 'grub pa'i thabs – method to accomplish aims; gang la gang 'dul – taming beings according to whatever is necessary; gar thabs – dance movements; gar thabs dGu – the nine moods of the héruka; gyad kyi 'dor thabs sa bGrad – feet set wide apart in the dPa bo *(hero or warrior)* stance; 'grig thabs – reconciliation or agreement; sGom thabs – method of meditation; sGrub thabs – means of accomplishment; bCos thabs – antidote or alleviation; 'jog thabs – method of settling in meditation; thabs mKhas – circumspection, ingenuity, or resourcefulness;thabs dag – abruptness; thabs dang sByar – resourcefulness; 'dul thabs – subjugation;brDa thabs rGyas pa – symbolic acts

These terms are themselves rich in meaning and every word could incite a commentary. Method is extravagantly capable. When we look at Da-thabs *(brDa thabs rGyas pa – symbolic acts)* for example, we are confronted with the oblique aspect of method – the method which emanates from yeshé 'cholwa or crazy wisdom. The Lama is capable of manifesting an incredible variety of modes and means in order to serve the needs of disciples – and some of these means are impossible to understand from the intellectual point of view. It would be easier to understand such methodology from the point of view of the arts and the effect that the arts have on those who see painting, listen to music, or read books.

The Lama is the 'master of method' and this facility extends to every aspect of his or her presentation via the three displays of the Lama: presence display, personality display, and life-circumstances display. Kyabjé Künzang Dorje Rinpoche is known also as Kyabjé Karma Gyalpo—Lord of Refuge – King of Activity—by those who understand his consummate versatility throughout the reach and range of what needs to be accomplished.

ASPIRATION

Thugmön, *(thugs sMon – thug-mön – thugs sMon pranidhana paramita – vectoral verve)* the mind of aspiration

– more generally referred to as mönlam *(sMon lam)*, the path of aspiration, is the innate vectoral verve which makes realisation a reality.

Aspiration is not hope *(re sMon)*. It is not wishful-thinking or expectation – nor is it: hunger, yearning, longing, pining, craving, flight of fancy, eagerness, fervour, zeal, intensity, vehemence, enthusiasm, obsession, fascination, addiction, vain hope, or obsession.

These 'emotivations' *(rang sNang ma dag pa'i kun sLong)* tend to predominate where there is a primitive level of experience in practice, characterised usually by lack of devotion and commitment. Emotivations such as ambition tend to be short-lived. They dissolve over time because there is no supporting foundation of practice on which they can depend for perseverance. Ambition—in this sense—concerns what we want, rather than that for which we are prepared to make all necessary sacrifices.

Pseudo-aspiration can be worn by some as an affected garment of superior status. Mr Casaubon—an independently wealthy cleric in George Eliot's novel 'Middlemarch'—constructed his life around pretensions to aspiration. He convinced those around him that he was engaged in erudite, complex research, which was beyond most people's comprehension. His wife Dorothea Brooke—excited by 'the moral superiority of scholarship'—imagines Mr Casaubon as 'a man who could understand the higher inward life ... who could illuminate principle with the widest knowledge'. Mr Casaubon's concept consciousness, however, is a recess where knowledge is subject to 'lifeless embalmment'.

On watching the BBC production of 'Middlemarch' with me, Ngak'chang Rinpoche was intrigued by the character and commented that Mr Casaubon—and persons of his disposition—are where intellectual white elephants go to die.

Mr Casaubon's work-in-progress, 'The Key to All Mythologies', is a futile and interminable undertaking – and he is utterly resistant to letting his wife help in any way whatsoever, in case she realises the sad truth that his work is both unpublishable and lacking in any significance to the world he wishes to address.

Aspiration is a quality which must be reliable – or else it is not aspiration. Those who speak of what they intend to accomplish and never accomplish it – do not have aspiration. So—in the initial stages of aspiration—discipline is required *(sMon gyi tshul khrims)* – the discipline of aspiration.

A publisher may well reject one's book – but at least it has to be completed and presented to publishers if the author is to be credited with aspiration. A bare century ago, no one would speak of their aspirations lightly, because once expressed it was anticipated that results would be forthcoming. If results were not forthcoming, the person who spoke of their aspirations would be discredited in the eyes of his or her peers. It is the same when one becomes the student of a Lama – something is expected. To take refuge is to aspire – and anyone who takes refuge should be seen to be making a valiant effort to behave according to the precepts and the eightfold path. Ngak'chang Rinpoche has often said that his respect for people rests on how they keep their word – whether they are reliable in accomplishing what they set out to accomplish.

Aspiration is the stable determination to achieve realisation – come what may – but not the determination to achieve realisation 'come who may'. One is not careless with regard to other aspirants. One does not step on others. One does not grind the fingers of others climbing the ladder. One does not jockey for position.

Aspiration is not the ruthless ambition which criticises other disciples of the Lama in order to secure superior rank and privileges. Practitioners who display aspiration are doggedly determined in relation to how their personal circumstances evolve. They prove themselves indomitable in the face of difficulties.

Aspiration is based on the previous paramitas, which is why aspiration is not usually found early in a practitioner's career. The steadfast strength of mind of aspiration cannot be developed before some sense of fruition has been gained in respect of the previous paramitas. Aspiration to the realised state means acting in the present – not in an hour's time, tomorrow, next week, next month or next year. This is mön'jug *(sMon jug)* – aspiration and application or aspiring and acting.

Aspiration can only exist in the present – and that is somewhat electrifying, somewhat inflammatory. It was Trungpa Rinpoche who instructed his students to Sit as if your hair were on fire and it is this quality which should pervade us as practitioners. This is where mön'jug becomes mön'jug gi sem *(sMon 'jug gi sems)* – the aspiration and application which arise from the nature of Mind.

The point-instant in which we realise that we have drifted from aspiration should be the point-instant of action – and a moment of joy. It is a waste of time to be self-deprecatory at this moment. The point-instant resolution to return to aspiration is an instantaneously-arising ornament of practice. It may occur many times in a day – and if we remember frequently that we have drifted from aspiration, we should take this as a sign of success rather than failure. This should be a continual occurrence for practitioners.

It will—on occasion—occur to us that we would rather stay with juicy yet unhelpful mind states, than return to aspiration. To remain stuck is the comfortable option – but, in that state of fixity, we may not necessarily understand that 'stuckness' as comfort. The stuckness of comfort is always replete with the referential qualities of solidity, permanence, separation, continuity, and definition – and we adhere to these like the tentacle suckers of an octopus.

There will always be situations where we would rather not be practising. This will occur in formal practice and on those occasions where we simply do not wish to act like practitioners. Recognition of the first moments of these phases—where we drift from aspiration—is crucial to the development of practice. At these points we need to be resolute – and to dwell within the push and pull gestalt of vectoral verve versus deliberate obfuscation. The time that we are able to reside in this extremely uncomfortable location—experiencing the raw texture of this gestalt—is most fruitful in allowing these patterns to unwind themselves. In being clearly seen – patterns unwind of themselves.

To aspire *(to non-duality)* is not the same as to be inspired, but the two are linked. Inspiration arises when we see someone or something outside ourselves that resonates with our desire to practise. When this resonance occurs – the volume of aspiration is amplified and, as Ngak'chang Rinpoche comments: ... in relation to the amplification of aspiration; when the Lama provides support for aspiration through inspiration – he or she has recourse to an alarming array of effects pedals. These are the buddhakarmas.

Aspiration goes beyond ordinary encouragement when fostered by the Lama – inasmuch as it is non-referential inspiration or vajra inspiration. Vajra inspiration is that which we find within ourselves as a result of practice in relation to the Lama. This is the case without knowing or even being concerned with how it came to be there.

In the Nyingma tradition there are three special gTérma lineages *(khyad par gyi brGyud pa gSum)* which are as follows:

1. The Kabab Lung-ten gi gyüdpa *(bKa' babs lung bsTan gyi brGyud pa)* – prophetic mandate lineage.
2. The Mönlam dBang-kur gi gyüdpa *(sMon lam dBang bsKur gyi brGyud pa)* – lineage of empowerment through aspiration.
3. The Khandro Tad-gya gi gyüdpa *(mKha' 'gro gTad rGya gyi brGyud pa)* – Mind mandate lineage of the khandros.

Aspiration is clearly far more than wishing in the sense of the Mönlam dBang-kur, and we can see that—once established—aspiration is the heart power of practice. We speak of ngön-gyi Mönlam *(sNgon gyi sMon lam)* – former aspirations; and ngön-gyi mönlam gyi dBang-gi *(sNgon gyi sMon lam gyi dBang gis)* – the force of past aspirations; and from this we can see that aspiration is our inheritance as well as the present energy toward the future. Dentsig möndrüp *(bden tsig gi smon pa grub pa)* – the 'power of prophecy' – links aspiration with the future in terms of knowing what will happen through ensuring that it happens. This is often misunderstood with regard to the Lama's prophecies. It is not that one's Lama's prophecy may not be 'literal predictions' – but the aspirational vector of one's Lama's intention carries through into one's own stream of practice – and one's own aspiration ensures that the prophecy is realised.

It would be useful perhaps to conclude here—in respect of aspiration—by mentioning the Namthar Go-sum *(rNam thar sGo gSum)* – the 'Three Portals of Emancipation': emptiness – tongpa-nyid *(sTong pa nyid),* aspirationlessness – mön'mèd *(sMon pa med pa),* and attributelessness – tshan-nyid 'med *(mtshan nyid 'med pa).* Mön 'mèd—aspirationlessness—is the integration of aspiration with the non-dual state in which effort is no longer necessary, and in which aspiration becomes primordial wisdom.

STRENGTH

I am still waiting for something to start. The life where everything is different, where I do not do things like this. But there is no magic, there is just a series of decisions in each moment and while I wait to feel transformed I am making all the same old decisions underground and pretending I am not and feeling bad that nothing is different.

This is how an apprentice described the nature of momentary feelings – and in so doing delightfully defined absence of strength: 'I am making all the same old decisions underground and pretending I am not and feeling bad that nothing is different.' It can be useful to explore the reasons for the absence of a quality in order to understand how that quality could gain ascendancy through practice. The lack of any quality is mainly due to the way in which we undermine ourselves. We wish to change – but we hang onto old patterns. We want a different situation – but act in all the ways which created the situation to which we have been accustomed for so long.

Strength *(tob – sTobs – power)* is an expression of confidence in our innate goodness – the confidence that when our elaborate patterns fall apart – someone will be left, rather than an 'empty shell of someone'. Strength is the confidence in the fact that we are not merely the meschuggas of our hopes and fears. Strength is the unrestrained willingness to leap over the edge of anything into a state of being which has not been carefully rehearsed. The leap is a non-referential leap – and therefore unselfconscious. The leap simply occurs.

Strength comes from acknowledgement of weakness – the ability or strength to be vulnerable. When cavalry charge the enemy, it is not that they are unaware of the immanent risk of death. The warrior is fully conversant with the reality of the situation – but the warrior simply acts in that knowledge. This is an act of bravery rather than 'an act'. An act is merely bravado – a mechanism implemented to conceal vulnerability.

To experience the power or strength to leap over the edge of change – we must acknowledge that we are wholly responsible for our emotional responses to *the way that things are in our lives*. Our life circumstances are subject to the dance of emptiness and form. Sometimes we experience the best possible luck – and at other times, the worst. Sometimes adventitious rewards ripen – and sometimes the most wretched conclusion that could occur – does just that.

Often there is *an element* of our own 'historical decision-making' embedded in the way that our circumstances pan out – and therefore we need to accept responsibility for that rather than bemoaning the swamp, desert, wasteland, or prison we may have assiduously created through wilfulness, embattlement, or intransigent myopia.

Our circumstances appear either to work out or not. We are not wholly responsible for every aspect of our circumstances but we are entirely responsible for our emotional responses in each moment.

We need strength to be open to the raw texture of our lives without recourse to refuge in positivism *(eternalism)* or despair *(nihilism)*. Each of these methods seeks to provide us with comfort – providing a buffer against the actuality of our lives.

Strength is required in terms of cooperating with the Lama's view of ourselves – cooperating with the Lama's advice which is consequent to their view. Strength is a state of complete openness – the condition in which one has the ability to offer no resistance to the nature of vajra relationship.

The degree of power is related to *that which contains it.* A firework is only powerful because the gun powder and other inflammables are contained by a cardboard shell. When the firework is ignited the resultant explosion depends on the rigidity of the containment. Ngak'chang Rinpoche used to play a game called 'genies' when he was a boy. This involved cutting open a firework and sprinkling the gun powder on the ground, standing astride it and then dropping a lighted match. He or one of his friends would then 'appear like a Genie' in a harmless puff of smoke and sparks. If Ngak'chang Rinpoche had chosen to hold the firework tightly in his hand – the result would have been the loss of his hand. Without the container – the firework loses its power.

Similarly, for a horse to move in a circle with sufficient power and strength to carry itself correctly, its energy must be contained by the rein, otherwise the energy is continually lost by the horse becoming front-heavy. When the horse becomes front-heavy it moves in an unbalanced way, almost dragging its quarters behind.

For practitioners the container is constructed by the precepts and vows. When a practitioner uses *the container of the vows,* their power is directed strongly and focused in a precise direction. The copious energy of an authentic practitioner is not dissipated in a brief puff of smoke – but rather their energy surges into the appropriate spacious method required by every circumstance.

PRIMORDIAL WISDOM

Yeshé *(ye shes – jnana paramita – primordial wisdom – pristine perspicacity)* is primordially good. Kunkhyen Chögyam Trungpa Rinpoche—in discussing the subject of 'basic goodness'—speaks of it as a reflection of primordial wisdom in our everyday lives. We all have basic goodness because we are beginninglessly enlightened. We spend our lives naturally manifesting basic goodness – yet we suppress it with referentiality – attempting to prove to ourselves that we are solid, permanent, separate, continuous, and defined. Ngak'chang Rinpoche talks of nascent experiences of non-dual realisation being like a light bulb which flickers on and off. Practitioners who apply serious commitment to practice allow basic goodness to manifest simply through being less obstructive to the sparkling through of basic goodness. They become like light bulbs which flicker with greater frequency.

The manifest destiny of primordial wisdom facilitates practitioners to allow other people to manifest at their best. They expect goodness. Primordial wisdom interrupts attempts to control people and their situations. Primordial wisdom is demonstrated through: relaxed appropriateness; unperturbed suitability; tranquil aptness; and unruffled precision.

Basic goodness—as manifest primordial wisdom—enables practitioners to encourage an ethos of openness and appreciation. Basic goodness promotes a sense of immediacy and it becomes apparent to practitioners that they are capable of approaching situations without need of pre-established structures or plans. Practitioners realise that they are naturally possessed of the ability to be present without restrictive concepts of past and future. They find themselves able to allow the basic goodness of others to become opportunities for the discovery of wider margins of the same.

Having a sense of basic goodness means that everyone can be approached freshly – but this does not require gullibility or naïveté. It requires that we avoid pre-empting every situation with respect to strategies based on the predictions of dualistic derangement. Basic goodness has no need to be proactive on the basis of suspicion. We can meet the basic goodness of others with disarming friendliness. If our view of the world is pervaded by basic goodness then we can be open and our decisions can be based on trust rather than on suspicion. We expect good behaviour from people – and we are therefore more likely to be met with good behaviour.

People whose basic goodness is less manifest will tend to

anticipate problems with people and situations. They will not feel safe with regard to entering situations in an unguarded manner. They anticipate problems because they are fearful and have learnt to be self-protective as their primary conduit of contact. Fearfulness always provokes the need to control.

Ngak'chang Rinpoche told me a story about his father once, which illustrates this tendency in societal terms. Rinpoche said that when he was at Art College his father had some concern about him in terms of the fact that he seemed to have no social life. Rinpoche replied that he did not socialise a great deal because he enjoyed his work and wanted to take full advantage of the Art College facilities – but that he was far from being a recluse. This was of course in contradiction to Rinpoche's attitude whilst at school – and so it was maybe not surprising that Rinpoche's father found his utter immersion in College work perplexing. Rinpoche's father then asked him—apparently wishing to be helpful—how he conducted himself at social gatherings. He asked: What is your opening gambit? Rinpoche was confused for a moment and replied that he had not yet found he had a need for one but would be interested to hear any suggestions his father might have. Rinpoche's father was somewhat confounded – being unable to understand how it was possible to walk into a room full of people and have no prearranged means of broaching conversation with them. The idea that it was possible simply to be in a room and not speak immediately – or not to be introduced seemed like chaos. Or simply to walk up to a group of people and listen to a conversation without joining in immediately. The idea of not introducing yourself at all – but merely speaking when it became a natural impulse with regard to the drift of the conversation seemed to Rinpoche's father to be no different from standing on a street corner. The modes of social mien Rinpoche explained were utter mysteries to his father. Admittedly Rinpoche's father was born in 1902. He was an old man when Rinpoche was growing up, and therefore his view was vaguely that of a Victorian Officer's Mess. Rinpoche's father was a major in the Royal Engineers and his social sense derived entirely from that situation – nonetheless this provides us with an illustration of reliance on pattern and bewilderment in the face of an open-ended situation.

A practitioner is not bewildered by chaos. I am not suggesting that Victorian etiquette and social mores are intrinsically deluded – we might easily find ourselves benefited by the adoption of more formal etiquette in this world of dishevelled slovenliness. It is more a question of the freedom to accept chaos and the freedom to trust the basic goodness of others.

Primordial wisdom is synonymous with Kun-zhi *(kun gZhi – alaya)*. Trungpa Rinpoche says that 'Kun-zhi is the fundamental state of existence, or consciousness before it is divided into 'I' and 'other' or into the various emotions.' It is the basic ground and its natural style is goodness. It is the awakened mind.

This is how it is expressed in Sutra, where duality is defined in terms of the division between self and other. It is expressed this way in Sutrayana as a method of working against the self-cherishing mind. On hearing this, one could make the mistake of thinking that entering the state of kun-zhi would dissolve our separateness as beings. With knowledge of kun-zhi, beings do not act separately from others – as if other beings were disconnected or irrelevant. The state of kun-zhi acknowledges all beings as intrinsically interrelated. From the perspective of Dzogchen, kun-zhi is the non-dual state.

The Ten Hindrances to Enlightenment show us what we need to get rid of. To assist us in the eradication of the hindrances are ten virtues to cultivate, listed above. These are the Ten Paramitas, which are translated as, the Ten Perfections of the Heart.

In the Ten Perfections you will see elements of the Five Precepts and The Noble Eightfold Middle Path. Alongside these important Dhammateachings are listed the ever important "energy" and "determination." If we want to succeed at anything, we can never underestimate the importance of persistence and determination.

Renunciation, listed above does not necessarily mean giving up your possessions and becoming a monk or nun. Renunciation can simply mean being content with what you have and maintaining a simple life and lifestyle. It can mean "counting your blessings" or doing something simple to put your mind at ease to allow you to pursue spiritual quests. It can also mean making some small sacrifices, such as choosing your vacation time from work to go to a vipassana retreat, instead of a cruise.

The Buddha spent many past lives as an ascetic monastic perfecting each of the ten perfections. He could not be re-born in his final life as theBuddha until all ten perfections were fully developed. Enlightenment is not something so simple as just sitting one day and all of a sudden feeling at "one with nature" and very "awake." There is a common danger in many Western countries where some practitioners and teachers say that they are enlightened when they have one momentary glimpse of jhanic pleasure in their meditation. They are mistaking some pleasurable jhanic states for enlightenment. Enlightenment is attainable, but no easy task and has the prerequisite of the ten paramitas.

PÂRAMITÂ

Pâramitâ or pâramî (*Pâli*) is "perfection" or "completeness." In Buddhism, the *pâramitâs* refer to the perfection or culmination of certain virtues. In Buddhism, these virtues are cultivated as a way of purification, purifying karma and helping the aspirant to live an unobstructed life, while reaching the goal of enlightenment.

Etymology

Scholar Donald Lopez describes the etymology of the term:

The term *pâramitâ,* commonly translated as "perfection," has two etymologies. The first derives it from the word parama, meaning "highest," "most distant," and hence, "chief," "primary," "most excellent." Hence, the substantive can be rendered "excellence" or "perfection." This reading is supported by the *Madhyântavibhâga* (V.4), where the twelve excellences (*parama*) are associated with the ten perfections (*pâramitâ*).

A more creative yet widely reported etymology divides

pâramitâ into *pâra* and *mita,* with *pâra* meaning "beyond," "the further bank, shore or boundary," and *mita,* meaning "that which has arrived," or *ita* meaning "that which goes." *Pâramitâ,* then means "that which has gone beyond," "that which goes beyond," or "transcendent." This reading is reflected in the Tibetan translation *pha rol tu phyin pa* ("gone to the other side").

Theravâda Buddhism

Theravâda Buddhism's teachings on the *pâramitâs* can be found in late canonical books and post-canonical commentaries.

Canonical sources

In the Pâli canon's *Buddhavamsa* the Ten Perfections (*dasa pâramiyo*) are (original terms in Pâli):

1. *Dâna pâramî* : generosity, giving of oneself
2. *Sîla pâramî* : virtue, morality, proper conduct
3. *Nekkhamma pâramî* : renunciation
4. *Paññâ pâramî* : transcendental wisdom, insight
5. *Viriya* (also spelled *vîriya*) *pâramî* : energy, diligence, vigour, effort
6. *Khanti pâramî* : patience, tolerance, forbearance, acceptance, endurance
7. *Sacca pâramî* : truthfulness, honesty
8. *Adhimmhâna* (*adhitthana*) *pâramî* : determination, resolution
9. *Mettâ pâramî* : loving-kindness
10. *Upekkhâ* (also spelled *upekhâ*) *pâramî* : equanimity, serenity

Two of the above virtues, *metta* and *upekkha* also comprise two of the four immeasurables (*brahmavihâra*).

Historicity

The Theravâdin teachings on *pâramitâs* can be found in canonical books (*Jâtaka, Apadâna, Buddhavamsa, Cariyâpimaka*) and post-canonical commentaries which were written to supplement the Pâli canon at a later time, and thus they are not an original part of the Theravâdin teachings. The oldest parts of the *Sutta Pimaka* (for example, *Majjhima Nikâya, Digha Nikâya, Samyutta Nikâya* and the *Anguttara Nikâya*) do not have any mention of the *pâramitâs* as a category (though they are all mentioned individually).

Some scholars even refer to the teachings of the *pâramitâs* as a semi-Mahâyâna teaching which was added to the scriptures at a later time, in order to appeal to the interests and needs of the lay community and to popularize their religion. However, these views rely on the early scholarly presumption of Mahâyâna originating with religious devotion and appeal to laity. More recently, scholars have started to open up early Mahâyâna literature which is very ascetic and expounds the ideal of the monk's life in the forest. Therefore, the practice of the *pâramitâs* is closer to the ideals of the ascetic tradition of the Sramama in Buddhism.

Traditional practice

Bodhi (2005) maintains that, in the earliest Buddhist texts (which he identifies as the first four *nikâyas*), those seeking the extinction of suffering (*nibbana*) pursued the noble eightfold path. As time went on, a backstory was provided for the multi-life development of theBuddha; as a result, the ten perfections were identified as part of the path for the bodhisattva (Pâli: *bodhisatta*). Over subsequent centuries, the *pâramîs* were seen as being significant for aspirants to both Buddhahood and arahantship. Thus, Bodhi (2005) summarizes:

It should be noted that in established Theravâda tradition the pâramîs are not regarded as a discipline peculiar to candidates for Buddhahood alone but as practices which must be fulfilled by all aspirants to enlightenment and deliverance, whether as Buddhas, paccekabuddhas, or disciples. What distinguishes the supreme bodhisattva from aspirants in the other two vehicles is the degree to which the pâramîs must be cultivated and the length of time they must be pursued. But the qualities themselves are universal requisites for deliverance, which all must fulfil to at least a minimal degree to merit the fruits of the liberating path.

Mahâyâna Buddhism

In Mahâyâna Buddhism, the Prajñapâramitâ Sûtras, the *Lotus Sutra* (*Skt., Saddharma Punarîka Sûtra*), and a large number of other texts, list the six perfections as (original terms in Sanskrit):

1. *Dâna pâramitâ*: generosity, giving of oneself
2. *Úîla pâramitâ* : virtue, morality, discipline, proper conduct
3. *Kcânti (kshanti) pâramitâ* : patience, tolerance, forbearance, acceptance, endurance
4. *Vîrya pâramitâ* : energy, diligence, vigor, effort
5. *Dhyâna pâramitâ* : one-pointed concentration, contemplation
6. *Prajñâ pâramitâ* : wisdom, insight

   Note that this list is also mentioned by the Theravâda commentator Dhammapala, who says it is equivalent to the above list of ten.

   In the Ten Stages (*Dasabhûmika*) Sutra, four more *pâramitâs* are listed:

7. *Upâya pâramitâ*: skilful means
8. *Pramidhâna pâramitâ*: vow, resolution, aspiration, determination
9. *Bala pâramitâ*: spiritual power
10. *Jñâna pâramitâ*: knowledge

Tibetan Buddhism

According to the perspective of Tibetan Buddhism, Mahâyâna practitioners have the choice of two practice paths: the path of perfection (Sanskrit:*pâramitâyâna*) or the path of tantra (Sanskrit:*tantrayâna*), which is the Vajrayâna.

Traleg Kyabgon Rinpoche renders "*pâramitâ*" into English as "transcendent action" and then frames and qualifies it:

When we say that *paramita* means "transcendent action," we mean it in the sense that actions or attitude are performed in a non-egocentric manner. "Transcendental" does not refer to some external reality, but rather to the way in which we conduct our lives and perceive the world - either in an egocentric or a non-egocentric way. The six *paramitas* are concerned with the effort to step out of the egocentric mentality.

The gyulü is said to be endowed with the six perfections (Sanskrit: *cad-pâramitâ*).

2

Five Principles of Peaceful Coexistence

The Five Principles of Peaceful Coexistence, known in India as the Panchsheel Treaty (from Sanskrit, *panch*:five, *sheel*:virtues), are a set of principles to govern relations between states. Their first formal codification in treaty form was in an agreement between China and India in 1954. They were enunciated in the preamble to the "Agreement (with exchange of notes) on trade and intercourse between Tibet Region of China and India", which was signed at Peking on 29 April 1954. This agreement stated the five principles as:

1. Mutual respect for each other's territorial integrity and sovereignty.
2. Mutual non-aggression.
3. Mutual non-interference in each other's internal affairs.
4. Equality and cooperation for mutual benefit.
5. Peaceful co-existence.

An underlying assumption of the Five Principles was that newly independent states after decolonization would be able to develop a new and more principled approach to international relations. The principles were emphasized by the Prime Minister of India, Jawaharlal Nehru, in a broadcast speech made at the time of the Asian Prime Ministers Conference at Colombo just a few days after the signing of the Sino-Indian treaty in Beijing. Nehru went so far as to say: "If these principles were recognized in the mutual relations of all countries, then indeed there would hardly be any conflict and certainly no war." The five principles were subsequently incorporated in modified form in a statement of ten principles issued in April 1955 at the historic Asian-African Conference in Bandung, Indonesia, which did more than any other meeting to form the idea that post-colonial states had something special to offer the world.

It has been suggested that the five principles had partly originated as the five principles of the Indonesian state. In June 1945 Sukarno, the Indonesian nationalist leader, had proclaimed five general principles, or pancasila, on which future institutions were to be founded. Indonesia became independent in 1949.

The Five Principles as they had been adopted in Colombo and elsewhere formed the basis of the Non-Aligned Movement, established in Belgrade in 1961.

The history of the first major enunciation of the Five Principles is not wholly encouraging. China has often emphasized its close association with the Five Principles. It had put them forward, as the Five Principles of Peaceful Coexistence, at the start of negotiations that took place in Delhi from December 1953 to April 1954 between the Delegation of the PRC Government and the Delegation of the Indian Government on the relations between the two countries with respect to the disputed territories of Aksai Chin and South Tibet. The 29 April 1954 agreement mentioned above was set to last for eight years. When it lapsed, relations were already souring, the provision for renewal of the agreement was not taken up, and the Sino-Indian War broke out between the two sides. However, in the 1970s, the Five Principles again came to be seen as important in Sino-Indian relations, and more generally as norms of relations between states. They have become widely recognized and accepted throughout the region.

FIVE PRINCIPLES OF PANCHSHEEL

After attaining the enlightenment, Gautam Buddha went to the holy city of Benares and shared his new understanding with other fellows who became his disciples immediately. This was considered as the beginning of the Buddhist community. Till his death, Buddha with his band of disciples spread the gospel of the Dhamma among all the classes comprised of beggars, kings and slave girls.

The Basic Teachings of Buddha which are core of Buddhism are-

Source of Buddha's Teachings

The Buddha's teachings have been reconstructed from stories, found mainly in the Sutta Pitaka. Although some stories describe his miraculous powers, others suggest that the Buddha tried to convince people through reason and persuasion rather than through displays of supernatural power. According to Buddhist philosophy, the world is transient (anicca) and constantly changing; it is also soulless (anatta) as there is nothing permanent or eternal in it. Within this transient world, sorrow (dukkha) is intrinsic to human existence. It is by following the path of moderation between severe penance and self-indulgence that human beings can rise above these worldly troubles. In the earliest forms of Buddhism, whether or not god existed was irrelevant.

Buddhist Teaching of Re-Birth

The Buddha regarded the social world as the creation of humans rather than of divine origin. Therefore, he advised kings and gahapatis to be humane and ethical. Individual effort was expected to transform social relations. The Buddha emphasized individual agency and righteous action as the means to escape from the cycle of rebirth and attain self-realization and nibbana, literally the extinguishing of the ego and desire - and thus end the cycle of suffering for those who renounced the world. According to Buddhist tradition, his last words to his followers were: "Be lamps unto yourselves as all of you must work out your own liberation."

Buddha's Teaching - The Way to Salvation

During the course of meditation, Gautam Buddha after attaining the enlightenment came out with the certain principles which have become the pillars of Buddhism. These teachings have also become the guidelines for the followers of Buddha. These principles can broadly be explained under the following categories.

1. The Four Noble Truths

The teachings of Buddha can be summarized under the category of Four Noble Truths which are as under:

a) Suffering is common - Birth, Sickness, Old age, Death etc.

b) Cause of Suffering - ignorance and greed.

c) End of Suffering – to cut off greed and ignorance.

d) Path to end Suffering - the Noble Eightfold Path is the way to end suffering.

2. The Noble Eightfold Path

The teachings of Buddha goes round and round like a great wheel that never stops, leading to the central point of the wheel, the only point which is fixed, Nirvana. The eight spokes on the wheel represent the eight parts of the Noble Eightfold Path which are as follows: 1) Right View; 2) Right Thought; 3) Right Speech; 4) Right Conduct; 5) Right Livelihood; 6) Right Effort; 7) Right Mindfulness; 8) Right Concentration.

The Panchshila

All the religions of the world are based on the fundamental principles of good conduct and prohibit their followers to indulge in the misconduct and misbehavior that may harm the society at large. So, the Panchshila of Buddha is comprised of the basic teachings of conduct which are as under:

1. No killing
   Respect for life
2. No stealing
   Respect for others' property
3. No sexual misconduct
   Respect for our pure nature

4. No lying
   Respect for honesty
5. No intoxicants
   Respect for a clear mind

THE PURPOSE OF BUDDHIST MORAL PRECEPTS

There are three fundamental modes of training in Buddhist practice: morality, mental culture, and wisdom. The English word morality is used to translate the Pali term *sila,* although the Buddhist term contains its own particular connotations. The word *sila* denotes a state of normalcy, a condition which is basically unqualified and unadulterated. When one practices*sila,* one returns to one's own basic goodness, the original state of normalcy, unperturbed and unmodified. Killing a human being, for instance, is not basically human nature; if it were, human beings would have ceased to exist a long time ago. A person commits an act of killing because he or she is blinded by greed, rage or hatred. Such negative qualities as anger, hatred, greed, ill will, and jealousy are factors that alter people's nature and make them into something other than their true self. To practice *sila* is thus to train in preserving one's true nature, not allowing it to be modified or overpowered by negative forces. This definition points to the objective of Buddhist morality rather than to the practice itself, but it does give us an idea of the underlying philosophy behind the training, as well as how the Buddhist moral precepts should be followed. These precepts are a means to an end, they are observed for a specific objective.

On the personal level, the observance of precepts serves as the preliminary groundwork for the cultivation of higher virtues or mental development. *Sila* is the most important step on the spiritual path. Without morality, right concentration cannot be attained, and without right concentration, wisdom cannot be fully perfected. Thus, morality not only enhances people's ethical values and fulfils their noble status as human beings, but it is crucial to their efforts toward the highest religious goal of *Nibbana.*

On the social level, *sila* contributes to harmonious and peaceful coexistence among community members and consequently helps to promote social growth and development. In a society where morality prevails and members are conscious of their roles, there will be general security, mutual trust, and close cooperation, these in turn leading to greater progress and prosperity. Without morality there will be corruption and disturbance, and all members of society are adversely affected. Most of the problems that society experiences today are connected, directly or indirectly, with a lack of good morality.

Questions of morality always concern the issues of right and wrong, good and evil. For a moral life to be meaningful these issues must not remain mere theoretical principles, but translated into practice. Good must be performed, evil must be given up. It is not enough to know what is good or evil, we also need to take proper action with respect to them. We need concrete guidelines to follow, and these are provided by the Buddhist moral precepts. Even the oft-quoted Buddhist ideals of abstention from evil, implementation of what is good, and perfect mental purification can be initially actualized through a consistent practice of moral precepts. The precepts help us to live those ideals; they teach us to do the right things and to avoid the wrong.

Buddhist moral precepts provide a wholesome foundation for personal and social growth. They are practical principles for a good life and the cultivation of virtues. If we understand the objectives of *sila* and realize its benefits, we will see moral precepts as an integral part of life rather than as a burden that we are compelled to shoulder. Buddhist moral precepts are not commandments imposed by force; they are a course of training willingly undertaken in order to achieve a desired objective. We do not practice to please a supreme being, but for our own good and the good of society. As individuals, we need to train in morality to lead a good and noble life. On the social level, we need to help maintain peace and harmony in society and facilitate the progress of the common good. The practice of moral precepts is essential in this regard.

Distinguishing good and evil

The problems of good and evil, right and wrong, have been dealt with in the discussion on *kamma*. Here it may suffice to give a brief summary on the subject.

To determine whether an action is good or evil, right or wrong, Buddhist ethics takes into account three components involved in a kammic action. The first is the intention that motivates the action, the second is the effect the doer experiences consequent to the action, and the third is the effect that others experience as a result of that action. If the intention is good, rooted in positive mental qualities such as love, compassion, and wisdom, if the result to the doer is wholesome (for instance, it helps him or her to become more compassionate and unselfish), and if those to whom the action is directed also experience a positive result thereof, then that action is good, wholesome, or skilful (*kusala*). If, on the other hand, the action is rooted in negative mental qualities such as hatred and selfishness, if the outcome experienced by the doer is negative and unpleasant, and if the recipients of the action also experience undesirable effects from the action or become more hateful and selfish, then that action is unwholesome or unskilful (*akusala*).

It is quite probable that on the empirical level an action may appear to be a mixture of good and bad elements, in spite of the intention and the way it is performed. Thus, an action committed with the best of intentions may not bring the desired result for either the doer or the recipient. Sometimes an action based on negative intentions may produce seemingly positive results (as stealing can produce wealth). Due to lack of knowledge and understanding, people may confuse one set of actions with an unrelated set of results and make wrong conclusions, or simply misjudge them on account of social values and conventions. This can lead to misconceptions about the law of *kamma* and loss of moral consciousness. This is why precepts are necessary in the practice of moral discipline: they provide definite guidelines and help to avoid some of the confusion that empirical observation and social conventions may entail.

Buddhist moral precepts are based on the Dhamma, and they reflect such eternal values as compassion, respect, self-restraint, honesty, and wisdom. These are values that are cherished by all civilizations, and their significance is universally recognized. Moral precepts that are based on such values or directed toward their realization will always be relevant to human society, no matter to what extent it has developed. Moreover, their validity can be empirically tested on the basis of one's own sensitivity and conscience, which are beyond factors of time and place. Killing, for instance, is objectionable when considered from the perspective of oneself being the victim of the action (although when other lives are subjected to the same act, its undesirability may not be felt as strongly). The same is true with regard to stealing, lying, and sexual misconduct. Because Buddhist moral precepts are grounded on these factors, their practicality remains intact even today, and their usefulness is beyond question.

Precepts for lay Buddhists

Observance of the five precepts constitutes the minimum moral obligation of a practicing lay Buddhist. These five precepts enjoin against killing living beings, taking what is not given (or stealing), sexual misconduct, false speech, and use of intoxicating drink or drugs.

The practice of Buddhist moral precepts deeply affects one's personal and social life. The fact that they represent a course of training which one willingly undertakes rather than a set of commandments wilfully imposed by a God or supreme being is likely to have a positive bearing upon one's conscience and awareness. On the personal level, the precepts help one to lead a moral life and to advance further on the spiritual path. Moreover, popular Buddhism believes that the practice of morality contributes to the accumulation of merits that both support one in the present life and ensure happiness and prosperity in the next. On the social level, observing the five precepts helps to promote peaceful coexistence, mutual trust, a cooperative spirit, and general peace and harmony in society. It also helps to maintain an atmosphere which is conducive to social progress and development, as we can see from the practical implications of each precept.

The first precept admonishes against the destruction of life. This is based on the principle of goodwill and respect for the right to life of all living beings. By observing this precept one learns to cultivate loving kindness and compassion. One sees others' suffering as one's own and endeavours to do what one can to help alleviate their problems. Personally, one cultivates love and compassion; socially, one develops an altruistic spirit for the welfare of others.

The second precept, not to take things which are not given, signifies respect for others' rights to possess wealth and property. Observing the second precept, one refrains from earning one's livelihood through wrongful means, such as by stealing or cheating. This precept also implies the cultivation of generosity, which on a personal level helps to free one from attachment and selfishness, and on a social level contributes to friendly cooperation in the community.

The third precept, not to indulge in sexual misconduct, includes rape, adultery, sexual promiscuity, paraphilia, and all forms of sexual aberration. This precept teaches one to respect one's own spouse as well as those of others, and encourages the practice of self-restraint, which is of utmost importance in spiritual training. It is also interpreted by some scholars to mean the abstention from misuse of senses and includes, by extension, non-transgression on things that are dear to others, or abstention from intentionally hurting other's feelings. For example, a young boy may practice this particular precept by refraining from intentionally damaging his sister's dolls. If he does, he may be said to have committed a breach of morality. This precept is intended to instill in us a degree of self-restraint and a sense of social propriety, with particular emphasis on sexuality and sexual behaviour.

The fourth precept, not to tell lies or resort to falsehood, is an important factor in social life and dealings. It concerns respect for truth. A respect for truth is a strong deterrent to inclinations or temptation to commit wrongful actions, while disregard for the same will only serve to encourage evil deeds. The Buddha has said: "There are few evil deeds that a liar is incapable of committing." The practice of the fourth precept, therefore, helps to preserve one's credibility, trustworthiness, and honour.

The last of the five Buddhist moral precepts enjoins against the use of intoxicants. On the personal level, abstention from intoxicants helps to maintain sobriety and a sense of responsibility. Socially, it helps to prevent accidents, such as car accidents, that can easily take place under the influence of intoxicating drink or drugs. Many crimes in society are committed under the influence of these harmful substances. The negative effects they have on spiritual practice are too obvious to require any explanation.

The five precepts

Theravada Buddhism preserves the Buddha's teachings and conducts religious ceremonies mainly in the original Pali language. The five precepts are also recited in Pali, and their meanings are generally known to most Buddhists. In the following the original Pali text is given in italics, and the corresponding English translation is given side by side:

1. *Panatipata veramani sikkhapadam samadiyami*: I observe the precept of abstaining from the destruction of life.
2. *Adinnadana veramani sikkhapadam samadiyami*: I observe the precept of abstaining from taking that which is not given.
3. *Kamesu micchacara veramani sikkhapadam samadiyami*: I observe the precept of abstaining from sexual misconduct.
4. *Musavada veramani sikkhapadam samadiyami*: I observe the precept of abstaining from falsehood.
5. *Suramerayamajjapamadatthana veramani sikkhapadam samadiyami*: I observe the precept of abstaining from intoxicants that cloud the mind and cause carelessness.

The refrain "I observe the precept of abstaining from..." which begins every precept clearly shows that these are not commandments. They are, indeed, moral codes of conduct that lay Buddhists willingly undertake out of clear understanding and conviction that they are good for both themselves and for society.

PRACTICAL APPLICATION OF THE FIVE PRECEPTS

Training is based on the axiomatic assumption that human beings have the potential for development. In order that this development may be realized, a concrete standard is needed by which people may train themselves. The five precepts are meant to fulfil this need.

For example, compassion is a spiritual quality that we all possess to some degree. However, without a conscious and persistent effort to develop it, this important quality may remain rudimentary and weak. By consciously practicing the first precept, we bring this compassion to a higher level of development and come a step closer to the realization of the Dhamma. In the process, our conduct becomes more refined and our mind becomes more sensitive to the problems and suffering of others. By practicing the second precept we not only purify our livelihood but train in generosity and non-attachment. The third precept has a direct connection with the training in sense restraint, which is an essential feature in higher spiritual development. In fact, enlightenment is not possible without mastery over the senses. The fourth precept deals with training in truthfulness and virtuous speech. The objective of this precept is not only the cultivation of respect for truth, but a way of life that is sincere and free from falsehood in every respect. Even the fifth precept, which enjoins against the use of intoxicants, is not merely negative, for the resultant effects that take place in the mind in terms of mental strength and moral integrity are very positive. The observance of this precept is also a natural precursor to the cultivation of mindfulness and wisdom, which are the essence of insight meditation. Each and every precept increases our awareness of how we may skillfully conduct ourselves in body and speech and helps us to see more clearly whether we are improving in this process of self-discipline.

We may summarize the five precepts in relation to the spiritual qualities that they are likely to produce and promote as follows. The first precept helps to promote goodwill, compassion, and kindness. The second can be instrumental in developing generosity, service, altruism, non-attachment, contentment, honesty, and right livelihood. The third precept helps to cultivate self-restraint, mastery over the emotions and senses, renunciation, and control of sensual desire. The fourth precept leads to the development of honesty, reliability, and moral integrity. The fifth precept helps to promote mindfulness, clarity of mind, and wisdom.

Self-reliance and responsibility are important features of the practice of Buddhist morality. Because these precepts are meant to be a course of training, it can hardly be expected that each and every practitioner will be able to follow them without committing the slightest error, any more than it can be expected of a music student not to make a single mistake in the course of his lessons. For people with certain temperaments or occupations, some precepts may appear more difficult to follow than the rest, but that should not be an obstacle to making an attempt to keep the precepts. If one is discouraged from practicing, one need simply consider that these precepts are a course of training; and training, by definition, implies imperfection and a gradual process of development.

However, for those who are new to Buddhism, it may be a good idea to begin with greater emphasis on those precepts that are easier to follow, bearing the others in mind for later development. For instance, the second and the third precepts obviously need to be practiced by virtue of necessity, for they are supported by laws and are in perfect harmony with customs and conventions in all civilized societies. There is, therefore, hardly an excuse for not practicing them. Having dealt with these two precepts in this way, the remaining three present much lighter and less daunting a task. In fact, if we understand the contents and meaning of the five precepts correctly, we may come to feel that it is more natural to observe them than not to.

Moral precepts and livelihood

It is not true to say that fishermen, farmers, or hunters cannot observe the first precept. Like people in other trades and occupations, they may not be able to observe all the precepts all the time or in all circumstances, given their family obligations and livelihood, but they can certainly practice them on special occasions, like holy days, or when they are not actually engaged in their professions. In fact, there may be more opportunities to practice than at first seems possible. We observe the precepts in accordance with our abilities, training by degrees until we are able to make the precepts part and parcel of our lives.

In the time of the Buddha there were people engaged in occupations that involved killing, such as hunters or fishermen. Farmers, too, were not free from killing, although the intention involved might not be as direct. For all of these people the precepts were there to be practiced, and some were better able to do so than others. Each person has the opportunity to practice to the best of his or her abilities until they become more mature and are spiritually ready to give up occupations or trades that involve unwholesome *kamma*.

One difficulty for some people is the use of alcoholic drinks: some feel discouraged from keeping the fifth precept because some of their friends drink or because they have business dealings with people who drink. Peer pressure and business objectives may be an obstacle to the observance of this precept, but this is by no means insurmountable. Most people are reasonable and do understand religious conscience. Sometimes, citing physicians' opinions may add weight to an excuse not to drink, but it is always best to be honest. In any case, a serious Dhamma practitioner should not allow trivial things like this to prevent him or her from trying to keep the precepts. There is always an opportunity to exert oneself if one is earnest in the practice.

Moral precepts and passivity

If one carefully studies the foregoing discussion on the five precepts, one will see that, although the Pali texts are worded in the negative "... abstaining from...", there is the positive commitment "I undertake to observe the precept..." in all of them. Negative expressions do not necessarily represent negative or passive attitudes of mind. Of course, misunderstandings may result from misinterpretations of the Buddhist moral precepts (as they arise in regard to other Pali technical terms like *Nibbana, dukkha, santutthi,* and *anatta*).

From the practical perspective Buddhist moral precepts do contain both positive and negative aspects. However, from the psychological point of view it is important for practitioners to first recognize that which is bad or wrong and which should be abstained from. Abstention from wrong or evil deeds is the most significant step toward real development in spirituality. Strangely enough, it often appears that people are so preoccupied with doing good, they forget the most important duty of refraining from evil. That is why even though one scientific accomplishment after another is being achieved, crime rates are soaring unchecked, and thinking people begin to question the benefits of those accomplishments. In religious circles, devotees passionately try to accumulate more and more merits without ever pausing to reflect whether there are things that should be cleansed from their minds. As long as this negative aspect is not attended to on a practical level, spiritual progress will not come about. On the other hand, consider a society in which people were determined not to do evil and who abstained from that which is bad and wrong; the result of such a 'negative' practice would indeed be most welcome. Even *Nibbana* is often negatively described as "the abandoning and destruction of desire and craving," and "the extinction of desire, the extinction of hatred, and the extinction of delusion," although it is positively the highest good.

Once wrong and evil deeds have been abandoned, it becomes more natural to do good. Since life means movement and action, any human expression which rejects evil is bound to be good and positive. If false speech is given up, whatever is spoken will naturally be truthful. Giving up of falsehood, which is a negative act, therefore constitutes in itself not only a negation, but a positive attitude and commitment. As the Buddha himself has admonished his followers:

"Abandoning false speech, one speaks the truth, becomes dependable, trustworthy, and reliable, and does not mislead the world. Abandoning malicious speech, one does not repeat there what has been heard here, nor does one repeat here what has been heard there, in order to sow the seeds of discord. One reconciles and unites those disunited and promotes closer bonds among friends. Unity is one's delight and joy, unity is one's love, it is the motive behind one's verbal expression. Abandoning harsh speech, one employs a speech which is blameless, pleasant, acceptable, heart-touching, civilized, and agreeable. Abandoning frivolous speech, one uses speech which is appropriate to the occasion, correct, purposeful, and in accordance with the Dhamma-Vinaya. One utters words that are worthy, opportune, reasonable, meaningful, and straightforward."

One important reason why the Buddhist moral precepts are phrased in negative terms is because the negative mode of expression tends to convey clearer and more specific injunctions which can be followed with ease. From a practical point of view, "Do not kill" carries stronger impact and a clearer definition than "Be kind to animals" and can be more conveniently practiced. From experience, however, we will see that anyone who consciously and constantly observes the first precept will naturally develop kindness toward people and animals. The second precept, which says, "Do not take what is not given," covers all forms of wrong livelihood, whether by deception, fraud, bribery or theft. By earnestly observing this precept, one will naturally take a positive step in earning one's livelihood in a righteous way. Through constant awareness and direct control of greed and avarice, which motivate wrong livelihood, one learns to develop generosity, altruism, and selfless service. These and other positive virtues result from the so-called negative actions of observing the moral precepts, clearly demonstrating how the precepts laid down by the Buddha can bear positive results, despite their wording and expression.

Moral dilemmas

The first of the five Buddhist moral precepts is based on the altruistic concept of universal love and compassion. It is not only a way of life and an exercise in personal morality, but also a part of the much larger scheme in spiritual discipline of which purity of body, speech, and mind are indispensable ingredients. As such it makes no exception in its practice, given the lofty ideal to which it is designed to lead. However, in real life situations, we may need a more practical attitude of mind to approach the problem in a more realistic manner.

First of all, we must recognize the fact that destruction of life is a negative act and the volition involved is an unwholesome one. By being honest with ourselves and by impartially contemplating the results that such acts bring, we can realize the wisdom of the first precept and consequently try to abstain from killing in any form. Perfection in the practice comes with spiritual maturity, and until perfection is attained, one needs to be aware of possible imperfections in the practice and try to improve oneself accordingly.

Because perfection in morality requires considerable effort and training, few can achieve it in the beginning. One need not, therefore, feel discouraged, but should learn how progress in the practice can be made through a systematized and graduated process of training. For instance, one may begin by resolving to abandon any killing that is not absolutely necessary. There are people who find pleasure in destroying other creatures, such as those who fish or hunt for sport. This type of killing is quite unnecessary and only demonstrates callousness. Others are engaged in sports which involve pain and suffering to animals and may even cost their lives, such as bull fights, cock fights, and fish fights — all senseless practices designed to satisfy sadistic impulses. One who wishes to train in the Dhamma should avoid having anything to do with this kind of entertainment. One may also resolve to show kindness to other people and animals in an objective and concrete way whenever it is possible to do so. While circumstances may prevent absolute abstention from killing, this may help to refine the mind and develop more sensitivity to the suffering of other beings. Trying to look for an alternative livelihood that does not involve destruction of life is a further step to be considered.

Keeping one's home free of pests or bugs by not creating conditions for their infestation helps reduce the necessity for exterminating them. Ecologically, this is a very commendable practice, since the adverse effects of chemical insecticides on the environment are well known. Prevention is, indeed, better than cure even concerning bugs and beetles. Cleanliness of habitat makes killing in such cases unnecessary. Even in the field of agriculture, insecticide-free farming is becoming increasingly popular and commercially competitive. If people are so inclined and compassion prevails, killing can be greatly avoided even in the real life situations of an ordinary householder with full family obligations and concerns.

In the unlikely event that killing is absolutely inevitable, it may be advisable to note the obvious distinction between killing out of cruelty and killing out of necessity. A person who goes out fishing for pleasure is cruel. While he may love children or make big donations for charitable institutions, as far as spirituality is concerned his mind is not refined enough to be sensitive to the pain and suffering of the poor creatures living in the river. A man who hunts for a living does so because it is necessary to maintain himself and his family. It would seem quite understandable that in the latter case the unwholesome effects would likely be much lighter than the former. The same thing is true in the case of killing for self defense. Killing dangerous animals, vermin, and insects accrues less kammically unwholesome consequences than killing a human being or an animal that serves man (such as a horse, a dog, or an elephant).

Buddhism, capital punishment and war

As a student of Buddhism, one may realize that each person practices Dhamma according to his or her ability and the opportunities that arise. A policeman on duty patrolling a crime-infested street or a soldier at a border outpost surveying suspicious movements inside hostile territory will experience totally different circumstances in spiritual endeavour from a monk sitting peacefully in his cloistered cell. Yet, what they do have in common is the opportunity to perform their duty. Each must therefore understand how the Dhamma can be best practiced, given the situation he is in. All of us are bounded up with certain duties, one way or another. Where policemen and soldiers are concerned, it would be naive to deny that their duties do include the possibility of killing.

It cannot be overemphasized, however, that destruction of life is, from a Buddhist standpoint, never justified. But in discussing the issue under question it is hardly appropriate not to distinguish between spiritual objectives and those of national security and administration. Capital punishment, for instance, is an instrument by which law and order may be effectively maintained for the common good of society, although Buddhism would not advocate that such a measure is conducive to the police officers' spiritual well-being. The principles and purposes on which the police and military institutions were established are as far apart from those on which Buddhist spiritual training was formulated as anything can be. Yet, Buddhism and those secular institutions do coexist now, as they did during the time of the Buddha. Important military chiefs and dignitaries are known to have been the Buddha's most devout followers. One does not, therefore, make the mistake of concluding that a person cannot be a Buddhist, or keep the Buddhist moral precepts for that matter, if he serves in the armed forces or police establishment. As has been said before there are more opportunities to practice the precepts than not to practice; this is true even where the above-mentioned professions are concerned.

Stealing from the rich to feed the poor

Helping the poor is a commendable effort, but stealing from the rich to fulfil that commitment can hardly be justified. If this were made into a standard practice, society would be in turmoil. Rights of possession would be ignored, and stealing would become the accepted norm. Finally, the practice would defeat itself, and thievery would be recognized as a charitable act. This is hardly a desirable state of affairs; it is something not even remotely resembling a moral condition.

One of the distinct features of the Buddhist moral precepts is the universal character in which they may be practiced with benefit by all members of society. For instance, non-stealing (second precept) can be universally observed with desirable results, and the practice will help to promote coexistence, peace, and harmony in society. If this precept were reversed and stealing were made a moral principle, we can immediately see that there would be so much conflict and confusion that society would eventually cease to function. Thus, stealing can never be made a moral act, no matter how ideal and noble the motivation.

Extramarital sex

This is a rather complex issue involving ramifications in emotional, social, and moral fields. The problem is a cause for concern in modern times, especially in the West where materialism has for so long been the philosophy of life.

The third moral precept advises against all forms of sexual misconduct, which include rape, adultery, promiscuity, paraphilia, and sexual perversions. Actually, the Buddhist commentary emphasizes adultery more than anything else, but if we take into account the purpose and intention of the precept, it is clear that the precept is intended to cover all improper behaviour with regard to sex. The broadest interpretation even purports to mean abstention from the misuse of the senses. The expression "misuse of the senses" is somewhat vague. It could refer to any morally unwholesome action committed under the influence of sensual desire or to the inability to control one's own senses. In any case there is no doubt that the third precept aims at promoting, among other things, proper sexual behaviour and a sense of social decency in a human civilization where monogamy is commonly practiced and self-restraint is a cherished moral value.

For one reason or another, many young people in love are not able to enter into married life as early as they wish. While marriage is still some distance in the future, or even an uncertain quantity, these people enter into relationships, of which sex forms a significant part. This happens not only among adults, who must legally answer to their own conduct, but also among teenagers who are still immature, emotionally unstable, and tend to act in irresponsible ways. Peer pressure and altered moral values are an important contributing factor to the escalation of the problem. The trend toward extramarital sex has become so common that it is now virtually taken for granted. Contubernal arrangements are becoming increasingly popular, and marriage is relegated to a place of insignificance, jeopardizing in the process the sanctity of family life.

In the context of these developments, the third precept becomes all the more relevant and meaningful. Unlike killing, which certain circumstances seem to warrant, there is hardly any plausible excuse for sexual promiscuity, except human weaknesses and inability to restrain the sexual urge. However, there is a distinction between sexual promiscuity and sexual relationship based on mutual trust and commitment, even if the latter were a relationship between two single adults. Thus one may begin to practice the third precept by resolving not to be involved in sexual activities without an earnest intention and serious commitment of both parties. This means that sex should not be consummated merely for the sake of sexuality, but should be performed with full understanding within the people involved and with mutual responsibility for its consequences. A certain level of maturity and emotional stability is necessary to ensure a healthy and productive sexual relationship between two partners. With the realization that there is a better and more noble path to follow than promiscuity, one may see the wisdom of self-restraint and the benefit of establishing a more lasting and meaningful relationship which, rather than impeding one's spiritual progress, may enhance it.

Finally, if anything else fails to convince people of the danger and undesirability of sexual promiscuity, perhaps the phenomenal AIDS epidemic will. This may seem beside the point, since moral precepts and moral integrity are matters that concern inner strength, fortitude, and conscientious practice, not fear and trepidation based on extraneous factors. It is, nevertheless, worthwhile to consider the connection between promiscuous behaviour and the AIDS epidemic and realize how strict observance of the third Buddhist moral precept could greatly reduce the risk of infection or spread of this deadly disease. Acceptance of this fact may also lead to an appreciation of the value of morality and moral precepts as laid down by the Buddha, consequently strengthening conviction in the Dhamma practice.

White lies

The practice of the fourth precept aims at inculcating a respect for truth in the mind, implying both one's own obligations as well as the rights of other people to truth. This is one of the most important components in developing sound social relationships, and it makes all documents, contracts, agreements, deeds, and business dealings meaningful. When we resort to falsehood, we not only become dishonest but also show disrespect to the truth. People who tell lies discredit themselves and become untrustworthy.

It is true that sometimes telling lies may prove more profitable than truth, especially from the material point of view. Because such gains are unwholesome and may cause harm in the long run, and because material profits are likely to lead to more falsehood and fabrication, it is imperative that the practice of the fourth precept be duly emphasized. Where a person's reputation and feelings are concerned, discretion should be exercised. Of course, there are instances where silence is more appropriate than speech, and one may choose this as an alternative to prevarication and falsehood.

Motivation is an important element in determining if one is transgressing the fourth precept and whether a given verbal expression constitutes a kammically unwholesome act. For instance, when an event is fictionalized for literary purposes, this may not be regarded as falsehood as such for the intention of the work is obvious and there is no attempt at falsification involved. Another example is the case of an invective, where an abusive expression is used (such as angrily calling someone a dog). This is a case of vituperation rather than fabrication or falsification, although it is, nonetheless, a kammically unwholesome act. Also, there is a clear distinction between expressing untruth with a selfish intention and with a well-meaning motive, as when a concocted story is told for instructional purposes or a white lie is told in order to keep an innocent child out of danger.

These latter two instances are even accepted as illustrations of the employment of skilful means. A story is told of a mother who returns home to find her house on fire. Her little son is playing in the house, unaware that its burning roof could collapse at any moment. He is so engrossed that he pays no attention to his mother, who is now in great distress, being unable to get into the house herself. So she calls out to her child, "Come quickly, my little one, I have some wonderful toys for you. All the toys you ever wanted to have are here!" In this instance the mother is using a skilful means that eventually saves the boy's life. Under certain circumstances, this may be the only alternative, but indiscriminate use of such means may lead to undesirable results. One needs to be judicious, therefore, in the practice of the precepts.

Sometimes speaking the truth may cause more harm than good, especially if it is done with malicious intent. A vindictive neighbour who spreads the scandals about the family next door may be speaking the truth, but she is neither doing anyone a service, nor is she practicing the Dhamma. A spy who sells his nation's sensitive classified information to an enemy may be speaking the truth, but he could cause much harm to his nation's security and jeopardize many innocent lives. The Buddha says, therefore, that one should speak the truth which is useful and conducive to the Dhamma, and should avoid that which is useless and is likely to cause unwholesome *kamma* to oneself and others.

Intoxicants

The fifth precept covers all intoxicants, including narcotics, that alter the state of consciousness and are physiologically addictive. The danger and negative effects of narcotics, such as cocaine and heroin, are too well known to need any further elaboration. Today they represent a serious health and social problem around the world.

Drinking intoxicants is not part of the Buddhist culture, although it seems to have become a widespread phenomenon in modern society. It is true that alcoholic consumption was prevalent before and during the time of the Buddha, but he never approved of the practice. The fact that something is commonly practiced does not necessarily mean that it is good and wholesome. Those who advocate drinking as a factor for promoting friendship forget to take account of the reality that so many friendships have been drowned in those intoxicants. The brawls, strife and unruly behaviour that often follow the consumption of alcoholic beverages represent an unequivocal testimony of the ignoble state to which human beings can be reduced to under the influence of intoxicants. Friendship founded on compassion and mutual understanding is much more desirable than that which is based on alcohol. Social drinking may produce a general euphoric atmosphere among drinkers (and probably a nuisance for nondrinkers), but it is never a necessary condition for interpersonal relationship. Often, people use this as an excuse to get drunk. The high rate of car accidents connected with drunk driving should serve as a strong reminder of the danger and undesirability of alcoholic consumption. On the other hand, it may be mentioned in passing that liquor does contain certain medicinal properties and can be used for medical purposes. Such use, if genuine and under qualified supervision, does not entail transgression of the fifth precept and is not considered a morally unwholesome act.

The most obvious danger of intoxicants is the fact that they tend to distort the sensibilities and deprive people of their self-control and powers of judgment. Under alcoholic influences, a person is likely to act rashly and without due consideration or forethought. Otherwise decent people may even commit murder or rape under the influence of alcohol, or cause all kinds of damage (such as fire, accident, and vandalism) to people or property. The Buddha described addiction to intoxicants as one of the six causes of ruin. It brings about six main disadvantages: loss of wealth, quarrels and strife, a poor state of health (liability to diseases), a source of disgrace, shameless and indecent behaviour, and weakened intelligence and mental faculties.

OTHER PRECEPTS

Occasionally, lay Buddhists may take the opportunity to observe the eight precepts as a means of developing higher virtues and self-control. Of course, these can be practiced as often as one wishes, but the special occasions on which they are normally observed are the holy days, especially the more important ones, the three month period of rains retreat, and special events connected with one's life. Sometimes, a Buddhist may observe them even as a token of gratitude and respect to a deceased relative or on the occasion of a birth anniversary of a monk he reveres. Four of these eight precepts are identical with the five precepts mentioned above. In order, they are as follows:

1. to abstain from the destruction of life
2. to abstain from stealing or taking what is not given
3. to abstain from sexual intercourse (to practice celibacy)
4. to abstain from falsehood
5. to abstain from alcoholic drinks
6. to abstain from partaking of food from afternoon till the following daybreak
7. to abstain from singing and entertainments, from decorating oneself and use of perfumes
8. to abstain from the use of large and luxurious beds.

3

Noble Eightfold Path

The Noble Eightfold Path is one of the principal teachings of the Buddha, who described it as the way leading to the cessation of suffering (*dukkha*) and the achievement of self-awakening. It is used to develop insight into the true nature of phenomena (or reality) and to eradicate greed, hatred, and delusion. The Noble Eightfold Path is the fourth of the Buddha's Four Noble Truths; the first element of the Noble Eightfold Path is, in turn, an understanding of the Four Noble Truths. It is also known as the *Middle Path* or *Middle Way*.

All eight elements of the Path begin with the word "right", which translates the word *samyañc* (in Sanskrit) or *sammâ* (in Pâli). These denote completion, togetherness, and coherence, and can also suggest the senses of "perfect" or "ideal". 'Samma' is also translated as "wholesome", "wise" and "skilful".

In Buddhist symbolism, the Noble Eightfold Path is often represented by means of the dharma wheel (dharmachakra), whose eight spokes represent the eight elements of the path.

INTRODUCTION TO NOBLE EIGHTFOLD PATH

The Noble Eightfold Path is, in the teachings of the Buddha, declared to be the way that leads to the end of *dukkha*, or suffering.

Essentially a practical guide of bringing about ethical and meditative discipline, the Noble Eightfold Path forms the fourth part of the Four Noble Truths, which have informed and driven much of the Buddhist tradition. As the name indicates, there are eight elements in the Noble Eightfold Path, and these are divided into three basic categories as follows:

- Wisdom (Sanskrit: *prajna,* Pali: *panna*)
  1. Right view
  2. Right intention
- Ethical conduct (Sanskrit: *uila,* Pali: *sila*)
  3. Right speech
  4. Right action
  5. Right livelihood
- Mental discipline (Sanskrit and Pali: *samadhi*)
  6. Right effort
  7. Right mindfulness
  8. Right concentration

In all of the elements of the Noble Eightfold Path, the word "right" is a translation of the word *samyanc* (Sanskrit) or *samma* (Pali), which denotes completion, togetherness, and coherence, and which can also carry the sense of "perfect" or "ideal".

Though the path is numbered one through eight, it is generally not considered to be a series of linear steps through which one must progress; rather, as the Buddhist monk and scholar Walpola Rahula points out, the eight elements of the Noble Eightfold Path "are to be developed more or less simultaneously, as far as possible according to the capacity of each individual. They are all linked together and each helps the cultivation of the others".

In Buddhist symbolism, the Noble Eightfold Path is often represented by means of the Dharma wheel (Sanskrit: *dharmacakra,* Pali: *dhammacakka*), whose eight spokes represent the eight elements of the path.

Wisdom (Prajna-Panna)

The "wisdom" subdivision of the Noble Eightfold Path is constituted by those elements that refer primarily to the mental or cognitive aspect of a Buddhist practitioner's practice.

Right View

Right view (*samyag-dicmi-samm-dimmhi*) can also be translated as "right perspective" or "right understanding". This element of the Noble Eightfold Path refers explicitly to the Four Noble Truths of Buddhism, stating that these must be fully understood by the Buddhist practitioner. In the *Mahasatipahana Sutta,* one of the Buddha Uakyamuni's discourses, right understanding is explained directly in terms of the Four Noble Truths:

> *And what, O bhikkhus, is right understanding? To understand suffering, to understand the origination of suffering, to understand extinction of suffering, to understand the path leading to the extinction of suffering; this is called right understanding.*

Additionally, right understanding is sometimes considered to encompass an understanding of the Buddhist idea of the non-permanence, or even non-existence, of the self, an idea known as *anatman* in Sanskrit and *anatta* in Pali. There are two stages for every stage of the eightfold path, a preliminary stage and the higher stages gradually obtained through the journey towards enlightenment. The preliminary stage of Right Views or right understanding is the knowledge of the Four Noble Truths. The higher stage requires more than the comprehension of the Four Noble Truths, it also includes the knowledge and understanding of the not-self doctrine, impermanence, dependent origination, the five aggregates, "karma", rebirth, and so on.

Right Intention

Right intention (*samyak-sackalpa-samm-saekappa*) can also be translated as "right thought", "right resolve", or "right aspiration" or the exertion of our own will to change. This element of the Noble Eightfold Path deals, fundamentally, with the Buddhist practitioner's reasons for practicing Buddhism, and with his or her outlook towards the world. It enjoins renunciation of worldly things and an accordant greater commitment to spiritual matters; good will; and a commitment to non-violence, or *ahias,* towards other living beings. In the *Magga-vibhanga Sutta,* it is simply explained as follows:

> *And what is right thought? Being resolved on renunciation, on freedom from ill will, on harmlessness: This is called right thought.*

Ethical Conduct (*Uila-Sila*)

The "ethical conduct" (Uila) subdivision of the Noble Eightfold Path is considered the cornerstone or foundation upon which unwholesome thoughts and practices end and higher meditative states begin.

In AN 11.2 Cetana Sutta (An Act of Will) Buddha states it is virtue (without clinging to virtue) which gives freedom from remorse, which leads to joy, serenity and subsequent rapturous states of meditation.

It is in the nature of things that freedom from remorse arises in a person endowed with virtue, consummate in virtue.

In Buddhism, this is also one of the Ten Recollections along with the Triple Gem.

> *"There is the case where the disciple of the noble ones recollects his own virtues, thus: '[They are] untorn, unbroken, unspotted, unsplattered, liberating, praised by the wise, untarnished, conducive to concentration.'*

This aspect of the Noble Eightfold Path is the most outward-oriented aspect of the Noble Eightfold Path insofar as it deals directly with a Buddhist practitioner's relationship with other members of his or her society.

Right Speech

Right speech (*samyag-vac-samma-vaca*), as the name implies, deals with the way in which a Buddhist practitioner would best make use of his or her words. In the Pali Canon, this aspect of the Noble Eightfold Path is explained as follows:

> *And what is right speech? Abstaining from lying, abstaining from divisive speech, abstaining from abusive*

speech, abstaining from idle chatter: This, monks, is called right speech.

Other discourses in the Canon elaborate:

"Abandoning false speech, he abstains from false speech. He speaks the truth, holds to the truth, is firm, reliable, no deceiver of the world...."

"Abandoning divisive speech he abstains from divisive speech. What he has heard here he does not tell there to break those people apart from these people here. What he has heard there he does not tell here to break these people apart from those people there. Thus reconciling those who have broken apart or cementing those who are united, he loves concord, delights in concord, enjoys concord, speaks things that create concord...."

"Abandoning abusive speech, he abstains from abusive speech. He speaks words that are soothing to the ear, that are affectionate, that go to the heart, that are polite, appealing and pleasing to people at large....

"Abandoning idle chatter, he abstains from idle chatter. He speaks in season, speaks what is factual, what is in accordance with the goal, the Dhamma, and the Vinaya. He speaks words worth treasuring, seasonable, reasonable, circumscribed, connected with the goal...."

Regarding telling the truth about mundane knowledge, the *Cunda Kammaraputta Sutta* (AN 10.176) ascribes to the Buddha the following elaboration:

"There is the case where a certain person, abandoning false speech, abstains from false speech. When he has been called to a town meeting, a group meeting, a gathering of his relatives, his guild, or of the royalty, if he is asked as a witness, 'Come & tell, good man, what you know': If he doesn't know, he says, 'I don't know.' If he does know, he says, 'I know.' If he hasn't seen, he says, 'I haven't seen.' If he has seen, he says, 'I have seen.' Thus he doesn't consciously tell a lie for his own sake, for the sake of another, or for the sake of any

reward. Abandoning false speech, he abstains from false speech."

Regarding telling the truth about spiritual knowledge, the *Canki Sutta* (MN 95) ascribes to the Buddha the following cautionary statements:

"If a person has conviction, his statement, 'This is my conviction,' safeguards the truth. But he doesn't yet come to the definite conclusion that 'Only this is true; anything else is worthless.'..."

"If a person likes something... holds an unbroken tradition... has something reasoned through analogy... has something he agrees to, having pondered views, his statement, 'This is what I agree to, having pondered views,' safeguards the truth. But he doesn't yet come to the definite conclusion that 'Only this is true; anything else is worthless.'..."

Walpola Rahula glosses this path factor by stating that not engaging in such "forms of wrong and harmful speech" ultimately means that "one naturally has to speak the truth, has to use words that are friendly and benevolent, pleasant and gentle, meaningful and useful".

Right Action

Right action (*samyak-karmanta-samma-kammanta*) can also be translated as "right conduct" and, as the name implies, deals with the proper way in which a Buddhist practitioner would act in his or her daily life. In the *Magga-vibhanga Sutta,* this aspect of the Noble Eightfold Path is explained as follows:

And what is right action? Abstaining from taking life, from stealing, & from illicit sex. This is called right action.

The *Cunda Kammaraputta Sutta* (AN 10.176) expands:

"And how is one made pure in three ways by bodily action?

"There is the case where a certain person, abandoning

the taking of life, abstains from the taking of life. He dwells with his rod laid down, his knife laid down, scrupulous, merciful, compassionate for the welfare of all living beings."

"Abandoning the taking of what is not given, he abstains from taking what is not given. He does not take, in the manner of a thief, things in a village or a wilderness that belong to others and have not been given by them."

"Abandoning sensual misconduct, he abstains from sensual misconduct. He does not get sexually involved with those who are protected by their mothers, their fathers, their brothers, their sisters, their relatives, or their Dhamma; those with husbands, those who entail punishments, or even those crowned with flowers by another man."

Together with the idea of *ahias* and right speech, right action constitutes the Five Precepts (Sanskrit: *pancauila,* Pali: *pancasila*), which form the fundamental ethical code undertaken by lay followers of Buddhism, and which are as follows:

1. To refrain from destroying living beings.
2. To refrain from stealing.
3. To refrain from sexual misconduct (adultery, rape, etc.).
4. To refrain from false speech (lying).
5. To refrain from intoxicants, which lead to heedlessness.

Right Livelihood

Right livelihood (*samyag-ajiva-samma-ajiva*) is based around the concept of *ahias,* or harmlessness, and essentially states that Buddhist practitioners ought not to engage in trades or occupations which, either directly or indirectly, result in harm to other living beings or systems. Such occupations include "trading in arms and lethal weapons, intoxicating drinks, poisons, killing animals, [and] cheating", among others. "Business in human beings"—such as slave trading and prostitution—is also forbidden, as are several other dishonest means of gaining wealth, such as "scheming, persuading, hinting, belittling, [and] pursuing gain with gain".

Mental Discipline (*Samadhi*)

The "mental discipline" subdivision of the Noble Eightfold Path is constituted by those elements that deal with how a Buddhist practitioner can best go about shaping his or her outlook towards the world.

Right Effort

Right effort (*samyag-vyayama-samma-vayama*) can also be translated as "right endeavour", and involves the Buddhist practitioner's continuous effort to, essentially, keep his or her mind free of thoughts that might impair his or her ability to realize or put into practice the other elements of the Noble Eightfold Path; for example, wishing ill towards another living being would contradict the injunction—contained in the "Right thought" element—to have good will towards others, and the "Right effort" element refers to the process of attempting to root out such an ill wish and replace it with a good wish.

And what, monks, is right effort?

(i) There is the case where a monk generates desire, endeavours, activates persistence, upholds & exerts his intent for the sake of the non-arising of evil, unskilful qualities that have not yet arisen.

(ii) He generates desire, endeavours, activates persistence, upholds & exerts his intent for the sake of the abandonment of evil, unskilful qualities that have arisen.

(iii) He generates desire, endeavours, activates persistence, upholds & exerts his intent for the sake of the arising of skilful qualities that have not yet arisen.

(iv) He generates desire, endeavours, activates persistence, upholds & exerts his intent for the maintenance, non-confusion, increase, plenitude, development, & culmination of skilful qualities that have arisen: This, monks, is called right effort." — SN 45.8

By making right effort, a Buddhist practitioner is considered to be engaging in an effort that is wholesome in terms of *karma;* that is, in terms of that effort's ultimate consequences to the practitioner. The four phases of Right Effort: (in simple English)

(1) make effort to prevent the evil that has not yet come.
(2) make effort to destroy the evil that has come.
(3) make effort to produce the good that has not yet come.
(4) make effort to cultivate the good that has come.

Right Mindfulness

Right mindfulness (*samyak-smrti-samma-sati),* also translated as "right memory", together with right concentration, is concerned broadly with the practice of Buddhist meditation. Roughly speaking, "mindfulness" refers to the practice of keeping the mind alert to phenomena as they are affecting the body and mind. In the *Magga-vibhanga Sutta,* this aspect of the Noble Eightfold Path is explained as follows:

And what, monks, is right mindfulness?

(i) There is the case where a monk remains focused on (his/her) *body* in and of itself... ardent, aware, and mindful... having already put aside worldly desire and aversion.
(ii) (He/she) remains focused on *feelings* in and of themselves... ardent, aware, and mindful... having already put aside worldly desire and aversion.
(iii) (He/she) remains focused on *the mind* in and of itself... ardent, aware, and mindful... having already put aside worldly desire and aversion.
(iv) (He/she) remains focused on *mental qualities* in and of themselves... ardent, aware, and mindful... having already put aside worldly desire and aversion.

This, monks, is called right mindfulness.

This is also an important aspect of what constitutes the concept of "self" or Buddhist concept of Atman:

"And how, Ananda, is a bhikkhu an island unto himself, a refuge unto himself, seeking no external refuge; with the Dhamma as his island, the Dhamma as his refuge, seeking no other refuge?

"When he dwells contemplating the body in the body, earnestly, clearly comprehending, and mindfully, after having overcome desire and sorrow in regard to the world; when he dwells contemplating feelings in feelings, the mind in the mind, and mental objects in mental objects, earnestly, clearly comprehending, and mindfully, after having overcome desire and sorrow in regard to the world, then, truly, he is an island unto himself, a refuge unto himself, seeking no external refuge; having the Dhamma as his island, the Dhamma as his refuge, seeking no other refuge. (DN 16 Maha-parinibbana Sutta)

Bhikkhu Bodhi, a monk of the Theravadin tradition, further glosses the concept of mindfulness as follows:

> *The mind is deliberately kept at the level of* bare attention, *a detached observation of what is happening within us and around us in the present moment. In the practice of right mindfulness the mind is trained to remain in the present, open, quiet, and alert, contemplating the present event. All judgments and interpretations have to be suspended, or if they occur, just registered and dropped.*

Right Concentration

Right concentration (*samyak-samadhi-samma-samadhi*), together with right mindfulness, is concerned broadly with the practice of Buddhist meditation.

And what, monks, is right concentration?

(i) Quite withdrawn from sensuality, withdrawn from unwholesome states, a monk enters in the first jhana: rapture and pleasure born from detachment, accompanied by movement of the mind onto the object and retention of the mind on the object.

(ii) With the stilling of directed thought and evaluation, (he/she) enters and remains in the second jhana: rapture and pleasure born of concentration; fixed single-pointed awareness free from movement of the mind onto the object and retention of the mind on the object; assurance.

(iii) With the fading of rapture, (he/she) remains in equanimity, mindful and fully aware, and physically sensitive of pleasure. (He/She) enters and remains in the third jhana which the Noble Ones declare to be

"Equanimous and mindful, (he/she) has a pleasurable abiding."

(iv) With the abandoning of pleasure and pain...as with the earlier disappearance of elation and distress...(he/she) enters and remains in the fourth jhana: purity of equanimity and mindfulness, neither in pleasure nor in pain.

This, monks, is called right concentration.

The Ninth and Tenth Elements

In the *Great Forty Sutra* (Mahacattarisaka Sutta), which appears in the Pali Canon, the Buddha explains that cultivation of the Eightfold Path leads to the development of two further stages once enlightenment has been reached. These also fall under the category of panna and are *Right Knowledge* (sammnga) and *Right Liberation* (or *Right Release*; sammavimutti). Some consider *Right Association* as an implicit ninth aspect of the Path. To further the foregoing, Bucknell & Martin (1986: p.6) state:

> *The Eightfold Path as described gives an impression of orderliness and completeness. However, closer study of the texts indicates that it is not after all a complete account of Gautama's course of practice. A number of suttas describe a Tenfold Path. This differs from the Eightfold Path in having two further stages following right concentration, namely right insight or knowledge or wisdom (sammnga) and right liberation (samma vimutti). These two extra stages are nowhere described, nor is any explanation given for their frequent omission. The tenth state, right liberation, is presumably to be equated with the final goal, nirvgna. However, the ninth stage, right insight, which appears from its position in the list to be of crucial importance, remains unaccounted for.*

The Noble Eightfold Path and Cognitive Psychology

From the standpoint of modern cognitive psychology, the Noble Eightfold Path can be seen as rooted in what is called cognitive dissonance, which is the perception of incompatibility between two cognitions. In the essay "Buddhism Meets Western Science", Gay Watson explains this dissonance as it relates to Buddhist teaching:

> *Buddhism has always been concerned with feelings, emotions, sensations, and cognition. The Buddha points both to cognitive and emotional causes of suffering. The emotional cause is desire and its negative opposite, aversion. The cognitive cause is ignorance of the way things truly occur, or of three marks of existence: that all things are unsatisfactory, impermanent, and without essential self.*

The Noble Eightfold Path is, from this psychological viewpoint, an attempt to resolve this dissonance by changing patterns of thought and behaviour. It is for this reason that the first element of the path is right understanding (*samm-dimmhi*), which is how one's mind views the world. Under the wisdom (*panna*) subdivision of the Noble Eightfold Path, this worldview is intimately connected with the second element, right thought (*samm-saekappa*), which concerns the patterns of thought and intention that controls one's actions. These elements can be seen at work, for example, in the opening verses of the *Dhammapada*:

> *Preceded by perception are mental states,*
> *For them is perception supreme,*
> *From perception have they sprung.*
> *If, with perception polluted, one speaks or acts,*
> *Thence suffering follows*
> *As a wheel the draught ox's foot.*
> *Preceded by perception are mental states,*
> *For them is perception supreme,*
> *From perception have they sprung.*
> *If, with tranquil perception, one speaks or acts,*
> *Thence ease follows*
> *As a shadow that never departs.*

Thus, by altering one's distorted worldview, bringing out "tranquil perception" in the place of "perception polluted", one is able to ease suffering. Watson points this out from a psychological standpoint:

> *Research has shown that repeated action, learning, and memory can actually change the nervous system physically, altering both synaptic strength and connections. Such changes may be brought about by cultivated change in emotion and action; they will, in turn, change subsequent experience.*

THE EIGHTFOLD PATH AND THE PRACTICE OF DHAMMA

Because the roots of ignorance are so intimately entwined with the fabric of the psyche, the unawakened mind is capable of deceiving itself with breathtaking ingenuity. The solution therefore requires more than simply being kind, loving, and mindful in the present moment. The practitioner must equip him-or herself with the expertise to use a range of tools to outwit, outlast, and eventually uproot the mind's unskilful tendencies. For example, the practice of generosity *(dana)* erodes the heart's habitual tendencies towards craving and teaches valuable lessons about the motivations behind, and the results of, skilful action. The practice of virtue *(sila)* guards one against straying wildly off-course and into harm's way. The cultivation of goodwill *(metta)* helps to undermine anger's seductive grasp. The ten recollections offer ways to alleviate doubt, bear physical pain with composure, maintain a healthy sense of self-respect, overcome laziness and complacency, and restrain oneself from unbridled lust. And there are many more skills to learn. The good qualities that emerge and mature from these practices not only smooth the way for the journey to Nibbana; over time they have the effect of transforming the practitioner into a more generous, loving, compassionate, peaceful, and clear-headed member of society. The individual's sincere pursuit of Awakening is thus a priceless and timely gift to a world in desperate need of help.

Discernment (panna)

The Eightfold Path is best understood as a collection of personal qualities to be developed, rather than as a sequence of steps along a linear path. The development of right view and right resolve (the factors classically identified with wisdom and discernment) facilitates the development of right speech, action, and livelihood (the factors identified with virtue). As virtue develops so do the factors identified with concentration (right effort, mindfulness, and concentration). Likewise, as concentration matures, discernment evolves to a still deeper level. And so the process unfolds: development of one factor fosters development of the next, lifting the practitioner in an upward spiral of spiritual maturity that eventually culminates in Awakening. The long journey to Awakening begins in earnest with the first tentative stirrings of right view — the discernment by which one recognizes the validity of the four Noble Truths and the principle of kamma. One begins to see that one's future well-being is neither predestined by fate, nor left to the whims of a divine being or random chance. The responsibility for one's happiness rests squarely on one's own shoulders. Seeing this, one's spiritual aims become suddenly clear: to relinquish the habitual unskilful tendencies of the mind in favour of skilful ones. As this right resolve grows stronger, so does the heartfelt desire to live a morally upright life, to choose one's actions with care. At this point many followers make the inward commitment to take the Buddha's teachings to heart, to become "Buddhist" through the act of taking refuge in the Triple Gem: the Buddha (both the historical Buddha and one's own innate potential for Awakening), the Dhamma (both the Buddha's teachings and the ultimate Truth towards which they point), and the Sangha (both the unbroken monastic lineage that has preserved the teachings since the Buddha's day, and all those who have achieved at least some degree of Awakening). With one's feet thus planted on solid ground, and with the help of an admirable friend or teacher *(kalyanamitta)* to guide the way, one is now well-equipped to proceed down the Path, following in the footsteps left by the Buddha himself.

Virtue (sila)

Right view and right resolve continue to mature through the development of the path factors associated with *sila,* or virtue — namely, right speech, right action, and right livelihood. These are condensed into a very practical form in the five precepts, the basic code of ethical conduct to which every practicing Buddhist subscribes: refraining from killing, stealing, sexual misconduct, lying, and using intoxicants. Even the monks' complex code of 227 rules and the nuns' 311 ultimately have these five basic precepts at their core.

Concentration (samadhi)

Having gained a foothold in the purification of one's outward behaviour through the practice of *sila,* the essential groundwork has been laid for delving into the most subtle and transformative aspect of the path: meditation and the development of *samadhi,* or concentration. This is spelled out in detail in the final three path factors: right effort, by which one learns how to favour skilful qualities of mind over unskilful ones; right mindfulness, by which one learns to keep one's attention continually grounded in the present moment of experience; and right concentration, by which one learns to immerse the mind so thoroughly and unwaveringly in its meditation object that it enters *jhana,* a series of progressively deeper states of mental and physical tranquillity.

Right mindfulness and right concentration are developed in tandem through *satipatthana* ("frames of reference" or "foundations of mindfulness"), a systematic approach to meditation practice that embraces a wide range of skills and techniques. Of these practices, mindfulness of the body (especially mindfulness of breathing) is particularly effective at bringing into balance the twin qualities of tranquillity *(samatha)* and insight *(vipassana),* or clear-seeing. Through persistent practice, the meditator becomes more adept at bringing the combined powers of *samatha-vipassana* to bear in an exploration of the fundamental nature of mind and body. As the meditator masters the ability to frame his immediate experience in terms of *anicca* (inconstancy), *dukkha,* and *anatta* (not-self), even the subtlest manifestations of these three characteristics of experience are brought into exquisitely sharp focus. At the same time, the root cause of *dukkha* — craving— is relentlessly exposed to the light of awareness. Eventually craving is left with no place to hide, the entire karmic process that fabricates *dukkha* unravels, the eightfold path reaches its noble climax, and the meditator gains, at long last, his or her first unmistakable glimpse of the Unconditioned — Nibbana.

Awakening

This first enlightenment experience, known as stream-entry *(sotapatti),* is the first of four progressive stages of Awakening, each of which entails the irreversible shedding or weakening of several fetters *(samyojana),* the manifestations of ignorance that bind a person to the cycle of birth and death. Stream-entry marks an unprecedented and radical turning point both in the practitioner's current life and in the entirety of his or her long journey in samsara. For it is at this point that any lingering doubts about the truth of the Buddha's teachings disappear; it is at this point that any belief in the purifying efficacy of rites and rituals evaporates; and it is at this point that the long-cherished notion of an abiding personal "self" falls away. The stream-enterer is said to be assured of no more than seven future rebirths (all of them favorable) before eventually attaining full Awakening. But full Awakening is still a long way off. As the practitioner presses on with renewed diligence, he or she passes through two more significant landmarks: once-returning *(sakadagati),* which is accompanied by the weakening of the fetters of sensual desire and ill-will, and non-returning *(agati),* in which these two fetters are uprooted altogether. The final stage of Awakening— *arahatta* — occurs when even the most refined and subtle levels of craving and conceit are irrevocably extinguished. At this point the practitioner — now an *arahant,* or "worthy one" — arrives at the end-point of the Buddha's teaching. With ignorance, suffering, stress, and rebirth having all come to their end, the arahant at last can utter the victory cry first proclaimed by the Buddha upon his Awakening:

"Birth is ended, the holy life fulfilled, the task done! There is nothing further for the sake of this world." [MN 36]

The arahant lives out the remainder of his or her life inwardly enjoying the bliss of Nibbana, secure at last from the possibility of any future rebirth. When the arahant's aeons-long trail of past kamma eventually unwinds to its end, the arahant dies and he or she enters into *parinibbana* — total Unbinding. Although language utterly fails at describing this extraordinary event, the Buddha likened it to what happens when a fire finally burns up all its fuel.

ORIGIN

According to discourses found in both the Theravada school's Pali canon, and some of the Âgamasin the Chinese Buddhist canon, the Noble Eightfold Path was rediscovered by Gautama Buddhaduring his quest for enlightenment. The scriptures describe an ancient path which has been followed and practiced by all the previous Buddhas. The Noble Eightfold Path is a practice said to lead its practitioner toward self-awakening and liberation. The path was taught by the Buddha to his disciples so that they, too, could follow it.

In the same way I saw an ancient path, an ancient road, traveled by the Rightly Self-awakened Ones of former times. And what is that ancient path, that ancient road, traveled by the Rightly Self-awakened Ones of former times? Just this noble eightfold path: right view, right aspiration, right speech, right action, right livelihood, right effort, right mindfulness, right concentration...I followed that path. Following it, I came to direct knowledge of aging & death, direct knowledge of the origination of aging & death, direct knowledge of the cessation of aging & death, direct knowledge of the path leading to the cessation of aging & death...Knowing that directly, I have revealed it to monks, nuns, male lay followers & female lay followers...—Nagara Sutta

The practice of the Noble Eightfold Path varies from one Buddhist school to another. Depending on the school, it may be practiced as a whole, only in part, or it may have been modified. Each Buddhist lineage implements the path in the manner most conducive to the development of the students drawn to that lineage.

Additionally, some sources give alternate definitions for the Noble Eightfold Path. The Ekottara Âgama in particular contains variant teachings of basic doctrines such as the Noble Eightfold Path, which are different from those found in the Pali Canon.

Threefold division

This presentation is called the "Three Higher Trainings" in Mahâyâna Buddhism: higher moral discipline, higher concentration and higher wisdom. "Higher" here refers to the fact that these trainings that lead to liberation and enlightenment are engaged in with the motivation ofrenunciation or bodhicitta.

Practice

According to the *bhikkhu* (monk) and scholar Walpola Rahula, the divisions of the noble eightfold path "are to be developed more or less simultaneously, as far as possible according to the capacity of each individual. They are all linked together and each helps the cultivation of the others." Bhikkhu Bodhi explains that "with a certain degree of progress all eight factors can be present simultaneously, each supporting the others. However, until that point is reached, some sequence in the unfolding of the path is inevitable."

According to the discourses in the Pali and Chinese canons, right view, right intention, right speech, right action, right livelihood, right effort, and right mindfulness are used as the support and requisite conditions for the practice of right concentration. Understanding of the right view is the preliminary role, and is also the forerunner of the entire Noble Eightfold Path. The practitioner should first try to understand the concepts of right view. Once right view has been understood, it will inspire and encourage the arising of right intention within the practitioner. Right intention will lead to the arising of right speech. Right speech will lead to the arising of right action. Right action will lead to the arising of right livelihood. Right livelihood will lead to the arising of right effort. Right effort will lead to the arising of right mindfulness. The practitioner must make the right effort to abandon the wrong view and to enter into the right view. Right mindfulness is used to constantly remain in the right view. This will help the practitioner restrain greed, hatred and delusion.

Once these support and requisite conditions have been established, a practitioner can then practice right concentration more easily. During the practice of right concentration, one will need to use right effort and right mindfulness to aid concentration practice. In the state of concentration, one will need to investigate and verify his or her understanding of right view. This will then result in the arising of right knowledge, which will eliminate greed, hatred and delusion. The last and final factor to arise is right liberation.

Wisdom

"Wisdom" (*prajñâ / paññâ*), sometimes translated as "discernment" at its preparatory role, provides the sense of direction with its conceptual understanding of reality. It is designed to awaken the faculty of penetrative understanding to see things as they really are. At a later stage, when the mind has been refined by training in moral discipline and concentration, and with the gradual arising of right knowledge, it will arrive at a superior right view and right intention.

Right view

Right view (*samyag-d[cmi / sammâ-dimmhi*) can also be translated as "right perspective", "right outlook" or "right understanding". It is the right way of looking at life, nature, and the world as they really are for us. It is to understand how our reality works. It acts as the reasoning with which someone starts practicing the path. It explains the reasons for our human existence, suffering, sickness, aging, death, the existence of greed, hatred, and delusion. Right view gives direction and efficacy to the other seven path factors. It begins with concepts and propositional knowledge, but through the practice of right concentration, it gradually becomes transmuted into wisdom, which can eradicate the fetters of the mind. An understanding of right view will inspire the person to lead a virtuous life in line with right view. In the Pâli and Chinese canons, it is explained thus:

> And what is right view? Knowledge with reference to suffering, knowledge with reference to the origination of suffering, knowledge with reference to the cessation of suffering, knowledge with reference to the way of practice leading to the cessation of suffering: This is called right view.

There are two types of right view:

1. View with taints: this view is mundane. Having this type of view will bring merit and will support the favourable existence of the sentient being in the realm of samsara.
2. View without taints: this view is supramundane. It is a factor of the path and will lead the holder of this view toward self-awakening and liberation from the realm of samsara.

Right view has many facets; its elementary form is suitable for lay followers, while the other form, which requires deeper understanding, is suitable for monastics. Usually, it involves understanding the following reality:

1. Moral law of karma: Every action (by way of body, speech, and mind) will have karmic results (a.k.a. reaction). Wholesome and unwholesome actions will produce results and effects that correspond with the nature of that action. It is the right view about the moral process of the world.
2. The three characteristics: everything that arises will cease (impermanence). Mental and body phenomena are impermanent, source of suffering and not-self.
3. Suffering: Birth, aging, sickness, death, sorrow, lamentation, pain, grief, distress, and despair are suffering. Not being able to obtain what one wants is

> also suffering. The arising of craving is the proximate cause of the arising of suffering and the cessation of craving is the proximate cause of the cessation of the suffering. The quality of ignorance is the root cause of the arising of suffering, and the elimination of this quality is the root cause of the cessation of suffering. The way leading to the cessation of suffering is the noble eightfold path. This type of right view is explained in terms of Four Noble Truths.

Right view for monastics is explained in detail in the *Sammâdimmhi Sutta* ("Right View Discourse"), in which Ven. Sariputta instructs that right view can alternately be attained by the thorough understanding of the unwholesome and the wholesome, the four nutriments, thetwelve *nidanas* or the three taints. "Wrong view" arising from ignorance (*avijja*), is the precondition for wrong intention, wrong speech, wrong action, wrong livelihood, wrong effort, wrong mindfulness and wrong concentration. The practitioner should use right effort to abandon the wrong view and to enter into right view. Right mindfulness is used to constantly remain in right view.

The purpose of right view is to clear one's path of the majority of confusion, misunderstanding, and deluded thinking. It is a means to gain right understanding of reality. Right view should be held with a flexible, open mind, without clinging to that view as a dogmatic position. In this way, right view becomes a route to liberation rather than an obstacle.

Right intention

Right intention (*samyak-saCkalpa/sammâ sankappa*) can also be known as "right thought", "right resolve", "right conception", "right aspiration" or "the exertion of our own will to change". In this factor, the practitioner should constantly aspire to rid themselves of whatever qualities they know to be wrong and immoral. Correct understanding of right view will help the practitioner to discern the differences between right intention and wrong intention. In the Chinese and Pali Canon, it is explained thus:

And what is right resolve? Being resolved on renunciation, on freedom from ill will, on harmlessness: This is called right resolve. It means the renunciation of the worldly things and an accordant greater commitment to the spiritual path; good will; and a commitment to non-violence, or harmlessness, towards other living beings.

Ethical conduct

For the mind to be unified in concentration, it is necessary to refrain from unwholesome deeds of body and speech to prevent the faculties of bodily action and speech from becoming tools of the defilements. Ethical conduct (*Úîla / Sîla*) is used primarily to facilitate mental purification.

Right speech

Right speech (*samyag-vâc / sammâ-vâcâ*), deals with the way in which a Buddhist practitioner would best make use of their words. In the Pali Canon, it is explained thus:

And what is right speech? Abstaining from lying, from divisive speech, from abusive speech, and from idle chatter: This is called right speech.

The *Samaññaphala Sutta, Kevatta Sutta* and *Cunda Kammaraputta Sutta* elaborate:

Abandoning false speech... He speaks the truth, holds to the truth, is firm, reliable, no deceiver of the world...

Abandoning divisive speech... What he has heard here he does not tell there to break those people apart from these people here...Thus reconciling those who have broken apart or cementing those who are united, he loves concord, delights in concord, enjoys concord, speaks things that create concord...

Abandoning abusive speech... He speaks words that are soothing to the ear, that are affectionate, that go to the heart, that are polite, appealing and pleasing to people at large...

Abandoning idle chatter... He speaks in season, speaks what is factual, what is in accordance with the goal, the Dhamma, and the Vinaya. He speaks words worth treasuring, seasonable, reasonable, circumscribed, connected with the goal...

The *Abhaya Sutta* elaborates:

In the case of words that the Tathagata knows to be unfactual, untrue, unbeneficial, unendearing and disagreeable to others, he does not say them.

In the case of words that the Tathagata knows to be factual, true, yet unbeneficial, unendearing and disagreeable to others, he does not say them.

In the case of words that the Tathagata knows to be factual, true, beneficial, yet unendearing and disagreeable to others, he has a sense of the proper time for saying them.

In the case of words that the Tathagata knows to be unfactual, untrue, unbeneficial, yet endearing and agreeable to others, he does not say them.

In the case of words that the Tathagata knows to be factual, true, but unbeneficial, yet endearing and agreeable to others, he does not say them.

In the case of words that the Tathagata knows to be factual, true, beneficial, and endearing and agreeable to others, he has a sense of the proper time for saying them. Why is that? Because the Tathagata has sympathy for living beings.

In every case, if it is not true, beneficial nor timely, one is not to say it. The Buddha followed this, for example, when asked questions of a purely *meta*physical nature, unrelated to the goal, path or discipline that he taught. When asked a question such as "Is the universe eternal?", the Buddha dismissed the topic with the response: "It does not further." (or: "The personal possibilities (goals) assigned you are not furthered by an answer to an ultimate question about the universe's fate.")

Right action

Right action (*samyak-karmânta / sammâ-kammanta*) can also be translated as "right conduct". As such, the practitioner should train oneself to be morally upright in one's activities, not acting in ways that would be corrupt or bring harm to oneself or to others. In the Chinese and Pali Canon, it is explained as:

And what is right action? Abstaining from taking life, from stealing, and from illicit sex [or sexual misconduct]. This is called right action. —Saccavibhanga Sutta

And what, monks, is right action? Abstaining from taking life, abstaining from stealing, abstaining from unchastity: This, monks, is called right action. —Magga-vibhanga Sutta

For the lay follower, the *Cunda Kammaraputta Sutta* elaborates:

And how is one made pure in three ways by bodily action? There is the case where a certain person, abandoning the taking of life, abstains from the taking of life. He dwells with his... knife laid down, scrupulous, merciful, compassionate for the welfare of all living beings. Abandoning the taking of what is not given, he abstains from taking what is not given. He does not take, in the manner of a thief, things in a village or a wilderness that belong to others and have not been given by them. Abandoning sensual misconduct, he abstains from sensual misconduct. He does not get sexually involved with those who are protected by their mothers, their fathers, their brothers, their sisters, their relatives, or their Dhamma; those with husbands, those who entail punishments, or even those crowned with flowers by another man. This is how one is made pure in three ways by bodily action.

For the monastic, the *Samaññaphala Sutta* adds:

Abandoning uncelibacy, he lives a celibate life, aloof, refraining from the sexual act that is the villager's way.

Right livelihood

Right livelihood (*samyag-âjîva / sammâ-âjîva*). This means that practitioners ought not to engage in trades or occupations which, either directly or indirectly, result in harm for other living beings. In the Chinese and Pali Canon, it is explained thus: And what is right livelihood? There is the case where a disciple of the noble ones, having abandoned dishonest livelihood, keeps his life going with right livelihood: This is called right livelihood. More concretely today interpretations include "work and career need to be integrated into life as a

Buddhist," it is also an ethical livelihood, "wealth obtained through rightful means" (Bhikku Basnagoda Rahula) - that means being honest and ethical in business dealings, not to cheat, lie or steal. As people are spending most of their time at work, it's important to assess how our work affects our mind and heart. So important questions include "How can work become meaningful? How can it be a support, not a hindrance, to spiritual practice — a place to deepen our awareness and kindness?"

The five types of businesses that should not be undertaken:

1. Business in weapons: trading in all kinds of weapons and instruments for killing.
2. Business in human beings: slave trading, prostitution, or the buying and selling of children or adults.
3. Business in meat: "meat" refers to the bodies of beings after they are killed. This includes breeding animals for slaughter.
4. Business in intoxicants: manufacturing or selling intoxicating drinks or addictive drugs.
5. Business in poison: producing or trading in any kind of poison or a toxic product designed to kill.

CONCENTRATION

Concentration ("samadhi") is achieved through concentrating the attention on a single meditation object. This brings the calm and collectedness needed to develop true wisdom by direct experience.

Right effort

Right effort (*samyag-vyâyâma / sammâ-vâyâma*) can also be translated as "right endeavour" or "right diligence". In this factor, the practitioners should make a persisting effort to abandon all the wrong and harmful thoughts, words, and deeds. The practitioner should instead be persisting in giving rise to what would be good and useful to themselves and others in their thoughts, words, and deeds, without a thought for the difficulty or weariness involved. In both the Chinese and the

Pali Canon, it is explained thus: And what, monks, is right effort?

(i) There is the case where a monk generates desire, endeavours, activates persistence, upholds and exerts his intent for the sake of the non-arising of evil, unskilful qualities that have not yet arisen.

(ii) He generates desire, endeavours, activates persistence, upholds and exerts his intent for the sake of the abandonment of evil, unskilful qualities that have arisen.

(iii) He generates desire, endeavours, activates persistence, upholds and exerts his intent for the sake of the arising of skilful qualities that have not yet arisen.

(iv) He generates desire, endeavours, activates persistence, upholds and exerts his intent for the maintenance, non-confusion, increase, plenitude, development, and culmination of skilful qualities that have arisen:

This, monks, is called right effort.

Although the above instruction is given to the male monastic order, it is also meant for the female monastic order and can be practiced by lay followers of both genders.

The above four phases of right effort mean to:

1. Prevent the unwholesome that has not yet arisen in oneself.
2. Let go of the unwholesome that has arisen in oneself.
3. Bring up the wholesome that has not yet arisen in oneself.
4. Maintain the wholesome that has arisen in oneself.

Right mindfulness

Right mindfulness (*samyak-sm[ti / sammâ-sati*), also translated as "right memory", "right awareness" or "right attention". Here, practitioners should constantly keep their minds alert to phenomena that affect the body and mind. They should be mindful and deliberate, making sure not to act or speak due to inattention or forgetfulness. In the Pali Canon, it is explained thus:

And what, monks, is right mindfulness?

(i) There is the case where a monk remains focused on the body in and of itself—ardent, aware, and mindful—putting away greed and distress with reference to the world.

(ii) He remains focused on feelings in and of themselves—ardent, aware, and mindful—putting away greed and distress with reference to the world.

(iii) He remains focused on the mind in and of itself—ardent, aware, and mindful—putting away greed and distress with reference to the world.

(iv) He remains focused on mental qualities (*dhammesu*) in and of themselves—ardent, aware, and mindful—putting away greed and distress with reference to the world.

This, monks, is called right mindfulness.

Although the above instruction is given to the male monastic order, it is also meant for the female monastic order and can be practiced by lay followers from both genders.

Bhikkhu Bodhi, a monk of the Theravada tradition, further explains the concept of mindfulness as follows:

The mind is deliberately kept at the level of *bare attention*, a detached observation of what is happening within us and around us in the present moment. In the practice of right mindfulness the mind is trained to remain in the present, open, quiet, and alert, contemplating the present event. All judgments and interpretations have to be suspended, or if they occur, just registered and dropped. The Maha Satipatthana Sutta also teaches that by mindfully observing these phenomena, we begin to discern its arising and subsiding and the Three Characteristics of Dharma in direct experience, which leads to the arising of insight and the qualities of dispassion, non-clinging, and release.

Right concentration

Right concentration (*samyak-samâdhi* / *sammâ-samâdhi*), as its Sanskrit and Pali names indicate, is the practice of concentration (*samadhi*). It is also known as right meditation. As such, the practitioner concentrates on an object of attention until reaching full concentration and a state of meditative absorption (*jhana*). Traditionally, the practice of samadhi can be developed through mindfulness of breathing (*anapanasati*), through visual objects (*kasina*), and through repetition of phrases (*mantra*). Jhana is used to suppress the five hindrances in order to enter into Samadhi. Jhana is an instrument used for developing wisdom by cultivating insight and using it to examine true nature of phenomena with direct cognition. This leads to cutting off the defilements, realizing the dhamma and, finally, self-awakening. During the practice of right concentration, the practitioner will need to investigate and verify their right view. In the process right knowledge will arise, followed by right liberation. In the Pali Canon, it is explained thus: And what is right concentration?

(i) Herein a monk aloof from sense desires, aloof from unwholesome thoughts, attains to and abides in the first meditative absorption [jhana], which is detachment-born and accompanied by applied thought, sustained thought, joy, and bliss.

(ii) By allaying applied and sustained thought he attains to, and abides in the second jhana, which is inner tranquillity, which isunification (of the mind), devoid of applied and sustained thought, and which has joy and bliss.

(iii) By detachment from joy he dwells in equanimity, mindful, and with clear comprehension and enjoys bliss in body, and attains to and abides in the third jhana, which the noble ones [ariyas] call "dwelling in equanimity, mindfulness, and bliss".

(iv) By giving up of bliss and suffering, by the disappearance already of joy and sorrow, he attains to, and abides in the fourth jhana, which is neither suffering nor bliss, and which is the purity of equanimity — mindfulness.

This is called right concentration.

Although this instruction is given to the male monastic order, it is also meant for the female monastic order and can be practiced by lay followers from both genders.

According to the Pali and Chinese canon, right concentration is dependent on the development of preceding path factors:

The Blessed One said: "Now what, monks, is noble right concentration with its supports and requisite conditions? Any singleness of mind equipped with these seven factors — right view, right resolve, right speech, right action, right livelihood, right effort, and right mindfulness — is called noble right concentration with its supports and requisite conditions. — Maha-cattarisaka Sutta

Acquired factors

In the *Mahâcattârîsaka Sutta* which appears in the Chinese and Pali canons, the Buddha explains that cultivation of the noble eightfold path leads to the development of two further factors, which are right knowledge, or insight (*sammâ-ñâGa*), and right liberation, or release (*sammâ-vimutti*). These two factors fall under the category of wisdom (*paññâ*).

Right knowledge and right liberation

Right knowledge is seeing things as they really are by direct experience, not as they appear to be, nor as the practitioner wants them to be, but as they truly are. A result of Right Knowledge is the tenth factor - Right liberation.

These two factors are the end result of correctly practicing the noble eightfold path, which arise during the practice of right concentration. The first to arise is right knowledge: this is where deep insight into the ultimate reality arises. The last to arise is right liberation: this is where self-awakening occurs and the practitioner has reached the pinnacle of their practice.

COGNITIVE PSYCHOLOGY

In the essay "Buddhism Meets Western Science", Gay Watson explains:

Buddhism has always been concerned with feelings, emotions, sensations, and cognition. The Buddha points both to cognitive and emotional causes of suffering. The emotional cause is desire and its negative opposite, aversion. The cognitive cause is ignorance of the way things truly occur, or of three marks of existence: that all things are unsatisfactory, impermanent, and without essential self.

The noble eightfold path is, from this psychological viewpoint, an attempt to change patterns of thought and behaviour. It is for this reason that the first element of the path is right understanding (*sammâ-dimmhi*), which is how one's mind views the world. Under the wisdom (*paññâ*) subdivision of the noble eightfold path, this worldview is intimately connected with the second element, right thought (*sammâ-samkappa*), which concerns the patterns of thought and intention that controls one's actions. These elements can be seen at work, for example, in the opening verses of the *Dhammapada*: The noble eightfold path is also the fourth noble truth.

All experience is preceded by mind,
Led by mind,
Made by mind.
Speak or act with a corrupted mind,
And suffering follows
As the wagon wheel follows the hoof of the ox.
All experience is preceded by mind,
Led by mind,
Made by mind.
Speak or act with a peaceful mind,
And happiness follows
Like a never-departing shadow.

Thus, by altering one's distorted worldview, bringing out "tranquil perception" in the place of "perception polluted", one is able to ease suffering. Watson points this out from a psychological standpoint:

Research has shown that repeated action, learning, and memory can actually change the nervous system physically, altering both synaptic strength and connections. Such changes may be brought about by cultivated change in emotion and action; they will, in turn, change subsequent experience.

4

Bhikkhuni Ptimokkha

THE BHIKKHUNIS' CODE OF DISCIPLINE

The Bhikkhuni Pmimokkha contains 311 rules. Of these, 181 are shared with the Bhikkhu Pâmimokkha: four Pârâjikas, seven Samghâdisesas, 18 Nissaggiya Pâcittiyas (NP), 70 Pâcittiyas, all 75 Sekhiyas, and all seven Adhikarama-samatha rules. In addition, the Bhikkhunî Pâmimokkha contains 13 Pâcittiya rules that are identical to rules for bhikkhus that are contained in the Khandhakas; one Prjika rule similar to a Bhikkhus' Samghâdisesa rule; one Pârâjika rule similar to a Bhikkhus' Pâcittiya rule; two Samghâdisesa rules similar to Bhikkhus' Khandhaka rules; two NP rules similar to Bhikkhus' NP rules; three Pâcittiyas similar to a Bhikkhus' Samghâdisesa; seven Pâcittiyas similar to Bhikkhus' Pâcittiyas; and eight Pâcittiyas similar to rules for bhikkhus that are contained in the Khandhakas. Also, the eight Pâmidesanîya rules for the bhikkhunîs are elaborations of a single Bhikkhus' Pcittiya rule.

Thus the Bhikkhuni Pmimokkha contains 85 rules for which there are no direct correspondences in the rules for the bhikkhus. Some writers have interpreted these added rules as sign of an attempt to oppress the bhikkhunîs unfairly, but it should be noted that:

1. more than one third of these extra rules were formulated to protect Bhikkhunis from being the direct recipients of the abusive or careless behaviour of other Bhikkhunis;

2. two of the extra rules (Pcittiyas 6 and 44) prevent Bhikkhunis from putting themselves in a position of servitude to bhikkhus or lay people;
3. according to the rules' origin stories, all but three of the extra rules (Pcittiyas 59, 94, and 95) were formulated only after Bhikkhunis complained to the bhikkhus about an errant Bhikkhuni's behaviour.

Tellingly, these last three exceptions were formulated after complaints initiated by the bhikkhus, and they touch directly on the formal subordination of the Bhikkhuni Community to the Bhikkhu Community. However, they are counterbalanced by two rules exclusive to the Bhikkhu Pmimokkha — NP 4 & 17 — that were formulated at the request of Bhikkhunis to prevent bhikkhus from abusing their position in the hierarchy in a way that would interfere with the Bhikkhunis' practice of the Dhamma. For a more detailed discussion of the checks and balances in the relationships between the two Communities.

In the following translation, I have marked the correspondences between the bhikkhus' and Bhikkhunis' rules in brackets. Where the brackets follow the number of the Bhikkhuni rule and simply contain a number, the corresponding bhikkhus' rule is in the same section in the Bhikkhu Pmimokkha as in the Bhikkhunî Pâmimokkha. Thus, under the Samghâdisesa rules, 7 [5] means that the Bhikkhunîs' Samghâdisesa 7 is identical with the Bhikkhus' Samghâdisesa 5. If the brackets follow the rule and simply contain a reference to a rule in the Mahavagga (Mv) or Cullavagga (Cv), the corresponding bhikkhus' rule is contained in the Khandhakas. If the brackets follow the rule and include the word "see" followed by a number, the corresponding bhikkhus' rule is similar rather than identical. Correspondences in the Sekhiya and AdhikaraGa-samatha sections are not marked, as these two sections are completely identical in the two Pâmimokkhas.

Rules marked with an asterisk (*) are identical with — or directly related to — vows included in the Eight Garudhammas, or Rules of Respect. On this topic, see *The Buddhist Monastic Code,* volume II, chapter 23. Some writers have argued that, because the rules in question are all pcittiya rules, and because the Rules of Respect impose a more stringent penalty than a simple confession for overstepping the vows, we must assume that the vows and their more stringent punishment were added later to the canon, in an attempt to oppress the Bhikkhunis. However, a standard principle throughout the Vinaya — formulated in AdhikaraGa-samatha 4 in both Pâmimokkhas — is that an offender cannot be penalized until he/she has confessed to an offense. In light of this principle, the confession required by the pcittiya rules would be a first, necessary step before imposing the half-month penance stipulated in the fifth vow.

The translation here is based on the complete Pali Bhikkhuni Pmimokkha in Mohan Wijayaratna, *Buddhist Nuns: The Birth and Development of a Women's Monastic Order*(BN), although there were many spots where I had to rely on the Thai edition of the Pali Canon to correct mistakes in BN. I have also consulted I.B. Horner's partial English translation of the Bhikkhuni Pmimokkha rules in *The Book of Discipline,* volume three (BD); the partial Thai translation included in Mahamakut's complete translation of the Pali Canon; the complete English translation in BN; and the complete translation in *The Pmimokkha,*edited by William Pruitt and translated by K. R. Norman (N). Where my translation differs from BD, I have marked it with a (§); where it differs from BN, a (¶); where it differs from N, a (•).

Parenthetical insertions in the rules, if otherwise unmarked, are based on the canonical word-commentary from the Bhikkhuni Vibhanga, the part of the Vinaya Pitaka that contains the Bhikkhuni Pmimokkha together with its explanatory material. If marked with the abbreviation "Comm:", parenthetical insertions in the rules are drawn from the Commentary, Buddhaghosa's Samantapasadika. Technical issues are explained in the endnotes.

PÂRÂJIKA

1 [1]. Should any Bhikkhuni willingly engage in sexual intercourse, even with a male animal, she is defeated and no longer in affiliation.

2 [2]. Should any Bhikkhuni, in what is reckoned a theft, take what is not given from an inhabited area or from the wilderness — just as when, in the taking of what is not given, kings arresting the criminal would flog, imprison, or banish her, saying, "You are a robber, you are a fool, you are benighted, you are a thief" — a Bhikkhuni in the same way taking what is not given is defeated and no longer in affiliation.

3 [3]. Should any Bhikkhuni intentionally deprive a human being of life, or search for an assassin for him, or praise the advantages of death, or incite him to die, saying, "My good man, what use is this evil, miserable life to you? Death would be better for you than life," or with such an idea in mind, such a purpose in mind, should in various ways praise the advantages of death or incite him to die, she also is defeated and no longer in affiliation.

4 [4]. Should any Bhikkhuni, without direct knowledge, boast of a superior human state, a truly noble knowledge and vision as present in herself, saying, "Thus do I know; thus do I see," such that regardless of whether or not she is cross-examined on a later occasion, she — being remorseful and desirous of purification — might say, "Ladies, not knowing, I said I know; not seeing, I said I see — vainly, falsely, idly," unless it was from over-estimation, she also is defeated and no longer in affiliation.

5. Should any Bhikkhuni, lusting, consent to a lusting man's rubbing, rubbing up against, taking hold of, touching, or fondling (her) below the collar-bone and above the circle of the knees, she also is defeated and no longer in affiliation for being "one above the circle of the knees."

6. Should any Bhikkhuni, knowing that (another) Bhikkhuni has fallen into an act (entailing) defeat, neither accuse her herself nor inform the group, and then — whether she (the other Bhikkhuni) is still alive or has died, has been expelled or gone over to another sect — she (this Bhikkhuni) should say, "Even before, ladies, I knew of this Bhikkhuni that 'This sister is of such-and-such a sort,' and I didn't accuse her myself nor did I inform the group," then she also is defeated and no longer

in affiliation for being "one who concealed a fault."

7. Should any Bhikkhuni follow a bhikkhu who has been suspended by a united Community (of bhikkhus) in line with the Dhamma, in line with the Vinaya, in line with the teacher's instructions, and who is disrespectful, has not made amends, has broken off his friendship (with the bhikkhus), the Bhikkhunis are to admonish her thus: "Lady, that bhikkhu has been suspended by a united Community in line with the Dhamma, in line with the Vinaya, in line with the teacher's instructions. He is disrespectful, he has not made amends, he has broken off his friendship. Do not follow him, lady."

And should that Bhikkhuni, thus admonished by the Bhikkhunis, persist as before, the Bhikkhunis are to rebuke her up to three times for the sake of relinquishing that. If while being rebuked up to three times she relinquishes that, that is good. If she does not relinquish that, then she also is defeated and no longer in affiliation for being "a follower of a suspended (bhikkhu+)."

8. Should any Bhikkhuni, lusting, consent to a lusting man's taking hold of her hand or touching the edge of her outer robe, or should she stand with him or converse with him or go to a rendezvous with him, or should she consent to his approaching her, or should she enter a hidden place with him, or should she dispose her body to him — (any of these) for the purpose of that unrighteous act (Comm: physical contact) — then she also is defeated and no longer in affiliation for "(any of) eight grounds."

SAMGHÂDISESA

1. Should any Bhikkhuni start litigation against a householder, a householder's son, a slave, or a worker, or even against a wandering contemplative: this Bhikkhuni, as soon as she has fallen into the first act of offence, is to be (temporarily) driven out, and it entails initial and subsequent meetings of the Community.

2. Should any Bhikkhuni knowingly give Acceptance *(upasampada)* to a woman thief sentenced to death, without

having obtained permission from the king or the Community or the (governing) council or the (governing) committee or the (governing) guild — unless the woman is allowable (i.e., already ordained in another sect or with other Bhikkhunis) — this Bhikkhuni, also, as soon as she has fallen into the first act of offence, is to be (temporarily) driven out, and it entails initial and subsequent meetings of the Community.

3. Should any Bhikkhuni go among villages alone or go to the other shore of a river alone or stay away for a night alone or fall behind her companion(s) alone: this Bhikkhuni, also, as soon as she has fallen into the first act of offence, is to be (temporarily) driven out, and it entails initial and subsequent meetings of the Community.

4. Should any Bhikkhuni — without having obtained permission from the Community who performed the act, without knowing the desire of the group — restore a Bhikkhuni whom a Community acting harmony in line with the Dhamma, in line with the Vinaya, in line with the teacher's instructions, has suspended: this Bhikkhuni, also, as soon as she has fallen into the first act of offence, is to be (temporarily) driven out, and it entails initial and subsequent meetings of the Community.

5. Should any Bhikkhuni, lusting, having received staple or non-staple food from the hand of a lusting man, consume or chew it: this Bhikkhuni, also, as soon as she has fallen into the first act of offence, is to be (temporarily) driven out, and it entails initial and subsequent meetings of the Community.

6. Should any Bhikkhuni say, "What does it matter to you whether this man is lusting or not, when you are not lusting? Please, lady, take what the man is giving — staple or non-staple food — with your own hand and consume or chew it": this Bhikkhuni, also, as soon as she has fallen into the first act of offence, is to be (temporarily) driven out, and it entails initial and subsequent meetings of the Community.

7 [5]. Should any Bhikkhuni engage in conveying a man's intentions to a woman or a woman's intentions to a man, proposing marriage or paramourage — even if only for a momentary liaison: this Bhikkhuni, also, as soon as she has

fallen into the first act of offence, is to be (temporarily) driven out, and it entails initial and subsequent meetings of the Community.

8 [8]. Should any Bhikkhuni — corrupt, aversive, disgruntled — charge a Bhikkhuni with an unfounded case entailing defeat, (thinking), "Perhaps I may bring about her fall from this celibate life," then regardless of whether or not she is cross-examined on a later occasion, if the issue is unfounded and the Bhikkhuni confesses her aversion: this Bhikkhuni, also, as soon as she has fallen into the first act of offence, is to be (temporarily) driven out, and it entails initial and subsequent meetings of the Community.

9 [9]. Should any Bhikkhuni — corrupt, aversive, disgruntled — using as a mere ploy an aspect of an issue that pertains otherwise, charge a Bhikkhuni with a case entailing defeat, (thinking), "Perhaps I may bring about her fall from this celibate life," then regardless of whether or not she is cross-examined on a later occasion, if the issue pertains otherwise, an aspect used as a mere ploy, and the Bhikkhuni confesses her aversion: this Bhikkhuni, also, as soon as she has fallen into the first act of offence, is to be (temporarily) driven out, and it entails initial and subsequent meetings of the Community.

10. Should any Bhikkhuni, angry and displeased, say, "I repudiate the Buddha, I repudiate the Dhamma, I repudiate the Sangha, I repudiate the Training. Since when were the Sakyan-daughter contemplatives the only contemplatives? There are other contemplatives who are conscientious, scrupulous, and desirous of training. I will practice the holy life in their company," the Bhikkhunis are to admonish her thus: "Lady, don't — angry and displeased — say, 'I repudiate the Buddha, I repudiate the Dhamma, I repudiate the Sangha, I repudiate the Training. Since when were the Sakyan-daughter contemplatives the only contemplatives? There are other contemplatives who are conscientious, scrupulous, and desirous of training. I will practice the holy life in their company.' Take delight, lady. The Dhamma is well-expounded. Follow the holy life for the right ending of suffering."

And should that Bhikkhuni, thus admonished by the Bhikkhunis, persist as before, the Bhikkhunis are to rebuke her up to three times for the sake of relinquishing that. If while being rebuked up to three times she relinquishes that, that is good. If she does not relinquish that, then this Bhikkhuni, also, as soon as she has fallen into the third act of offence, is to be (temporarily) driven out, and it entails initial and subsequent meetings of the Community.

11. Should any Bhikkhuni, overthrown in even a trifling issue, angry and displeased, say, "The Bhikkhunis are biased through favoritism, biased through aversion, biased through delusion, biased through fear," the Bhikkhunis are to admonish her thus: "Lady, don't — overthrown in even a trifling issue, angry and displeased — say, 'The Bhikkhunis are biased through favoritism, biased through aversion, biased through delusion, biased through fear. It may be that you, lady, are biased through favoritism, biased through aversion, biased through delusion, biased through fear."

And should that Bhikkhuni, thus admonished by the Bhikkhunis, persist as before, the Bhikkhunis are to rebuke her up to three times for the sake of relinquishing that. If while being rebuked up to three times she relinquishes that, that is good. If she does not relinquish that, then this Bhikkhuni, also, as soon as she has fallen into the third act of offence, is to be (temporarily) driven out, and it entails initial and subsequent meetings of the Community.

12. In case Bhikkhunis are living entangled, depraved in their conduct, depraved in their reputation, depraved in their notoriety (depraved in their livelihood), exasperating the Bhikkhuni Community, hiding one another's faults, the Bhikkhunis are to admonish them thus: "The sisters are living entangled, depraved in their conduct, depraved in their reputation, depraved in their notoriety. Split up (your group), ladies. The Community recommends strict isolation for the sisters."

And should those Bhikkhunis, thus admonished by the Bhikkhunis, persist as before, the Bhikkhunis are to rebuke them up to three times times for the sake of relinquishing that. If while being rebuked up to three times by the Bhikkhunis they relinquish that, that is good. If they do not relinquish that, then these Bhikkhunis, also, as soon as they have fallen into the third act of offence, are to be (temporarily) driven out, and it entails initial and subsequent meetings of the Community.

13. Should any Bhikkhuni say (to the Bhikkhunis criticized in the preceding case), "Live entangled, ladies. Don't live separately. There are other Bhikkhunis in the Community with the same conduct, the same reputation, the same notoriety, exasperating the Bhikkhuni Community, hiding one another's faults, but the Community doesn't say anything to them. It's simply because of your weakness (lack of partisans) that the Community — with contempt, scorn, intolerance, and threats — says, 'The sisters are living entangled, depraved in their conduct, depraved in their reputation, depraved in their notoriety. Split up (your group), ladies. The Community recommends strict isolation for the sisters,'" the Bhikkhunis are to admonish her thus: "Lady, don't say, 'Live entangled, ladies. Don't live separately. There are other Bhikkhunis in the Community with the same conduct, the same reputation, the same notoriety, exasperating the Bhikkhuni Community, hiding one another's faults, but the Community doesn't say anything to them. It's simply because of your weakness that the Community — with contempt, scorn, intolerance, and threats — says, "The sisters are living entangled, depraved in their conduct, depraved in their reputation, depraved in their notoriety. Split up (your group), ladies. The Community recommends strict isolation for the sisters."'"

And should that Bhikkhuni, thus admonished by the Bhikkhunis, persist as before, the Bhikkhunis are to rebuke her up to three times for the sake of relinquishing that. If while being rebuked up to three times she relinquishes that, that is good. If she does not relinquish that, then this Bhikkhuni, also, as soon as she has fallen into the third act of offence, is to be (temporarily) driven out, and it entails initial and subsequent meetings of the Community.

14 [10]. Should any Bhikkhuni agitate for a schism in a united Community, or should she persist in taking up an issue conducive to schism, the Bhikkhunis are to admonish her thus: "Do not, lady, agitate for a schism in a united Community or persist in taking up an issue conducive to schism. Let the lady be reconciled with the Community, for a united Community, on courteous terms, without dispute, with a common recitation, dwells in peace."

And should that Bhikkhuni, thus admonished by the Bhikkhunis, persist as before, the Bhikkhunis are to rebuke her up to three times so as to desist. If while being rebuked up to three times she desists, that is good. If she does not desist, then this Bhikkhuni, also, as soon as she has fallen into the third act of offence, is to be (temporarily) driven out, and it entails initial and subsequent meetings of the Community.

15 [11]. Should Bhikkhunis — one, two, or three — who are followers and partisans of that Bhikkhuni, say, "Do not, ladies, admonish that Bhikkhuni in any way. She is an exponent of the Dhamma, she is an exponent of the Vinaya. She acts with our consent and approval. She knows, she speaks for us, and that is pleasing to us," the Bhikkhunis are to admonish them thus: "Do not say that, ladies. That Bhikkhuni is not an exponent of the Dhamma and she is not an exponent of the Vinaya. Do not, ladies, approve of a schism in the Community. Let the ladies' (minds) be reconciled with the Community, for a united Community, on courteous terms, without dispute, with a common recitation, dwells in peace."

And should those Bhikkhunis, thus admonished by the Bhikkhunis, persist as before, the Bhikkhunis are to rebuke them up to three times times for the sake of relinquishing that. If while being rebuked up to three times by the Bhikkhunis they relinquish that, that is good. If they do not relinquish that, then these Bhikkhunis, also, as soon as they have fallen into the third act of offence, are to be (temporarily) driven out, and it entails initial and subsequent meetings of the Community.

16 [12]. In case a Bhikkhuni is by nature difficult to admonish — who, when being legitimately admonished by the

Bhikkhunis with reference to the training rules included in the (Pmimokkha) recitation, makes herself unadmonishable, (saying,) "Do not, ladies, say anything to me, good or bad; and I won't say anything to the ladies, good or bad. Refrain, ladies, from admonishing me" — the Bhikkhunis are to admonish her thus: "Let the lady not make herself unadmonishable. Let the lady make herself admonishable. Let the lady admonish the Bhikkhunis in accordance with what is right, and the Bhikkhunis will admonish the lady in accordance with what is right; for it is thus that the Blessed One's following is nurtured: through mutual admonition, through mutual rehabilitation."

And should that Bhikkhuni, thus admonished by the Bhikkhunis, persist as before, the Bhikkhunis are to rebuke her up to three times for the sake of relinquishing that. If while being rebuked up to three times she relinquishes that, that is good. If she does not relinquish that, then this Bhikkhuni, also, as soon as she has fallen into the third act of offence, is to be (temporarily) driven out, and it entails initial and subsequent meetings of the Community.

17 [13]. In case a Bhikkhuni living in dependence on a certain village or town is a corrupter of families, a woman of depraved conduct — whose depraved conduct is both seen and heard about, and the families she has corrupted are both seen and heard about — the Bhikkhunis are to admonish her thus: "You, lady, are a corrupter of families, a woman of depraved conduct. Your depraved conduct is both seen and heard about, and the families you have corrupted are both seen and heard about. Leave this monastery, lady. Enough of your staying here."

And should that Bhikkhuni, thus admonished by the Bhikkhunis, say about the Bhikkhunis, "The Bhikkhunis are biased through favoritism, biased through aversion, biased through delusion, biased through fear, in that for this sort of offense they banish some and do not banish others," the Bhikkhunis are to admonish her thus: "Do not say that, lady. The Bhikkhunis are not biased through favoritism, are not biased through aversion, are not biased through delusion, are not biased through fear. You, lady, are a corrupter of families, a woman of depraved conduct. Your depraved conduct is both seen and heard about, and the families you have corrupted are both seen and heard about. Leave this monastery, lady. Enough of your staying here."

And should that Bhikkhuni, thus admonished by the Bhikkhunis, persist as before, the Bhikkhunis are to rebuke her up to three times for the sake of relinquishing that. If while being rebuked up to three times she relinquishes that, that is good. If she does not relinquish that, then this Bhikkhuni, also, as soon as she has fallen into the third act of offence, is to be (temporarily) driven out, and it entails initial and subsequent meetings of the Community.

NISSAGGIYA PÂCITTIYA

Part One: The Bowl Chapter

1. Should any Bhikkhuni make a bowl-hoard (have more than one bowl in her possession), it is to be forfeited and confessed.

2. Should any Bhikkhuni, having determined an out-of-season cloth to be an in-season cloth, distribute it, it is to be forfeited and confessed.

3. Should any Bhikkhuni, having exchanged robe-cloth with another Bhikkhuni, later say to her, "Here, lady. This is your robe-cloth. Bring me that robe-cloth of mine. What was yours is still yours. What was mine is still mine. Bring me that one of mine. Take yours back," and then snatch it back or have it snatched back, it is to be forfeited and confessed.

4. Should any Bhikkhuni, having had one thing requested, (then send it back and) have another thing requested, it is to be forfeited and confessed.

5. Should any Bhikkhuni, having had one thing bought, (then send it back and) have another thing bought, it is to be forfeited and confessed.

6. Should any Bhikkhuni, using a fund intended for one

purpose, dedicated to one purpose for a Community, have something else bought, it is to be forfeited and confessed.

7. Should any Bhikkhuni, having herself asked for a fund intended for one purpose, dedicated to one purpose for a Community, use it to have something else bought, it is to be forfeited and confessed.

8. Should any Bhikkhuni, using a fund intended for one purpose, dedicated to one purpose for a group, have something else bought, it is to be forfeited and confessed.

9. Should any Bhikkhuni, having herself asked for a fund intended for one purpose, dedicated to one purpose for a group, use it to have something else bought, it is to be forfeited and confessed.

10. Should any Bhikkhuni, having herself asked for a fund intended for one purpose, dedicated to one purpose for an individual, use it to have something else bought, it is to be forfeited and confessed.

Part Two: The Robe-cloth Chapter

11. When a Bhikkhuni is asking for a heavy cloth, one worth four "bronzes" at most may be asked for. If she asks for more than that, it is to be forfeited and confessed.

12. When a Bhikkhuni is asking for a light cloth, one worth two and a half "bronzes" at most may be asked for. If she asks for more than that, it is to be forfeited and confessed.

13 [1]. When a Bhikkhuni has finished her robe and the frame is destroyed (her kathina privileges are in abeyance), she is to keep extra robe-cloth ten days at most. Beyond that, it is to be forfeited and confessed.

14 [2]. When a Bhikkhuni has finished her robe and the frame is destroyed (her kathina privileges are in abeyance): If she dwells apart from (any of) her five robes even for one night — unless authorized by the Bhikkhunis — it is to be forfeited and confessed.

15 [3]. When a Bhikkhuni has finished her robe and the frame is destroyed (her kathina privileges are in abeyance):

Should out-of-season robe-cloth accrue to her, she may accept it if she so desires. Having accepted it, she is to make it up immediately (into a cloth requisite). But should it not be enough, she may lay it aside for a month at most if she has an expectation for filling the lack. If she should keep it beyond that, even when she has an expectation (for further cloth), it is to be forfeited and confessed.

16 [6]. Should any Bhikkhuni ask for robe-cloth from a man or woman householder unrelated to her, except at the proper occasion, it is to be forfeited and confessed. Here the proper occasion is this: The Bhikkhuni's robe has been snatched away or destroyed. This is the proper occasion here.

17 [7]. If that unrelated man or woman householder presents the Bhikkhuni with many robes (pieces of robe-cloth), she is to accept at most (enough for) an upper and a lower robe. If she accepts more than that, it is to be forfeited and confessed.

18 [8]. In case a man or woman householder unrelated (to the Bhikkhuni) prepares a robe fund for the sake of a Bhikkhuni, thinking. "Having purchased a robe with this robe fund, I will clothe the Bhikkhuni named so-and-so with a robe:" If the Bhikkhuni, not previously invited, approaching (the householder) should make a stipulation with regard to the robe, saying, "It would be good indeed, sir, if you clothed me (with a robe), having purchased a robe of such-and-such a sort with this robe fund" — out of a desire for something fine — it is to be forfeited and confessed.

19 [9]. In case two householders — men or women — unrelated (to the Bhikkhuni) prepare separate robe funds for the sake of a Bhikkhuni, thinking, "Having purchased separate robes with these separate robe funds of ours, we will clothe the Bhikkhuni named so-and-so with robes": If the Bhikkhuni, not previously invited, approaching (them) should make a stipulation with regard to the robe, saying, "It would be good indeed, sirs, if you clothed me (with a robe), having purchased a robe of such-and-such a sort with these separate robe funds, the two (funds) together for one (robe)" — out of a desire for something fine — it is to be forfeited and confessed.

20 [10]. In case a king, a royal official, a brahman, or a householder sends a robe fund for the sake of a Bhikkhuni via a messenger, (saying,) "Having purchased a robe with this robe fund, clothe the Bhikkhuni named so-and-so with a robe": If the messenger, approaching the Bhikkhuni, should say, "This is a robe fund being delivered for the sake of the lady. May the lady accept this robe fund," then the Bhikkhuni is to tell the messenger: "We do not accept robe funds, my friend. We accept robes (robe-cloth) as are proper according to season."

If the messenger should say to the Bhikkhuni, "Does the lady have a steward?" then, Bhikkhunis, if the Bhikkhuni desires a robe, she may indicate a steward — either a monastery attendant or a lay follower — (saying,) "That, sir, is the Bhikkhunis' steward."

If the messenger, having instructed the steward and going to the Bhikkhuni, should say, "I have instructed the steward the lady indicated. May the lady go (to her) and she will clothe you with a robe in season," then the Bhikkhuni, desiring a robe and approaching the steward, may prompt and remind her two or three times, "I have need of a robe." Should (the steward) produce the robe after being prompted and reminded two or three times, that is good.

If she should not produce the robe, (the Bhikkhuni) should stand in silence four times, five times, six times at most for that purpose. Should (the steward) produce the robe after (the Bhikkhuni) has stood in silence for the purpose four, five, six times at most, that is good.

If she should not produce the robe (at that point), should she then produce the robe after (the Bhikkhuni) has endeavored further than that, it is to be forfeited and confessed.

If she should not produce (the robe), then the Bhikkhuni herself should go to the place from which the robe fund was brought, or a messenger should be sent (to say), "The robe fund that you, venerable sirs, sent for the sake of the Bhikkhuni has given no benefit to the Bhikkhuni at all. May the you be united with what is yours. May what is yours not be lost." This is the proper course here.

Part Three: The Gold and Silver Chapter

21 [18]. Should any Bhikkhuni take gold and silver, or have it taken, or consent to its being deposited (near her), it is to be forfeited and confessed.

22 [19]. Should any Bhikkhuni engage in various types of monetary exchange, it (the income) is to be forfeited and confessed.

23 [20]. Should any Bhikkhuni engage in various types of trade, (the article obtained) is to be forfeited and confessed.

24 [22]. Should any Bhikkhuni with an alms bowl having less than five mends ask for another new bowl, it is to be forfeited and confessed. The bowl is to be forfeited by the Bhikkhuni to the company of Bhikkhunis. That company of Bhikkhunis' final bowl should be presented to the Bhikkhuni, (saying,) "This, Bhikkhuni, is your bowl. It is to be kept until broken." This is the proper course here.

25 [23]. There are these tonics to be taken by sick Bhikkhunis: ghee, fresh butter, oil, honey, sugar/molasses. Having been received, they are to be used from storage seven days at most. Beyond that, they are to be forfeited and confessed.

26 [25]. Should any Bhikkhuni — having herself given robe-cloth to (another) Bhikkhuni and then being angered and displeased — snatch it away or have it snatched away, it is to be forfeited and confessed.

27 [26]. Should any Bhikkhuni, having requested thread, have robe-cloth woven by weavers, it is to be forfeited and confessed.

28 [27]. In case a man or woman householder unrelated (to the Bhikkhuni) has robe-cloth woven by weavers for the sake of a Bhikkhuni, and if the Bhikkhuni, not previously invited (by the householder), having approached the weavers, should make stipulations with regard to the cloth, saying, "This cloth, friends, is to be woven for my sake. Make it long, make it broad, make it tightly woven, well woven, well spread, well scraped, well smoothed, and perhaps I may reward you with a little something"; and should that Bhikkhuni, having said that,

reward them with a little something, even as much as almsfood, it (the cloth) is to be forfeited and confessed.

29 [28]. Ten days prior to the third-month Kattika full moon, should robe-cloth offered in urgency accrue to a Bhikkhuni, she is to accept it if she regards it as offered in urgency. Once she has accepted it, she may keep it throughout the robe season. Beyond that, it is to be forfeited and confessed.

30 [30]. Should any Bhikkhuni knowingly divert to herself gains that had been allocated for a Community, they are to be forfeited and confessed.

PÂCITTIYA

Part One: The Garlic Chapter

1. Should any Bhikkhuni eat garlic, it is to be confessed.

2. Should any Bhikkhuni have the hair in the "confining places" (armpits and pelvic areas) removed, it is to be confessed.

3. (Genital) slapping (even to the extent of consenting to a blow with a lotus-leaf) is to be confessed.

4. (The insertion of) a dildo is to be confessed.

5. When a Bhikkhuni is giving herself an ablution, is to be given only to the depth of two finger joints (and using no more than two fingers). Beyond that, it is to be confessed.

6. Should any Bhikkhuni, when a bhikkhu is eating, attend on him with water or a fan, it is to be confessed.

7. Should any Bhikkhuni, having requested raw grain or having had it requested, having roasted it or having had it roasted, having pounded it or having had it pounded, having cooked it or having had it cooked, then eat it, it is to be confessed.

8. Should any Bhikkhuni toss or get someone else to toss excrement or urine or trash or leftovers over a wall or a fence, it is to be confessed.

9. Should any Bhikkhuni toss or get someone else to toss excrement or urine or trash or leftovers on living crops, it is to be confessed.

10. Should any Bhikkhuni go to see dancing or singing or instrument-playing, it is to be confessed.

Part Two: The Darkness Chapter

11. Should any Bhikkhuni stand or converse with a man, one on one, in the darkness of the night without a light, it is to be confessed.

12. Should any Bhikkhuni stand or converse with a man, one on one, in a concealed place, it is to be confessed.

13. Should any Bhikkhuni stand or converse with a man, one on one, in the open air, it is to be confessed.

14. Should any Bhikkhuni — along a road, in a cul-de-sac, or at a crossroads — stand or converse with a man one on one, or whisper in his ear, or dismiss the Bhikkhuni who is her companion, it is to be confessed.

15. Should any Bhikkhuni, having gone to family residences before the meal (before noon), having sat down on a seat, depart without taking the owner's leave, it is to be confessed.

16. Should any Bhikkhuni, having gone to family residences after the meal (between noon and sunset), sit or lie down on a seat without asking the owner's permission, it is to be confessed.

17. Should any Bhikkhuni, having gone to family residences in the wrong time (between sunset and dawn), having spread out bedding or having had it spread out, sit or lie down (there) without asking the owner's permission, it is to be confessed.

18. Should any Bhikkhuni, because of a misapprehension, because of a misunderstanding, malign another (Bhikkhuni), it is to be confessed.

19. Should any Bhikkhuni curse herself or another (Bhikkhuni) with regard to hell or the holy life, it is to be confessed.

20. Should any Bhikkhuni weep, beating and beating herself, it is to be confessed.

Part Three: The Naked Chapter

21. Should any Bhikkhuni bathe naked, it is to be confessed.

22. When a Bhikkhuni is making a bathing cloth, it is to be made to the standard measurement. Here the standard is this: four spans — using the sugata span — in length, two spans in width. In excess of that, it is to be cut down and confessed.

23. Should any Bhikkhuni, having unsewn (another) Bhikkhuni's robe or having had it unsewn, and then later — when there are no obstructions — neither sew it nor make an effort to have it sewn within four or five days, it is to be confessed.

24. Should any Bhikkhuni exceed her five-day outer robe period, it is to be confessed.

25. Should any Bhikkhuni wear a robe that should be given back (one that she has borrowed from another Bhikkhuni without asking her permission), it is to be confessed.

26. Should any Bhikkhuni put an obstruction in the way of a group's receiving robe-cloth, it is to be confessed.

27. Should any Bhikkhuni block a robe-cloth distribution that is in accordance with the rule, it is to be confessed.

28. Should any Bhikkhuni give a contemplative robe (a robe that has been marked so as to be allowable for a bhikkhu or Bhikkhuni) to a householder, a male wanderer, or female wanderer, it is to be confessed.

29. Should any Bhikkhuni let the robe-season (the period for receiving kathina-donations) pass on the basis of a weak expectation for cloth, it is to be confessed.

30. Should any Bhikkhuni block the dismantling of the kathina privileges in accordance with the rule, it is to be confessed.

Part Four: The Sharing Chapter

31. Should two Bhikkhunis share a single bed, it is to be confessed.

32. Should two Bhikkhunis share a single blanket or sleeping mat, it is to be confessed.

33. Should any Bhikkhuni intentionally cause annoyance to (another) Bhikkhuni, it is to be confessed.

34. Should any Bhikkhuni not attend to her ailing student nor make an effort to have her attended to, it is to be confessed.

35. Should any Bhikkhuni, having given living space to another Bhikkhuni, then — angry and displeased — evict her or have her evicted, it is to be confessed.

36. Should any Bhikkhuni live entangled with a householder or a householder's son, the Bhikkhunis are to admonish her thus: "Lady, don't live entangled with a householder or a householder's son. Live alone, lady. The Community recommends strict isolation for the lady."

And should that Bhikkhuni, thus admonished by the Bhikkhunis, persist as before, the Bhikkhunis are to rebuke her up to three times for the sake of relinquishing that. If while being rebuked up to three times she relinquishes that, that is good. If she does not relinquish that, it is to be confessed.

37. Should any Bhikkhuni, without joining a caravan of merchants, set out within the local king's territory on a journey considered dubious and risky, it is to be confessed.

38. Should any Bhikkhuni, without joining a caravan of merchants, set out outside the local king's territory on a journey considered dubious and risky, it is to be confessed.

39. Should any Bhikkhuni set out on a journey during the Rains-residence, it is to be confessed.

40. Should any Bhikkhuni, having completed the Rains-residence, not depart on a journey of at least five or six leagues, it is to be confessed.

Part Five: The Picture Gallery Chapter

41. Should any Bhikkhuni go to see a royal pleasure house or a picture gallery (any building decorated for amusement) or a park or a pleasure grove or a lotus pond, it is to be confessed.

42. Should any Bhikkhuni make use of a dais or a throne, it is to be confessed.

43. Should any Bhikkhuni spin yarn (thread), it is to be confessed.

44. Should any Bhikkhuni do a chore for a lay person, it is to be confessed.

45. Should any Bhikkhuni — when told by a Bhikkhuni, "Come, lady. Help settle this issue," and having answered, "Very well" — then, when there are no obstructions, neither settle it nor make an effort to have it settled, it is to be confessed.

46. Should any Bhikkhuni give, with her own hand, staple or non-staple food to a householder, a male wanderer, or a female wanderer, it is to be confessed.

47. Should any Bhikkhuni use a menstrual cloth without having forfeited it (after her previous period), it is to be confessed.

48. Should any Bhikkhuni depart on a journey without having forfeited her dwelling space, it is to be confessed.

49. Should any Bhikkhuni study lowly arts (literally, bestial knowledge), it is to be confessed.

50. Should any Bhikkhuni teach lowly arts, it is to be confessed. [Cv.V.33.2]

Part Six: The Monastery Chapter

51. Should any Bhikkhuni, without asking permission, knowingly enter a monastery containing a bhikkhu, it is to be confessed.

52. Should any Bhikkhuni revile or insult a bhikkhu, it is to be confessed.*

53. Should any Bhikkhuni, in a fit of temper, revile a group (the Bhikkhuni Community), it is to be confessed.

54. Should any Bhikkhuni, having eaten and turned down an offer (of further food), chew or consume staple or non-staple food (elsewhere), it is to be confessed.

55. Should any Bhikkhuni be stingy with regard to families (supporters), it is to be confessed.

56. Should any Bhikkhuni spend the Rains-residence in a dwelling where there are no bhikkhus (nearby), it is to be confessed.*

57. Should any Bhikkhuni, having completed the Rains-residence, not invite (criticism) from both Communities with regard to three matters — what they have seen, heard, or suspected (her of doing) — it is to be confessed.*

58. Should any Bhikkhuni not go for the exhortation or for the (meeting that defines) affiliation (i.e., the Uposatha), it is to be confessed.*

59. Every half-month a Bhikkhuni should request two things from the Bhikkhu Community: the asking of the date of the Uposatha and the approaching for exhortation. In excess of that (half-month), it is to be confessed.*

60. Should any Bhikkhuni, without having informed a Community or a group (of Bhikkhunis), alone with a man have a boil or scar that has appeared on the lower part of her body (between the navel and the knees) burst or cut open or cleaned or smeared with a salve or bandaged or unbandaged, it is to be confessed.

Part Seven: The Pregnant Woman Chapter

61. Should any Bhikkhuni sponsor (the Acceptance *(upasampada)* of) a pregnant woman, it is to be confessed.

62. Should any Bhikkhuni sponsor (the Acceptance of) a woman who is still nursing, it is to be confessed.

63. Should any Bhikkhuni sponsor (the Acceptance of) a trainee who has not trained for two years in the six precepts, it is to be confessed.*

64. Should any Bhikkhuni sponsor (the Acceptance of) a trainee who has not trained for two years in the six precepts and who has not been authorized by a Community, it is to be confessed.

65. Should any Bhikkhuni sponsor (the Acceptance of) a married woman who (has been married) less than twelve years, it is to be confessed.

66. Should any Bhikkhuni sponsor (the Acceptance of) a married woman who (has been married) fully twelve years but who has not trained for two years in the six precepts, it is to be confessed.

67. Should any Bhikkhuni sponsor (the Acceptance of) a married woman who (has been married) fully twelve years and who has trained for two years in the six precepts but who has not been authorized by a Community, it is to be confessed.

68. Should any Bhikkhuni, having sponsored (the Acceptance of) her student, neither assist her (in her training) nor have her assisted for (the next) two years, it is to be confessed.

69. Should any Bhikkhuni not attend to her preceptor for two years, it is to be confessed.

70. Should any Bhikkhuni, having sponsored (the Acceptance of) her student, neither take her away nor have her taken away for at least five or six leagues, it is to be confessed.

Part Eight: The Maiden Chapter

71. Should any Bhikkhuni sponsor (the Acceptance of) a maiden (unmarried woman/female novice) less than twenty years old, it is to be confessed.

72. Should any Bhikkhuni sponsor (the Acceptance of) a maiden fully twenty years old but who has not trained for two years in the six precepts, it is to be confessed.

73. Should any Bhikkhuni sponsor (the Acceptance of) a maiden fully twenty years old who has trained for two years in the six precepts but who has not been authorized by a Community, it is to be confessed.

74. Should any Bhikkhuni sponsor (an Acceptance) when she has less than twelve years (seniority), it is to be confessed.

75. Should any Bhikkhuni, even if she has fully twelve years (seniority) sponsor (an Acceptance) when she has not been authorized by a Community (of Bhikkhunis), it is to be confessed.

76. Should any Bhikkhuni — having been told, "Enough, lady, of your sponsoring (Acceptance) for the time being," and having answered, "Very well" — later complain, it is to be confessed.

77. Should any Bhikkhuni — having said to a trainee, "If you give me a robe, I will sponsor you (for Acceptance)," — then, when there are no obstructions, neither sponsor her (Acceptance) nor make an effort to have her sponsored (for Acceptance), it is to be confessed.

78. Should any Bhikkhuni — having said to a trainee, "If you attend to me for two years, I will sponsor you (for Acceptance)," — then, when there are no obstructions, neither sponsor her (Acceptance) nor make an effort to have her sponsored (for Acceptance), it is to be confessed.

79. Should any Bhikkhuni sponsor (the Acceptance of) a trainee who is entangled with men, entangled with youths, temperamental, a cause of grief, it is to be confessed.

80. Should any Bhikkhuni sponsor (the Acceptance of) a trainee without getting permission from her parents or her husband, it is to be confessed.

81. Should any Bhikkhuni sponsor (the Acceptance of) a trainee by means of stale giving of consent, it is to be confessed.

82. Should any Bhikkhuni sponsor (Acceptances — act as a preceptor) in consecutive years, it is to be confessed.

83. Should any Bhikkhuni sponsor (Acceptances — act as a preceptor for) two (trainees) in one year, it is to be confessed.

Part Nine: The Sunshade and Leather Footwear Chapter

84. Should any Bhikkhuni, not being ill, use a sunshade and leather footwear (outside a monastery), it is to be confessed.

85. Should any Bhikkhuni, not being ill, ride in a vehicle, it is to be confessed.

86. Should any Bhikkhuni wear a hip ornament, it is to be confessed.

87. Should any Bhikkhuni wear a woman's ornament, it is to be confessed.

88. Should any Bhikkhuni (not being ill) bathe with perfumes and paint, it is to be confessed.

89. Should any Bhikkhuni (not being ill) bathe with scented sesame powder, it is to be confessed.

90. Should any Bhikkhuni (not being ill) have another Bhikkhuni rub or massage her, it is to be confessed.

91. Should any Bhikkhuni (not being ill) have a trainee rub or massage her, it is to be confessed.

92. Should any Bhikkhuni (not being ill) have a female novice rub or massage her, it is to be confessed.

93. Should any Bhikkhuni (not being ill) have a woman householder rub or massage her, it is to be confessed.

94. Should any Bhikkhuni sit down in front of a bhikkhu without asking permission, it is to be confessed.*

95. Should any Bhikkhuni ask a question (about the Suttas, Vinaya, or Abhidhamma) of a bhikkhu who has not given leave, it is to be confessed.*

96. Should any Bhikkhuni enter a village without her vest, it is to be confessed.

Part Ten: The Lie Chapter

97 [1]. A deliberate lie is to be confessed.

98 [2]. An insult is to be confessed.

99 [3]. Divisive tale-bearing among Bhikkhunis is to be confessed.

100 [4]. Should any Bhikkhuni have an unordained person recite Dhamma line by line (with her), it is to be confessed.

101 [5]. Should any Bhikkhuni lie down together (in the same dwelling) with an unordained woman for more than two or three consecutive nights, it is to be confessed.

102 [6]. Should any Bhikkhuni lie down together (in the same dwelling) with a man, it is to be confessed.

103 [7]. Should any Bhikkhuni teach more than five or six sentences of Dhamma to a man, unless a knowledgeable woman is present, it is to be confessed.

104 [8]. Should any Bhikkhuni report (her own) superior human state to an unordained person, when it is factual, it is to be confessed.

105 [9]. Should any Bhikkhuni report (another) Bhikkhuni's serious offense to an unordained person — unless authorized by the Bhikkhunis — it is to be confessed.

106 [10]. Should any Bhikkhuni dig soil or have it dug, it is to be confessed.

Part Eleven: The Living Plant Chapter

107 [11]. The damaging of a living plant is to be confessed.

108 [12]. Evasive speech and causing frustration are to be confessed.

109 [13]. Complaining about or criticizing (a Community official) is to be confessed.

110 [14]. Should any Bhikkhuni set a bed, bench, mattress, or stool belonging to the Community out in the open — or have it set out — and then on departing neither put it away nor have it put away, or should she go without taking leave, it is to be confessed.

111 [15]. Should any Bhikkhuni set out bedding in a dwelling belonging to the Community — or have it set out — and then on departing neither put it away nor have it put away, or should she go without taking leave, it is to be confessed.

112 [16]. Should any Bhikkhuni knowingly lie down in a dwelling belonging to the Community so as to intrude on a Bhikkhuni who arrived there first, (thinking), "Whoever finds it confining will go away" — doing it for just that reason and no other — it is to be confessed.

113 [17]. Should any Bhikkhuni, angry and displeased, evict a Bhikkhuni from a dwelling belonging to the Community — or have her evicted — it is to be confessed.

114 [18]. Should any Bhikkhuni sit or lie down on a bed or bench with detachable legs on an (unplanked) loft in a dwelling belonging to the Community, it is to be confessed.

115 [19]. When a Bhikkhuni is building a large dwelling, she may apply two or three layers of facing to plaster the area around the window frame and reinforce the area around the door frame the width of the door opening, while standing where there are no crops to speak of. Should she apply more than that, even if standing where there are no crops to speak of, it is to be confessed.

116 [20]. Should any Bhikkhuni knowingly pour water containing living beings — or have it poured — on grass or on clay, it is to be confessed.

Part Twelve: The Food Chapter

117 [31]. A Bhikkhuni who is not ill may eat one meal at

a public alms center. Should she eat more than that, it is to be confessed.

118 [32]. A group meal, except at the proper occasions, is to be confessed. Here the proper occasions are these: a time of illness, a time of giving cloth, a time of making robes, a time of going on a journey, a time of embarking on a boat, a great occasion, a time when the meal is supplied by contemplatives. These are the proper occasions here.

119 [34]. In case a Bhikkhuni arriving at a family residence is presented with cakes or cooked grain-meal, she may accept two or three bowlfuls if she so desires. If she should accept more than that, it is to be confessed. Having accepted the two-or-three bowlfuls and having taken them from there, she is to share them among the Bhikkhunis. This is the proper course here.

120 [37]. Should any Bhikkhuni chew or consume staple or non-staple food at the wrong time, it is to be confessed.

121 [38]. Should any Bhikkhuni chew or consume stored-up staple or non-staple food, it is to be confessed.

122 [40]. Should any Bhikkhuni take into her mouth an edible that has not been given — except for water and tooth-cleaning sticks — it is to be confessed.

123 [42]. Should any Bhikkhuni say to a Bhikkhuni, "Come, lady, let's enter the village or town for alms," and then — whether or not she has had (food) given to her — dismiss her, saying, "Go away, lady. I don't like sitting or talking with you. I prefer sitting or talking alone" — doing it for just that reason and no other — it is to be confessed.

124 [43]. Should any Bhikkhuni sit intruding on a family "with its meal," it is to be confessed.

125 [44]. Should any Bhikkhuni sit in private on a secluded seat with a man, it is to be confessed.

126 [45]. Should any Bhikkhuni sit in private, alone with a man, it is to be confessed.

Part Thirteen: The Go-calling Chapter

127 [46]. Should any Bhikkhuni, being invited for a meal

and without taking leave of an available Bhikkhuni, go calling on families before or after the meal, except at the proper times, it is to be confessed. Here the proper times are these: a time of giving cloth, a time of making robes. These are the proper times here.

128 [47].A Bhikkhuni who is not ill may accept (make use of) a four-month invitation to ask for requisites. If she should accept (make use of) it for beyond that — unless the invitation is renewed or is permanent — it is to be confessed.

129 [48]. Should any Bhikkhuni go to see an army on active duty, unless there is a suitable reason, it is to be confessed.

130 [49]. There being some reason or another for a Bhikkhuni to go to an army, she may stay two or three (consecutive) nights with the army. If she should stay beyond that, it is to be confessed.

131 [50]. If a Bhikkhuni staying two or three nights with an army should go to a battlefield, a roll call, the troops in battle formation, or to see a review of the (battle) units, it is to be confessed.

132 [51]. The drinking of alcohol or fermented liquor is to be confessed.

133 [52]. Tickling with the fingers is to be confessed.

134 [53]. The act of playing in the water is to be confessed.

135 [54]. Disrespect is to be confessed.

136 [55]. Should any Bhikkhuni try to frighten another Bhikkhuni, it is to be confessed.

Part Fourteen: The Fire Chapter

137 [56]. Should any Bhikkhuni who is not ill, seeking to warm herself, kindle a fire or have one kindled — unless there is a suitable reason — it is to be confessed.

138 [57]. Should any Bhikkhuni bathe at intervals of less than half a month, except at the proper occasions, it is to be confessed. Here the proper occasions are these: the last month and a half of the hot season, the first month of the rains, these two and a half months being a time of heat, a time of fever;

(also) a time of illness; a time of work; a time of going on a journey; a time of wind or rain. These are the proper times here.

139 [58]. When a Bhikkhuni receives a new robe, any one of three means of discoloring it is to be applied: green, brown, or black. If a Bhikkhuni should make use of a new robe without applying any of the three means of discoloring it, it is to be confessed.

140 [59]. Should any Bhikkhuni, having herself placed robe-cloth under shared ownership*(vikappana)* with a bhikkhu, a Bhikkhuni, a female trainee, a male novice, or a female novice, then make use of the cloth without the shared ownership's being rescinded, it is to be confessed.

141 [60]. Should any Bhikkhuni hide (another) Bhikkhuni's bowl, robe, sitting cloth, needle box, or belt — or have it hidden — even as a joke, it is to be confessed.

142 [61]. Should any Bhikkhuni intentionally deprive an animal of life, it is to be confessed.

143 [62]. Should any Bhikkhuni knowingly make use of water containing living beings, it is to be confessed.

144 [63]. Should any Bhikkhuni knowingly agitate for the reviving of an issue that has been rightfully dealt with, it is to be confessed.

145 [66]. Should any Bhikkhuni knowingly and by arrangement travel together with a caravan of thieves, even for the interval between one village and the next, it is to be confessed.

146 [68]. Should any Bhikkhuni say the following: "As I understand the Dhamma taught by the Blessed One, those acts the Blessed One says are obstructive, when engaged in are not genuine obstructions," the Bhikkhunis are to admonish her thus: "Do not say that, lady. Do not misrepresent the Blessed One, for it is not good to misrepresent the Blessed One. The Blessed One would not say anything like that. In many ways, lady, the Blessed One has described obstructive acts, and when engaged in they are genuine obstructions."

And should that Bhikkhuni, thus admonished by the Bhikkhunis, persist as before, the Bhikkhunis are to rebuke her up to three times for the sake of relinquishing that. If while being rebuked up to three times she relinquishes that, that is good. If she does not relinquish that, it is to be confessed.

Part Fifteen: The View Chapter

147 [69]. Should any Bhikkhuni knowingly commune, affiliate, or lie down in the same dwelling with a Bhikkhuni professing such a view who has not acted in compliance with the rule, who has not abandoned that view, it is to be confessed.

148 [70]. And if a female novice should say the following: "As I understand the Dhamma taught by the Blessed One, those acts the Blessed One says are obstructive, when engaged in are not genuine obstructions," the Bhikkhunis are to admonish her thus: "Do not say that, lady novice. Do not misrepresent the Blessed One, for it is not good to misrepresent the Blessed One. The Blessed One would not say anything like that. In many ways, lady, the Blessed One has described obstructive acts, and when engaged in they are genuine obstructions."

And should that female novice, thus admonished by the Bhikkhunis, persist as before, the Bhikkhunis are to admonish her thus: "From this day forth, lady novice, you are not to claim the Blessed One as your teacher, nor are you even to have the opportunity the other female novices get — that of sharing dwellings two or three nights with the Bhikkhunis. Away with you! Get lost!"

Should any Bhikkhuni knowingly support, receive services from, consort with, or lie down in the same dwelling with a female novice thus expelled, it is to be confessed.

149 [71]. Should any Bhikkhuni, admonished by the Bhikkhunis in accordance with a rule, say, "Ladies, I will not train myself under this training rule until I have put questions about it to another Bhikkhuni, experienced and learned in the discipline," it is to be confessed. Bhikkhus, [the Buddha is apparently addressing the bhikkhus who will inform the Bhikkhunis of this training rule] a Bhikkhuni in training should

understand, should ask, should ponder. This is the proper course here.

150 [72]. Should any Bhikkhuni, when the Pmimokkha is being recited, say, "Why are these lesser and minor training rules recited when they lead only to anxiety, bother, and confusion?" the criticism of the training rules is to be confessed.

151 [73]. Should any Bhikkhuni, when the Pmimokkha is being recited every half-month, say, "Just now have I learned that this case, too, is handed down in the Pâmimokkha, is included in the Pmimokkha, and comes up for recitation every half-month"; and if the bhikkhunîs should know, "That bhikkhunî has already sat through two or three recitations of the Pâmimokkha, if not more," the bhikkhunî is not exempted for being ignorant. Whatever the offense she has committed, she is to be dealt with in accordance with the rule; and in addition, her deceit is to be exposed: "It is no gain for you, lady, it is ill-done, that when the Pmimokkha is being recited, you do not pay attention, properly taking it to heart." As for the deception (§), it is to be confessed.

152 [74]. Should any Bhikkhuni, angered and displeased, give a blow to (another) Bhikkhuni, it is to be confessed.

153 [75]. Should any Bhikkhuni, angered and displeased, raise the palm of her hand against (another) Bhikkhuni, it is to be confessed.

154 [76]. Should any Bhikkhuni charge a Bhikkhuni with an unfounded Samghâdisesa (offense), it is to be confessed.

155 [77]. Should any Bhikkhuni purposefully provoke anxiety in (another) Bhikkhuni, (thinking,) "This way, even for just a moment, she will have no peace" — doing it for just that reason and no other — it is to be confessed.

156 [78]. Should any Bhikkhuni stand eavesdropping on Bhikkhunis when they are arguing, quarreling, and disputing, thinking, "I will overhear what they say" — doing it for just that reason and no other — it is to be confessed.

Part Sixteen: The In-accordance -with-the-Rule Chapter

157 [79]. Should any Bhikkhuni, having given consent (by

proxy) to a transaction carried out in accordance with the rule, later complain (about the act), it is to be confessed.

158 [80]. Should any Bhikkhuni, when deliberation is being carried on in the Community, get up from her seat and leave without having given consent, it is to be confessed.

159 [81]. Should any Bhikkhuni, (acting as part of) a united Community, give robe-cloth (to an individual Bhikkhuni) and later complain, "The Bhikkhunis apportion the Community's gains according to friendship," it is to be confessed.

160 [82]. Should any Bhikkhuni knowingly divert to an individual gains that had been allocated for a Community, it is to be confessed.

161 [84]. Should any Bhikkhuni pick up or have (someone) pick up a valuable or what is considered a valuable, except in a monastery or in a dwelling, it is to be confessed. But when a Bhikkhuni has picked up or had (someone) pick up a valuable or what is considered a valuable (left) in a monastery or in a dwelling, she is to keep it, (thinking,) "Whoever it belongs to will (come and) fetch it." This is the proper course here.

162 [86]. Should any Bhikkhuni have a needle box made of bone, ivory, or horn, it is to be broken and confessed.

163 [87]. When a Bhikkhuni is having a new bed or bench made, it is to have legs (at most) eight fingerbreadths long — using sugata fingerbreadths — not counting the lower edge of the frame. In excess of that it is to be cut down and confessed.

164 [88]. Should any Bhikkhuni have a bed or bench upholstered, it (the upholstery) is to be torn off and confessed.

165 [90]. When a Bhikkhuni is having a skin-eruption covering cloth made, it is to be made to the standard measurement. Here the standard is this: four spans — using the sugata span — in length, two spans in width. In excess of that, it is to be cut down and confessed.

166 [92]. Should any Bhikkhuni have a robe made the size of the sugata robe or larger, it is to be cut down and confessed. Here, the size of the sugata robe is this: nine spans — using the sugata span — in length, six spans in width. This is the size of the sugata's sugata robe.

PÂMIDESANÎYA

1. Should any Bhikkhuni, not being ill, ask for ghee and consume it, she is to acknowledge it: "Lady, I have committed a blameworthy, unsuitable act that ought to be acknowledged. I acknowledge it."

2-8. Should any Bhikkhuni, not being ill, ask for oil... honey... sugar/molasses... fish... meat... milk... curds and consume it, she is to acknowledge it: "Lady, I have committed a blameworthy, unsuitable act that ought to be acknowledged. I acknowledge it." [Bhikkhus' Pcittiya 39]

SEKHIYA

Part One: The 26 Dealing with Proper Behaviour

1. {2} I will wear the lower robe {upper robe} wrapped around (me): a training to be observed.

3. {4} I will go {sit} well-covered in inhabited areas: a training to be observed.

5. {6} I will go {sit} well-restrained in inhabited areas: a training to be observed.

7. {8} I will go {sit} with eyes lowered in inhabited areas: a training to be observed.

9. {10} I will not go {sit} with robes hitched up in inhabited areas: a training to be observed.

11. {12} I will not go {sit} laughing loudly in inhabited areas: a training to be observed.

13. {14} I will go {sit} (speaking) with a lowered voice in inhabited areas: a training to be observed.

15. {16} I will not go {sit} swinging my body in inhabited areas: a training to be observed.

17. {18} I will not go {sit} swinging my arms in inhabited areas: a training to be observed.

19. {20} I will not go {sit} swinging my head in inhabited areas: a training to be observed.

21. {22} I will not go {sit} with arms akimbo in inhabited areas: a training to be observed.

23. {24} I will not go {sit} with my head covered in inhabited areas: a training to be observed.

25. I will not go tiptoeing or walking just on the heels in inhabited areas: a training to be observed.

26. I will not sit clasping the knees in inhabited areas: a training to be observed.

Part Two: The 30 Dealing with Food

27. I will receive almsfood appreciatively: a training to be observed.

28. I will receive almsfood with attention focused on the bowl: a training to be observed.

29. I will receive almsfood with bean curry in proper proportion: a training to be observed.

30. I will receive almsfood level with the edge (of the bowl): a training to be observed.

31. I will eat almsfood appreciatively: a training to be observed.

32. I will eat almsfood with attention focused on the bowl: a training to be observed.

33. I will eat almsfood methodically: a training to be observed.

34. I will eat almsfood with bean curry in proper proportion: a training to be observed.

35. I will not eat almsfood taking mouthfuls from a heap: a training to be observed.

36. I will not hide bean curry and foods with rice out of a desire to get more: a training to be observed.

37. Not being ill, I will not eat rice or bean curry that I have requested for my own sake: a training to be observed.

38. I will not look at another's bowl intent on finding fault: a training to be observed.

39. I will not take an extra-large mouthful: a training to be observed.

40. I will make a rounded mouthful: a training to be observed.

41. I will not open the mouth when the mouthful has yet to be brought to it: a training to be observed.

42. I will not insert the whole hand into the mouth while eating: a training to be observed.

43. I will not speak with the mouth full of food: a training to be observed.

44. I will not eat from lifted balls of food: a training to be observed.

45. I will not eat nibbling at mouthfuls of food: a training to be observed.

46. I will not eat stuffing out the cheeks: a training to be observed.

47. I will not eat shaking (food off) the hand: a training to be observed.

48. I will not eat scattering lumps of rice about: a training to be observed.

49. I will not eat sticking out the tongue: a training to be observed.

50. I will not eat smacking the lips: a training to be observed.

51. I will not eat making a slurping noise: a training to be observed.

52. I will not eat licking the hands: a training to be observed.

53. I will not eat licking the bowl: a training to be observed.

54. I will not eat licking the lips: a training to be observed.

55. I will not accept a water vessel with a hand soiled by food: a training to be observed.

56. I will not, in an inhabited area, throw away bowl-rinsing water that has grains of rice in it: a training to be observed.

Part Three: The 16 Dealing with Teaching Dhamma

57. I will not teach Dhamma to a person with an umbrella in her hand who is not ill: a training to be observed.

58. I will not teach Dhamma to a person with a staff in her hand who is not ill: a training to be observed.

59. I will not teach Dhamma to a person with a knife in her hand who is not ill: a training to be observed.

60. I will not teach Dhamma to a person with a weapon in her hand who is not ill: a training to be observed.

61. {62} I will not teach Dhamma to a person wearing non-leather {leather} footwear who is not ill: a training to be observed.

63. I will not teach Dhamma to a person in a vehicle who is not ill: a training to be observed.

64. I will not teach Dhamma to a person lying down who is not ill: a training to be observed.

65. I will not teach Dhamma to a person who sits clasping her knees and who is not ill: a training to be observed.

66. I will not teach Dhamma to a person wearing headgear who is not ill: a training to be observed.

67. I will not teach Dhamma to a person whose head is covered (with a robe or scarf) and who is not ill: a training to be observed.

68. Sitting on the ground, I will not teach Dhamma to a person sitting on a seat who is not ill: a training to be observed.

69. Sitting on a low seat, I will not teach Dhamma to a person sitting on a high seat who is not ill: a training to be observed.

70. Standing, I will not teach Dhamma to a person sitting who is not ill: a training to be observed.

71. Walking behind, I will not teach Dhamma to a person walking ahead who is not ill: a training to be observed.

72. Walking beside a path, I will not teach Dhamma to a person walking on the path who is not ill: a training to be observed.

Four: The 3 Miscellaneous Rules

73. Not being ill, I will not defecate or urinate while standing: a training to be observed.

74. Not being ill, I will not defecate, urinate, or spit on living crops: a training to be observed.

75. Not being ill, I will not defecate, urinate, or spit in water: a training to be observed.

ADHIKARAGA-SAMATHA

1. *A face-to-face verdict should be given.* This means that the transaction settling the issue must be carried out in the presence of the Community, in the presence of the individuals, and in the presence of the Dhamma and Vinaya.

2. *A verdict of mindfulness may be given.* This is the verdict of innocence given in an accusation, based on the fact that the accused remembers fully that she did not commit the offense in question.

3. *A verdict of past insanity may be given.* This is another verdict of innocence given in an accusation, based on the fact that the accused was out of her mind when she committed the offense in question and so is absolved of any responsibility for it.

4. *Acting in accordance with what is admitted.* This refers to the ordinary confession of offenses, where no formal interrogation is involved. The confession is valid only if in accord with the facts, e.g., a Bhikkhuni actually commits a pcittiya offense and then confesses it as such, and not as a stronger or lesser offense. If she were to confess it as a dukkata or a Samghâdisesa, that would be invalid.

5. *Acting in accordance with the majority.* This refers to cases in which Bhikkhunis are unable to settle a dispute unanimously, even after all the proper procedures are followed, and — in the words of the Canon — are "wounding one another with weapons of the tongue." In cases such as these, decisions can be made by majority vote.

6. *Acting for her (the accused's) further punishment.* This refers to cases where a Bhikkhuni admits to having committed the offense in question only after being formally interrogated about it. She is then to be reproved for her actions, made to remember the offense and to confess it, after which the Community carries out a "further punishment" transaction

against her as an added punishment for being so uncooperative as to require the formal interrogation in the first place.

7. *Covering over as with grass.* This refers to situations in which both sides of a dispute realize that, in the course of their dispute, they have done much that is unworthy of a contemplative. If they were to deal with one another for their offenses, the only result would be greater divisiveness. Thus if both sides agree, all the Bhikkhunis gather in one place. (According to the Commentary, this means that all Bhikkhunis in the Community territory*(sima)* must attend. No one should send her consent, and even sick Bhikkhunis must go.) A motion is made to the entire group that this procedure will be followed. One member of each side then makes a formal motion to the members of her faction that she will make a confession for them. When both sides are ready, the representative of each side addresses the entire group and makes the blanket confession, using the form of a motion and one announcement (*ñatti-dutiya-kamma*).

5

The Bhikkhus' Rules

A GUIDE FOR LAYPEOPLE

The Theravadin Buddhist Monk's Rules: The Teaching of the Buddha is concerned with more than intellectual knowledge for it needs to be experienced as truth in one's own life. The Buddha often called his Teaching the Dhamma-Vinaya and when he passed away he left these as the guide for all of us who followed. As Venerable Thiradhammo writes:

> *In simple terms we could say that while Dhamma represented the principles of Truth, the Vinaya represented the most efficacious lifestyle for the realization of that Truth. Or, the Vinaya was that way of life which enshrined the principles of Truth in the practicalities of living within the world." (HS Part 2)*

For the bhikkhu, the Vinaya helps to highlight actions and speech, and show up their significance. It brings an awareness of how he is intervening in the world, how he is affecting other people. For better? For worse? With what intention?

Of course, such an awareness is necessary for every human being, not just Buddhist monks. This is why the Buddha bequeathed to us the Five, the Eight and the Ten Precepts—as well as the bhikkhu's 227 rules of the Paatimokkha. These precepts and rules remain as pertinent today as they were 2,500 years ago for they restore the focus back to the human being, to how actions and words affect individuals and the world. While the particulars may have changed, the fundamentals remain the same.

Those who take the Buddha's Teaching seriously become ever more aware of their actions and speech, and how they match up against the Five Precepts. They then might start to realize the advantage in occasionally keeping the Eight Precepts-perhaps on the weekly Observance Day—and become more interested in the bhikkhu's Rule and how its precepts come together into a whole way of life.

This compilation, therefore, is for anyone interested in bhikkhus and how to relate to them. Some might think that the Theravaada lineage follows an overly traditionalist approach but then, it does happen to be the oldest living major tradition. A slight caution therefore for anyone completely new to the ways of monasticism, for it is an approach to dealing with life that may appear radically different for this modern day and age. The best introduction, perhaps essential for a true understanding, is meeting with a practicing bhikkhu who should manifest and reflect the peaceful and joyous qualities of the bhikkhu's way of life.

Buddhist monks and nuns first received the going-forth into the Holy Life from the Buddha himself, more than two and a half thousand years ago in India. Since then, their influence has been felt over much of Asia. The countries of Sri Lanka and South East Asia have been profoundly affected by the Theravadin School of Buddhism, which looks back to the original Teachings as recorded in the Pali scriptures.

Buddhism was often first introduced to a new country when bhikkhus were invited to come and teach the new religion by the indigenous ruler. This process now continues throughout the world, although the invitation nowadays comes more often from local Buddhists.

Buddhism is justly admired for its appreciation of tolerance and broad-mindedness, with a history generally unblemished by heretical infighting. This has resulted in a wide spectrum of practices, from the old Theravaada to the Zen of Japan and the Vajrayana of Tibet. Even between the different Theravadin countries and Schools there are slight variations in the ways the bhikkhus understand and practice the Vinaya Rule. Such differences have sometimes confused lay devotees so this book is also an attempt to offer a clearer understanding about the responsibilities of the Theravadin bhikkhu's life and those of the lay devotee.

When the Buddha was about to finally pass away and leave his followers, rather than appoint an individual to take his place he said this:

> *"Whatever Dhamma and Vinaya I have pointed out and formulated for you, that will be your Teacher when I am gone." (Mahaaparinibbaana Sutta, [D.16])*

More than twenty-five centuries have now gone by; empires have come and gone, great movements and ideologies have flared up and been lost. Yet on a deeper level under all of this, the Dhamma and Vinaya have been quietly guiding the communities of Buddhist monks. Why has it withstood the test of time so well? Why has it been so successful? Perhaps it is because the Lord Buddha understood the basic human condition of every time or place; he knew our predicament and failings, and he could show the way out to those of us who follow so long after him.

BECOMING A BHIKKHU

In the Pali texts, when a man decided to become a bhikkhu, he is often quoted as saying:

> *"Confined is the household life, a path of dust; the going forth is open and spacious. Not easy is it living in a house to lead the religious life absolutely fulfilled and purified, as polished as mother-of-pearl. Suppose I were to shave off my hair and beard, clothe myself in ochre robes and go forth from homelife into homelessness?" (HS ch.19)*

However, anyone wishing to become a bhikkhu must fulfil certain conditions about which he will be questioned during the actual ordination procedure. The candidate must be male and at least twenty years old. He must never have committed any grievous crimes and, if previously ordained, he must not have been guilty of any Defeater (Paaraajika) offences or have entered some other religion without disrobing first. He should also be of good reputation; fit and healthy enough to carry out the duties of a bhikkhu; not in debt; not subject to government service; and have permission from parents or guardian.

The Ordination ceremony requires a prescribed boundary (siima), a preceptor (upajjhaaya) and a quorum of bhikkhus to validate the formal Sangha Act. In the formal procedure the candidate is examined as to the necessary qualities and, if all the bhikkhus are satisfied, they receive him into the Sangha, the Community of Bhikkhus.

It is in this way that yet another link is added to the bhikkhu-lineage. Henceforth, the new bhikkhu can participate (and make up the necessary quorum) in future assemblies and help receive other new bhikkhus-as bhikkhus have continued to do for two and a half thousand years.

When a candidate requests full admission to the Community (after the saamanera ordination) he does not make any 'lifetime vows' but offers himself for training and instruction under his Preceptor's guidance. At the end of the ordination ceremony, the Preceptor will immediately instruct the new bhikkhu (or arrange that he is properly taught) about the Paatimokkha Rule and the other principles that all bhikkhus should follow and observe.

For the first five years a bhikkhu is called navaka ('new one') and he must live 'dependent' (nissaya) on a senior bhikkhu-either his preceptor or teacher (aacariya)-training in the ways of a bhikkhu. The preceptor and the new monk should be kind and helpful to each other, in almost a father-and-son relationship. A new bhikkhu who no longer lives under his preceptor must take another senior bhikkhu as his teacher and depend on him instead.

For the next five years after his navaka period, the bhikkhu is called majjhima, ('one in the middle') and he is allowed to live by himself if he is accomplished in certain qualities.

When a bhikkhu has completed ten Rains he is called Thera, which can be translated as 'an elder who is worthy of respect.' If he is also accomplished in certain extra qualities. He is allowed to give ordination as preceptor, to be a teacher, and have young monks live in dependence on him.

Ordination in South East Asia

Throughout South East Asia, it is very common for young men to become bhikkhus (or novices) for a short period of their life. Traditionally this occurs during the three months of the Rains Retreat, after which they disrobe and return to lay life, hopefully knowing and appreciating much more about the bhikkhu life-and probably having friends still in the monastery whom they can visit for advice. In Thailand this means that while a small proportion of bhikkhus will spend all their life in the robe, many more Thai men will have tasted the life.

Such an ordination is also a rite of passage, for it is a family, even a village event with many people joining in to see the young man off into this new stage of his life. The new monk will frequently visit his former home on his daily alms round so his ordination has a wider influence, showing the continuing possibility of living the 'Holy Life' started by the Lord Buddha so long ago.

It may also be considered a way for the young man to show his gratitude to his parents and grandparents, for they are thought to participate and share in the 'merit' he makes through his ordination. Also, some men might ordain for a time before marriage-one way for the young man to prove his maturity to his fiancee-and then again later in life after retirement.

The Rains Retreat

The bhikkhu's year is structured around the three months from July to October. In Asia this is the time of the monsoon season-the central period of the agricultural year-when the paddy fields are flooded and the main rice crop is planted. In the Buddha's time (and until modern times), people were less likely to travel around during this period because the roads were bad and there was a danger of crop damage. So the bhikkhus likewise suspended their mendicant wanderings and had to settle in one place.

A bhikkhu must make a formal determination to be resident at dawn every day in that place for the whole three month period. (There are exceptional circumstances when he may be allowed to be away, but even then he should return within seven days.) These three months are often a special time of study or meditation and so are sometimes known as the Rains Retreat or Rains Residence. This is also the normal time when the young men of South East Asia become monks for the traditional three month period.

A bhikkhu often measures the length of time he has been a monk according to how many Rains Residences he has undertaken. Therefore instead of saying he has been 'ordained seven years' he might say he has been ordained for 'seven Rains.'

Disrobing

Living the bhikkhu-life properly, following the Buddha's Teaching, requires full commitment and sustained effort. If this is lost and his Dhamma friends cannot rekindle his interest, the bhikkhu is always at liberty to return to lay life. There are no lifetime vows, so perhaps living a good lay life is better than being lax in keeping the bhikkhu's rules. Nevertheless, in some countries there is a cultural expectation of 'ordaining for life' and a corresponding stigma attached to disrobing.

"A bhikkhu who is tired of the practice of the Brahma-cariya [Holy Life] and wishes to return to the state of being a lay man may do this by taking leave of the training..." (EV,IIIp 237)

Disrobing is finalized by the monk clearly proclaiming his change of status before another bhikkhu or lay person. Once the other person understands his statement, he is no longer a bhikkhu. In Thailand there is often a formal ceremony for this that ends with the former monk undertaking the Five Precepts to replace the 227 Paatimokkha Rule. (This is also considered a step downwards, for the ideal way is certainly to continue with the Holy Life 'for as long as life lasts.')

In those countries where temporary ordinations are 'rites of passage,' some men may ordain and disrobe several times in their life-before marriage and after retirement, for example. However, there seems to be a tradition that bhikkhus do not disrobe and go forth again more than seven times, but this rarely occurs.

If a bhikkhu commits a Defeater Offence there is no need for him formally to disrobe because he is automatically expelled by his wrongful action and is no longer a bhikkhu from that moment. He can never reordain during that lifetime.

Buddhist Nuns

This book is really only concerned with bhikkhus. 27 In the Theravaada lineage it seems that the bhikkhunii ordination lineage for women given by the Buddha-equivalent to bhikkhu-ordination for men-was lost in Sri Lanka with the fall of Anuradhapura in Sri Lanka in the eleventh century C.E. and finally with the fall of Pagan in the thirteenth century C.E. Bhikkhuniis originally observed 311 Paatimokkha Rules, and there are whole sections of the Pali Vinaya texts devoted to the their rules.

The Vinaya and the Patimokkha

The Pali Vinaya texts are contained in five large volumes. The Sutta-Vibhanga division comprises the two books that contain the 227 Paatimokkha Rules (and those for bhikkhuniis) with the stories of their origin and other explanations. The next two books, the Mahaavagga and Cullavagga of the Khandhaka division:

> *"...contain a great variety of procedural material dealing with such important Sangha functions as giving the Going Forth and Acceptance, the recitation of the Paatimokkha and the keeping of the Rains Residence, as well as a great deal of material relating to bhikkhu's requisites, such as lodgings, medicines, clothing, etc." (HS ch. 7)*

The last book (the Parivaara) is a form of appendix or supplement.

So the 227 Paatimokkha Rules are a part of the greater Vinaya. As Ven. Thiradhammo remarks:

> *"...the Paatimokkha is more like the bare bones or skeleton of the Vinaya Pitaka [Basket]. Without reference to the explanations of the Sutta-Vibhanga or the elaboration of the Khandhakas this skeleton has no viable application!" (HS ch.7)*

The Buddha laid down that on full and new moon days all the bhikkhus in residence in the same community must come together in a formal meeting. If there is a quorum of at least four bhikkhus, they should listen to the full Paatimokkha Rule. A competent bhikkhu who has learned this by heart will recite it in the Pali language for the Community so that they can remind themselves of their responsibilities in keeping the major 227 Rules. The complete recitation may take anywhere from thirty-five minutes to an hour, depending on the skill of the reciting bhikkhu.

Before the Paatimokkha recitation begins, each bhikkhu should admit to any offences that he knows he has committed by formally telling another monk (or monks). Once this is accomplished, the monk is considered 'pure' and can listen to the recitation of the rules. (The recitation includes questions, asking if any bhikkhu present is guilty of the offences.) In many communities it is normal for each bhikkhu to make a 'general confession' of all possible offences to another bhikkhu before listening to the Paatimokkha recitation.

Different offences are of different seriousness but the most common faults committed by carelessness or mistake can be cleared by 'confession' to another bhikkhu. Admitting to one's mistake and agreeing to do better in the future is the way of growth and progress towards the elimination of all carelessness and absentmindedness.

Offences

When a bhikkhu breaks his precepts or rules it is called

an offence (aapatti). Such offences are committed by action or word, although intention is (almost always) a decisive factor. Just thinking about doing something wrong is unskilful and may lead to future problems but it is not an offence. We will be examining some of these rules in the following pages.

Major Rule Groups of the Patimokkha

(a) *The Four Paaraajika-The Defeaters:* The new bhikkhu is told about the Paaraajika Offences immediately after ordination, so he fully knows that they are the most serious of all the offences and that the consequences of transgressing them causes him to be no longer a bhikkhu. The nature of the act that breaks any of these four Paaraajika rules clearly reveals that the bhikkhu is no longer interested in developing the subtle and refined way of Dhamma. The alternative of voluntarily disrobing is always available if he feels he can no longer keep the Rule and this is considered a much better way to handle this sort of overwhelming desire.

A monk automatically falls from being a bhikkhu by committing any of these four offences of Defeat: sexual-intercourse, murder, major-theft, or falsely claiming supernormal abilities. A bhikkhu who falls into any of these four Defeater offences thereby severs himself irrevocably from the bhikkhu community and is no longer considered a bhikkhu.

The text portrays it with some vivid similes showing their irreparable nature: as 'a man with his head cut off'; as 'a withered leaf fallen from its stem'; as 'a palm tree cut down'; as 'a broken stone.' For while all the other offences can be remedied, these four are terminal.

(b) *The Thirteen Sanghaadisesa-Requiring Formal Meetings of the Community:* This is a very serious class of offence. However, any offending bhikkhu can be rehabilitated through confession and supervised probation. Finally, the bhikkhu needs to be reinstated by a specially convened Community (Sangha) meeting of at least twenty monks.

(c) *The Two Aniyata-Indefinite or Undetermined:* The Bhikkhu Community (together with the bhikkhu concerned) have to decide which rule, if any, has been infringed.

(d) *The 30 Nissaggiya Paacittiya-Confession with Forfeiture:* These rules are often concerned with bhikkhus being greedy and excessive in their demand for offerings, or with bhikkhus obtaining requisites through improper means. This oppresses lay donors and, classically, led them to comment: "How can these recluses... not knowing moderation ask for... ?" The rules of this category also guide bhikkhus on how they should take care of requisites and restrain the bhikkhus from obtaining items that by their very nature are inappropriate.

This offence can be cleared by forfeiture of the improper item to another bhikkhu(s) and formal confession of the offence.

The other classes of offences can usually be resolved by a simple 'confession' to another bhikkhu(s). They are:

(e) The 92 Paacittiya-Expiation through Confession.

All these offences can be cleared through confession to another bhikkhu.

(f) The Four Paa.tidesaniiya-to be Acknowledged.

(g) The 75 Sekhiyavatta-Trainings.

These are normally classified as offences of 'wrongdoing' (dukkata). There are two aspects to these 'rules of training' which are mainly about etiquette and good manners. First, they are a 'gauge' for the bhikkhu's mindfulness so that he becomes aware of his behaviour. Second, there is the external perspective of an observer watching the bhikkhu's activity and noticing the care and refinement with which he moves, eats, etc.

(h) The Seven Adhikaranasamatha-Settlement of Issues.

These are general procedures (rather than offences) for dealing with disputes, accusations, offences and duties.

In the full Vinaya texts there is also the class of 'grave' (thullaccaya) offence. This is a 'derived offence' from the most serious rules of Paaraajika and Sanghaadisesa (groups (a) and (b) above) to cover those circumstances when the full offence is not quite carried out but the conduct is still grave enough to be at fault. There is also the dubbhaasita offence of wrong speech.

Committing Offences

The Lord Buddha would not set down a rule until the situation demanded it, so the Pali often supplies the 'origin story' about how the different rules came about. Certain characters often reappear in the thick of misdeeds and mischief. For instance, one keeps on coming across Venerable Udaayin or the notorious 'group-of-six' monks. Their behaviour required attention and rectification from the Buddha, who then made it into a general rule for all the bhikkhus:

> *"'In that case, bhikkhus, I will formulate a training rule for the bhikkhus with ten aims in mind: the excellence of the Community, the peace of the Community, the curbing of the shameless, the comfort of the well-behaved bhikkhus, the restraint of [defilements] related to the present life, the prevention of [defilements] related to the next life, the arousing of faith in the faithless, the increase in the faithful, the establishment of the true Dhamma, and the fostering of discipline."' (BMC p.5)*

Later circumstances may have required the Buddha to make amendments or special exceptions and the rule would then have been adjusted accordingly. There are also many other minor offences mentioned in the original Pali texts, which have been further enlarged upon by later Commentaries. So the range of rules has become very extensive, and their observance and interpretation correspondingly wide.

Note that it was often lay people's criticism that brought the monk's wrong doings to the attention of the Buddha. (However, also notice how such criticism was often too hasty in blaming all monks rather than just the original delinquent.)

Modernization? The Great Standards

More than two and a half thousand years have passed since the Vinaya rules were originally set down by the Buddha, and many things have markedly changed since then. Should the rules be modernized and brought up to date? How can this be done?

Already during His lifetime, the Buddha made special allowances for different regions (or desa) outside the 'Middle Country' of North India-where He lived and taught. These dealt with both the workings of the Community-for example, a smaller quorum for ordination is allowed in distant parts where there are fewer monks-and practical measures, such as special dispensation for footwear and bathing. So there is a precedent for adapting to conditions, but this does not mean the abolishing of any rules.

The Lord Buddha also left us a set of principles that can still be used as a standard to judge new circumstances. These are known as 'The Great Standards.' Properly used they should protect against a wholesale dilution of the Rule.

This is how the Great Standards are formulated:

> *"Bhikkhus, whatever I have not objected to, saying, 'This is not allowable,' if it fits in with what is not allowable, if it goes against what is allowable, that is not allowable for you.*
>
> *"Whatever I have not objected to, saying, 'This is not allowable,' if it fits in with what is allowable, if it goes against what is not allowable, that is allowable for you.*
>
> *"And whatever I have not permitted, saying, 'This is allowable,' if it fits in with what is not allowable, if it goes against what is allowable, that is not allowable for you.*
>
> *"And whatever I have not permitted, saying, 'This is allowable,' if it fits in with what is allowable, if it goes against what is not allowable, that is allowable for you."*

> *Treated with care, these Great Standards should enable bhikkhus to live according to the Vinaya Rule in, for example, isolated communities in non-Buddhist countries with nontropical climates. They form a touchstone for modern conditions and substances.*

Strictness and Blaming Others

Among the unenlightened, finding fault with others (rather than dealing with one's own problems) often seems to be one of our most damaging habitual tendencies. We are able to twist whatever we want to this purpose. (Including the book that you are reading.) For bhikkhus there are many cautions:

> *"... those [monks] who follow the Vinaya blindly... tend to be proud and arrogant, regarding themselves as better behaved and more strict than others, and despising other bhikkhus as inferior. This in itself is unbecoming and worthy of censure; and when such bhikkhus have to associate with others whom they feel to be deficient in observing the Vinaya, they do it grudgingly and with a sense of distaste, and thus bring even more trouble on themselves.*

"As for the bhikkhu who behaves in the correct manner, he is bound to feel cheerful because he senses that his behaviour is becoming." (OP p.11)

"One who knows the Vinaya well, knows just how far the Vinaya goes. He will thus know what is definite and what is open to interpretation. He will know that a monk who practices contrary to what is clearly stated in the Vinaya... is rightly called alajjii [shameless]. But he will remain tolerant and in perfect harmony with those who follow a different practice from his own on matters not clearly covered by the Vinaya..." (AB)

Disparate interpretations of the Vinaya rules can lead different communities into claiming that only their understanding is correct and everyone else is wrong. The Buddhist Monastic Code has this to say:

"There is, of course, a danger in being too independent in interpreting the tradition, in that strongly held opinions can lead to disharmony in the Community.... At the same time,... there are many areas on which the Vibhanga [section of the Vinaya] is unclear and lends itself to a variety of equally valid interpretations. For proof of this, we need only look at the various traditions that have developed in the different Theravadin countries, and even within each country.

For some reason, although people tend to be very tolerant of different interpretations of the Dhamma, they can be very intolerant of different interpretations of the Vinaya and can get into heated arguments over minor issues having very little to do with the training of the mind."

Venerable Thanissaro continues by emphasizing:

"...that any interpretation based on a sound reading of the [Pali] Canon should be respected: that each bhikkhu should follow the interpretations of the Community in which he is living, as long as they do not conflict with the Canon, so as to avoid conflict over minor matters in daily life; and that he should also show respect for the differing interpretations of other Communities where they too do not conflict with the Canon, so as to avoid the pitfalls of pride and narrow-mindedness."(BMC p.15)

In the modern West we find ourselves with the unusual (unique?) situation of having Buddhist monasteries and temples of so many different countries and traditions so close at hand. We should appreciate this abundance and variety, deciding which establishment suits our needs and then not worry about the shortcomings of other places.

RIGHT LIVELIHOOD FOR A BHIKKHU

Teaching Dhamma

The bhikkhu's life should be wholly preparing him to gain insight into Dhamma. Only then will he have the wisdom to communicate anything of real value to others when the time is appropriate and the audience properly receptive. (A monk will usually wait for an invitation to speak on Dhamma, so there is no question about him proselytizing.) Teaching Dhamma, however, is not easy. If it is badly done, it can cause more misunderstanding than understanding.

The fourth Confession Rule came to be set down when the group-of-six monks taught Dhamma to lay people by rote, which caused the lay followers to feel disrespect for the monks:

> *"If a bhikkhu teaches Dhamma to an unordained person (one who is not a bhikkhu), repeating it together word by word, it is [an offence of Confession.]" (Paac. 4; Nv p.14)*

> *"To rehearse the Dhamma word by word... was the method to teach others to memorize when there were no books. This method was formerly used in (Thai) temples and popularly known by the name 'studying books in the evening.' The aim of prohibiting pronouncing (Scripture) together is clearly shown in the original story of this training-rule which was to prevent the pupils from looking down on the teacher." (Paat. 1969 Ed. p.159)*

Sixteen of the Sekhiya Training rules set down how and to whom a bhikkhu should teach Dhamma. These rules are also concerned with the etiquette of showing respect, respect not only for the bhikkhu but more importantly for the Dhamma that he is teaching. (The Great Standards would imply here that modern ways of showing respect and disrespect would be similarly covered by these rules.) These rules prohibit a bhikkhu from teaching anyone he considers to be showing disrespect to the Dhamma. Here is a summary of these Sekhiya Trainings:

"I will not teach Dhamma to someone who is not sick but who:

- has an umbrella; a wooden stick (club); weapon in their hand.

- is wearing (wooden-soled) sandals/shoes; is in a vehicle; is on a bed (or couch); is sitting clasping the knees; has a head wrapping (turban); whose head is covered; who is sitting on a seat while I am sitting on the ground; who is sitting on a high seat while I am sitting on a low seat; who is sitting while I am standing; who is walking in front of me while I am walking behind; who is walking on a pathway while I am walking beside the pathway."

How these rules are observed may diverge in different communities. Some will strictly follow the above while others will be more flexible according to modern conditions. As Venerable Brahmavangso remarks:

> *"...These Sekhiyas ensure that one teaches Dhamma only to an audience which shows respect. One may not expound from a soapbox in the marketplace... to the indifference of passers by. However it is common these days in the West for a seated audience, wearing their shoes and maybe even a hat, to respectfully listen to a speaker standing at a lectern... and as the audience is considered to be behaving respectfully according to the prevailing norms there seems no reason why a monk may not teach Dhamma in such a situation." (AB)*

Robbery by False Pretences: If a bhikkhu lies about his spiritual attainments, it may be ground for the offence of 'Defeat.' The originating circumstances for this Rule occurred during a famine when food was scarce and many bhikkhus found alms food difficult to obtain. A group of these monks devised a scheme where they told lay people of each other's attainments of 'superior human states,' often deliberately lying to impress them. The faithful lay people gave alms to such 'special' bhikkhus thinking that it would bring greater merit so they and their families went without food in order to feed those monks. Later, when the Buddha knew of this he rebuked them and described them as the worst of the 'Five Great Thieves'-immoral monks who obtain their alms food as a robber does. He set down:

> *"A bhikkhu who boasts of ['superior human states."] which he has not in fact attained, commits [an offence*

of Defeat.]" (Paar. 4; Nv p.5)

"Deliberately lying to another person that one has attained a superior human state is [an offence of Defeat.]" (Summary Paar. 4; BMC p.86)

The Commentary classes 'superior human states' (uttarimanussadhamma) as either: meditative absorption (jhaana), and certain psychic powers (abhinnaa) 112 or the path and fruit leading up to Nibbaana.

A deliberate lie is normally an offence of Confession (Paac. 1) but this deliberate false avowal of meditative attainment is classed as the most serious 'Defeater' Offence. This shows how much more damaging it was considered to be. When a 'guru-like' bhikkhu falsely puts himself forward as enlightened, his lies can be destructive not only to himself and his followers but to the whole of Buddhism.

"It may be hard to imagine in the present time why falsely claiming superior human conditions should be judged so severely. However, by reflecting that bhikkhus are totally dependent upon the generosity and goodwill of believing lay people, one may be able to appreciate the situation better. By falsely claiming high spiritual attainments a bhikkhu is equivalent to a swindler or defrauder, but in the worst way, since this involves spiritual fraud-dealing with the most precious and profound aspects of human existence."(HS ch.15)

A bhikkhu commits no offence when he has no intention to make superior claims, even if it is wrongly understood or misconstrued that way. If a bhikkhu is insane, psychotically believing his own delusions of grandeur and making extravagant claims of his own enlightenment, he receives exemption from any offence.

The eighth Confession rule is closely connected with this one of Defeat but there the 'announcement' is true. Even so, indulging in such disclosures to lay people requires confession especially when, as in the origin-story, a bhikkhu does so just to obtain more alms. The Lord Buddha criticized the showing off of even genuine supernormal attainments:

"To tell an unordained person of one's actual superior human attainments is [an offence of Confession.]" (Rule Summary, Paac. 8; BMC p.288)

Proper Behaviour Outside the Monastery: A bhikkhu can teach in many ways, not just by speech. There is the famous occasion mentioned in the Pali texts when the future right-hand disciple of Buddha, Saariputta, first saw a bhikkhu going on alms round:

"Saariputta the wanderer saw Ven. Assaji going for alms in Raajagaha: gracious... his eyes downcast, his every movement consummate. On seeing him, the thought occurred to him: 'Surely, of those in this world who are arahants or have entered the path to arahantship, this is one. What if I was to approach him and question him... "(BMC p.490)

Ven. Assaji's countenance and demeanour were a 'teaching' so impressive that Saariputta went and became a bhikkhu and a great arahant.

When a bhikkhu goes into a public place, he stands out because of the robes he wears. Whatever he does is noticed and reflects back on his community and the Sangha in general. As Venerable Thiradhammo writes:

"The bhikkhu lifestyle is for the sole purpose of realizing Nibbana. In striving towards this end, it was recognized that certain kinds of behaviour are detrimental, distracting or simply unhelpful, and are also unsuitable for an alms-mendicant. Many kinds of improper behaviour are not actually immoral, but rather put energy in the wrong direction or are expressions of a careless attitude. Some kinds of behaviour can lead to lay people's loss of faith, some are immature or childish, some bad or ugly, and some, quite malicious or nasty." (HS ch.17)

Therefore, there are a number of training rules to remind the bhikkhu about correct deportment. The first twenty-six Sekhiya Training rules cover proper behaviour in public places.

They may also explain the sometimes seemingly antisocial behaviour of a bhikkhu, who may not look one in the face or immediately say a "Good Morning." Here is a selection:

> *"When in inhabited areas, I will... wear the under and upper robe properly; be properly covered; go well restrained as to my movements; keep my eyes looking down; sit with little sound [of voice]."*

"When in inhabited areas, I will not... hitch up my robes; go or sit laughing loudly; go or sit fidgeting; swing my arms; shake my head; put my arms akimbo; cover my head with a cloth; walk on tiptoe; sit clasping the knees."

There is always an exception in the Sekhiya Training Rules for "one who is ill" so that a bhikkhu may, for example, cover his head when the weather is unbearably cold or the sun dangerously hot. The same applies to footwear, which normally should not be worn in inhabited areas.

Socializing and Wrong Resort: 'Going out on the town' is not appropriate for bhikkhus and is covered in several rules. The eighty-fifth Confession Rule, describes how the 'group-of-six' monks went to the village in the afternoon and sat around gossiping, so that lay people compared them to householders. Going outside the monastery (other than on the morning alms round) was therefore regulated with this rule:

> *"Entering a village, town, or city during the period after noon until the following dawn, without having taken leave of an available bhikkhu-unless there is an emergency-is [an offence of Confession.] (Summary Paac. 85; BMC p.470)*

Persons or places of 'wrong resort' for a bhikkhu are divided into six sorts (EV,II,pp.178-180). These are spending too much time socializing with 'unmarried women'-widows and spinsters (divorcees) or with bhikkhuniis. 'Wrong resort' also includes keeping company with sex-aberrants (pandaka). with prostitutes, and going to taverns.

A bhikkhu is prohibited from going to see and hear dancing, singing, and music. (In modern circumstances this will also concern films, videos, TV, etc.) This is similar to the Eight and Ten Precepts.

"In the Buddha's time one could only hear music at a live performance-hence seeing singing and music. However, following the Great Standards, it would seem appropriate to include contemporary forms of entertainment such as dancing, singing and music on television, videos, radios, tape-recorders and stereos. Most comprehensively, this applies to seeing or hearing any kind of entertainment like a 'pleasure-enjoying householder.' Listening or seeing for education is another matter." (HS ch.17)

Wrong Ways of Behaviour: Playful and wrong conduct (anaacaara) for a bhikkhu is, for example, playing like a child with toys or games, etc.; or making garlands of flowers, etc.

Bhikkhus are also prohibited from studying or speaking on 'low animal-like knowledge' (tiracchaana-vijjaa).

"The explanation of [low animal-like knowledge] seems to cover all general subjects which are not related to the Dhamma of bhikkhus. [These are:] knowledge of enchantments making men and women love each other; knowledge for making this or that person fall into disaster; knowledge for using spirits or showing various kinds of magic; knowledge of prediction, such as knowing beforehand lottery results; knowledge leading to self-delusion, such as transmuting mercury to gain the supernatural, as in the transmuting of silver and copper into gold.

"These knowledges are ['low animal-like knowledge'] because they are knowledge of doubtful things which are deceptive or deluding, not being true knowledge. A teacher of this is a deceiver and a pupil is one who practices to deceive, or he is just a foolish, deluded person." (EV,II,pp.120-121)

Wrong Livelihood

Wrong livelihood for a bhikkhu is divided into two:

One category concerns a bhikkhu searching for a living in a way that is also considered wrong by worldly norms. For example, robbing or deceiving others by claiming to be enlightened and receiving gifts and support because of people's belief.

The second category involves making a living that is wrong according to the Vinaya. For example: begging or asking from an unsuitable person or at an unsuitable time; thinking to gain something by giving a little but hoping for much in return; investing to gain interest; making a living by trade, for instance, giving medical treatment for reward.

Also to seek reward from:

"the ceremony for [chanting] paritta (verses of protection), that is, making holy water and the sacred thread, the blowing of a charmed formula onto a person by a bhikkhu is also prohibited... It is allowed only to recite the paritta [protection verses], but this also occurs later and is not found in the Pali [texts]... [This is wrong livelihood and a] bhikkhu who seeks his living in this way is called alajjii, 'one who has no shame.'" (EV,II,p.129)

'Corrupting Families': The very serious Sanghaadisesa Rule (requiring formal meetings of the Community) of 'corrupting families' concerns the proper relationship that bhikkhus should develop with lay followers.

It originated when two of the oft-transgressing 'group-of-six' monks neglected their Dhamma practice and behaved improperly in order to become popular with lay people. The lay people came to enjoy the sociable, playful monks so much that when more composed, right-practicing monks came by they were considered snobbish and dull.

"If a bhikkhu corrupts families-in other words he flatters and fawns on lay people-and other bhikkhus drive him away from the monastery, and in return he criticizes them and if another bhikkhu then tells him that he must not do this, but he will not listen, a Sangha should recite the [formal admonishment] to induce him to abandon this mode of behaviour. If he does not abandon it, it [entails initial and subsequent meetings of the Community]" (Sangh. 13; Nv p.7)

A bhikkhu guilty of habitually indulging in these practices

(sometimes called 'vile and low conduct' or paapasamaacaara) should be 'banished' from his particular Community until he reforms.

Of course, a bhikkhu may concern himself in lay people's affairs if it relates to religious duties. Also:

> *"the business of one's mother and father, or of persons who prepare to be ordained, called pandupalaasa (lit., yellow leaves, ready to fall off the tree), or of one's own veyyaavaccakara (steward, supporter, pupil) can be done by him even though these are apart from religious duties." (EV,II,pp.121-122)*

The relationship between the bhikkhu and his supporter should be a very special one:

> *"...A bhikkhu who is complete in good conduct does not lower himself to become the intimate of a family in the same way as a lay man may do. He is not aggressive or destructive but shows a heart of loving-kindness and conducts himself in a moderate way, thus causing good faith and reverence to arise in them towards himself. He is then called kulapasaadako (one in whom families have faith). He is the splendour of the [Teaching]...*
>
> *"Bhikkhus who are not strict lower themselves to become vile men but bhikkhus who are over-strict are not interested in showing [compassion] in helping householders in various ways." (EV,II,pp.123-124)*

A bhikkhu's wrong mode of livelihood also includes:

> *"running messages and errands for kings, ministers of state, householders, etc. A modern example would be participating in political campaigns." (BMC p.152)*

Intruding on Families: The meaning of one of the Confession rules is uncertain-as can be seen by the different translations below-but it might explain why visiting bhikkhus may be reluctant to intrude into a family's space.

The Forty-third Confession Rule (Paac. 43) arose from Ven. Upananda's visit to a man and his wife who were sitting in their bedroom together. The husband told his wife to give Ven.

Upananda a meal and when that was finished requested him to leave.

The wife noticed that her husband was becoming sexually excited, and not wishing to participate, asked Ven. Upananda to stay. He stayed. This happened three times after which the husband stormed out of the house indignant at Ven. Upananda's behaviour.

The Rule has been understood in rather different ways:

> *"Should any bhikkhu intrude upon and sit down in (the bedroom of) a family with both persons, (the man and the wife, present, one of whom does not agree to his remaining), it entails Confession." (Paac. 43; Paat. 1969 Ed. p.163)*

> *"To sit down intruding on a man and a woman in their private quarters-when one or both are sexually aroused, and when another bhikkhu is not present-is [an offence of Confession.]" (Summary Paac. 43; BMC p.385)*

> *"If a bhikkhu sits down, intruding on a family while they are taking food, it is [an offence of Confession.]" (Paac. 43; NVp19)*

> *"A monk who intrudes into and sits down in a house where husband and wife are by themselves enjoying each other's company, commits [an offence of Confession.]" (Paac. 43; BBC p.128)*

6

Patimokkha

MAHAVAGGA

(Rules for Foot-clothing, Seats, Vehicles, etc.)

1.

1. At that time the blessed Buddha dwelt at Ragagaha at the Vulture's Peak.

Now at that time Seniya Bimbisara, the king of Magadha, held rule and sovranty over eighty thousand townships. And at that time there was at Kampa a Setthi's son named Sona Kolivisa, delicately nurtured, on the soles of whose feet hair had grown.

Now when Seniya Bimbisara, the king of Magadha, was holding an assembly of the eighty thousand overseers over those townships, he sent a message to Sona Kolivisa on some matter of business, saying, 'Let Sona come hither. I desire Sona's presence!'

2. Then spake the parents of Sona Kolivisa to him thus: 'The king, dear Sona, wishes to see thy feet. But stretch not out thy feet, dear Sona, towards the king. Take thy seat cross-legged before the king, that the king may see thy feet as thou sittest there.' And they carried Sona Kolivisa in a palankeen (to Ragagaha).

And Sona Kolivisa went to the place where Seniya Bimbisara, the king of Magadha, was. And when he had come there, and had bowed down before Seniya Bimbisara, the king of Magadha, he took his seat cross-legged before the king. And Seniya Bimbisara, the king of Magadha, saw that hair had grown on the soles of the feet of Sona Kolivisa.

3. Now after Seniya Bimbisara, the king of Magadha, had instructed the eighty thousand overseers over those townships in the things of this world he exhorted them, saying, 'Ye have now received from me instruction in the things of this world. Go now, and wait upon the Blessed One. The Blessed One himself shall instruct you in the things of eternity.'

Then the eighty thousand overseers over those townships went on to the Vulture's Peak.

4. Now at that time the venerable Sagata was the attendant on the Blessed One. And the eighty thousand overseers over those townships went to the place where the venerable Sagata was. And when they were come there they spake thus to the venerable Sagata:

> *The eighty thousand overseers over the townships are come here, Sir, to visit the Blessed One. It were well, Sir, that we should be granted an audience of the Blessed One.'*

Then do you, Sirs, stay here yet a moment, while I let the Blessed One know.'

5. Then the venerable Sagata disappeared down the steps from before the very eyes of the eighty thousand overseers over those townships, and appeared before the Blessed One, and spake to the Blessed One, and said:

> *'Lord, the eighty thousand overseers over the townships are come here to visit the Blessed One. Let the Blessed One do as seemes to him fit.'*

Do thou then, Sagata, make a seat ready in the shade of the house.'

6. 'Even so, Lord!' said the venerable Sagata, in assent, to the Blessed One. And taking a chair, he disappeared from before the Blessed One, and reappeared up the steps before the very eyes of those eighty thousand overseers over those townships, and made ready a seat in the shade of the house.

And the Blessed One came out of the house and sat down on the seat made ready in the shade thereof.

7. Then those eighty thousand overseers over the townships went up to the place where the Blessed One was. And when they had come there they bowed down before the Blessed One and took their seats on one side. But those eighty thousand overseers over the townships paid more respect in their hearts to the venerable Sagata than to the Blessed One.

And the Blessed One perceived by his mind the thoughts of the minds of those eighty thousand overseers over the townships; and he addressed the venerable Sagata, and said: 'Show them now, Sagata, a still greater wonder, beyond the power of men.'

'Even so, Lord!' said the venerable Sagata, in assent, to the Blessed One. And rising up into the air he walked, and stood, and sat, and lay down, and gave forth smoke and fire, and disappeared in the sky.

8. Then the venerable Sagata, when he had shown in the open sky wonders of various kinds beyond the power of men, fell down with his head at the feet of the Blessed One, and said to the Blessed One:

> *My teacher, Lord, is the Blessed One; and I am the disciple. My teacher, Lord, is the Blessed One; and I am the disciple.'*

Then those eighty thousand overseers over the townships thinking, 'Wonderful is it, most marvellous! If even the pupil be so mighty and so powerful, how much more then the master!' paid more respect in their hearts to the Blessed One than to the venerable Sagata.

9. Then the Blessed One perceived by his mind the thoughts of the minds of those eighty thousand overseers over the townships, and held to them a discourse in due order; that is to say, he spake to them of giving, of righteousness, of heaven, of the danger, the worthlessness, the depravity of lusts, and of the advantages of renunciation. And when the Blessed One perceived that they had become pliant, softened, unprejudiced, upraised and believing in heart, then he proclaimed that which

is the special doctrine of the Buddhas; (that is to say), Suffering, its Origin, its Cessation, and the Path.

Just as a clean cloth, from which all stain has been washed away, would readily take the dye, just even so did those eighty thousand overseers over the townships obtain, even while sitting there, the pure and spotless Eye of the Truth; (that is to say, the knowledge that) whatsoever has a beginning, in that is inherent also the necessity of dissolution.

10. And having seen the Truth, having mastered the Truth, having understood the Truth, having penetrated the Truth, having overcome uncertainty, having dispelled all doubts, having gained full knowledge, dependent on nobody else for the knowledge of the doctrine of the Teacher, they said to the Blessed One: 'Glorious, Lord! glorious, Lord! Just as if one should set up, Lord, what had been overturned, or should reveal what had been hidden, or should point out the way to one who had lost his way, or should bring a lamp into the darkness, in order that those who had eyes might see visible things, thus has the Blessed One preached the doctrine in many ways. We take our refuge, Lord, in the Blessed One, and in the Dhamma, and in the fraternity of Bhikkhus; may the Blessed One receive us from this day forth while our life lasts as his disciples who have taken their refuge in Him.'

11. And Sona Kolivisa thought: As I understand the Dhamma proclaimed by the Blessed One, it is not easy to a person living as a layman to lead a wholly perfect and pure and altogether consummate life of holiness. What if I were to cut off my hair and beard, and to put on yellow robes, and give up the world, and go forth into the houseless state.'

And those eighty thousand overseers over the townships, having expressed their joy and delight at the words of the Blessed One, rose from their seats, respectfully saluted the Blessed One, and passing round him with their right sides towards him, went away.

12. And Sona Kolivisa, soon after those eighty thousand overseers over the townships had departed, went to the place where the Blessed One was. And when he had come there he

bowed down before the Blessed One and took his seat on one side. Sitting on one side Sona Kolivisa said to the Blessed One: 'As I understand the Dhamma proclaimed by the Blessed One (&c., as in § 11, down to:) and go forth into the houseless state. I desire, Lord, to cut off my hair and beard, and to put on yellow robes, and to give up the world, and to go forth into the houseless state. May the Blessed One, Lord, ordain me.'

Thus Sona Kolivisa received from the Blessed One the pabbaggaand Upasampada ordinations. And the venerable Sona, soon after his Upasampada, dwelt in the Sitavana grove.

13. As he, with eager determination, was walking up and down there, his feet were injured, and the place in which he walked became covered with blood, like a slaughterhouse for oxen. Then in the mind of the venerable Sona, who had gone apart and was plunged in meditation, there sprung up this thought:

> *'Though I have become one of those disciples of the Blessed One who live in the exercise of strenuous determination, yet my heart has not been set free from the Asavas through absence of craving. And there is much wealth laid up for me at home. It is possible both to enjoy that wealth, and to do good deeds. Let me now, then, returning to the lower state, enjoy my wealth and do good deeds.'*

14. Now the Blessed One perceived in his mind the thought of the heart of the venerable Sona; and as quickly as a strong man can stretch forth his arm, or can draw it back again when it has been stretched forth, he disappeared from the hill of the Vulture's Peak, and appeared in the Sitavana grove. And the Blessed One, as he was passing through the sleeping-places (of the Bhikkhus), came up, with a multitude of Bhikkhus, to the place where the venerable Sona had walked up and down.

When the Blessed One saw that the place where the venerable Sona had walked up and down was covered with blood, he addressed the Bhikkhus, and said: 'Whose walking-place is this, O Bhikkhus, which is covered with blood, like a slaughterhouse for oxen?'

'As the venerable Sona, Lord, was walking up and down here with eager determination, his feet were injured; and so this place has become covered with blood, like a slaughterhouse for oxen.'

15. Then the Blessed One went on to the house in which the venerable Sona was living, and sat down there on a seat made ready for him. And the venerable Sona bowed down before the Blessed

One, and took his seat on one side. And when he was thus seated, the Blessed One addressed the venerable Soma, and said: 'Is it not true, Sona, that in your mind, when you had gone apart and were plunged in meditation, there sprung up this thought: "Though I have become (&c., as in § 13, down to the end)?"'

'Even so, Lord!'

'Now what think you, Sona,—you were skilled, were you not, when you formerly lived in the world, in the music of the lute?'

'That was so, Lord!'

'Now what think you, Sona,—when the strings of your lute were too much stretched, had your lute then any sound, was it in a fit state to be played upon?'

'Not so, Lord!'

16. 'Now what think you, Sona,—when the strings of your lute were too loose, had your lute then any sound, was it in a fit state to be played upon?' 'Not so, Lord!'

Now what think you, Sona,—when the strings of your lute were neither too much stretched nor too loose, but fixed in even proportion, had your lute sound then, was it then in a fit state to be played upon?'

Yes, Lord!'

'And just so, Sona, does too eager a determination conduct to self-righteousness, and too weak a determination to sloth.

17. Do thou, therefore, O Sona, be steadfast in evenness of determination, press through to harmony of your mental powers. Let that be the object of your thought!'

Even so, Lord!' said the venerable Sona, and hearkened to the word of the Blessed One.

And when the Blessed One had exhorted the venerable Sona with this exhortation, then, as quickly as a strong man can stretch forth his arm, or can draw it back again when it has been stretched forth, he vanished from the presence of the venerable Sona in the Sitavana grove, and reappeared on the hill of the Vulture's Peak.

18. Thenceforward the venerable Sona was stead-fast in evenness of determination, he pressed through to harmony of his mental powers, that did he take as the object of his thought. And the venerable Sona remaining alone and separate, earnest, zealous, and resolved, attained ere long to that supreme goal of the higher life for the sake of which noble youths go out from all and every household gain and comfort to become houseless wanderers—yea, that supreme goal did he, by himself, and while yet in this visible world, bring himself to the knowledge of, and continue to realise, and to see face to face! And he became conscious that rebirth was at an end, that the higher life had been fulfilled, that all that should be done had been accomplished, and that after this present life there would be no beyond!

So the venerable Sona became yet another among the Arahats.

19. Now when the venerable Sona had attained to Arahatship there occurred to him the thought: 'Let me now make known my Insight in the presence of the Blessed One!'

Then the venerable Sona went to the place where the Blessed One was, and bowed down before the Blessed One, and took his seat on one side. And when he was thus seated, the venerable Sona said to the Blessed One:

20. 'Whatsoever Bhikkhu, Lord, is an Arahat whose Asavas are rooted out, who has lived the life, who has accomplished the task, who has laid aside every burden, who has gained the end he had in view, who has quite broken the fetter of a craving for (future) existence, who is completely set free by insight, six things does he reach up unto —unto renunciation, unto the love

of solitude, unto kindness of heart, unto the destruction of craving, unto the destruction of thirst, unto the getting free from delusions.

21. 'Now it may be, Lord, that it might occur, regarding this matter, to some brother, thus: "For the sake of faith merely has this brother attained unto renunciation." But not thus, Lord, should this matter be regarded. For the Bhikkhu in whom the Asavas are rooted out, who has lived the life, who has accomplished the task, he looks not upon himself as one who has anything yet to do, or to gather up, of (the fruit of his past) labour; but he attains to renunciation by the destruction of lust, by the very condition of the absence of lust; he attains to renunciation by the destruction of ill-will, by the very condition of the absence of ill-will; he attains to renunciation by the destruction of delusions, by the very condition of the absence of delusions.

22. 'Now it may, be, Lord, that it might occur, regarding this matter, to some brother, thus: "Seeking after gain, hospitality, and fame bath this brother attained to the love of solitude." But not thus.

23. 'Now it may be, Lord, that it might occur, regarding this matter, to some brother, thus: "Returning, verily, to the dependence upon works, as if that were the true essence (of spiritual welfare), has this brother attained to kindness of heart." But not thus.

24. 'He attains to the destruction of craving by the destruction of lust. He attains to the absence of thirst (&c., as in § 21). He attains to the absence of delusions (&c., as in § 21, down to the end).

25. 'When a Bhikkhu, Lord, has thus become fully emancipated in heart, even though many objects visible to the sight should enter the path of his eye, yet they take not possession of his mind: undefined is his mind, firm, immovable; and he sees into the (manner which that impression) passes away —even though many objects audible to the ear, assemble to the nostrils, tastable to the tongue, feelable by the body, sensible to the intellect should enter the path of the ear, the

nose, the tongue, the skin, the intellect, yet they take not possession of his mind: undefined is his mind, firm, immovable, and he sees into the (manner in which that impression) passes away.

26. 'Just, Lord, as if there be a mountain of rock, undivided, solid, one mass, and much wind and rain should fall upon it from the direction of the East, or of the West, or of the North, or of the South, yet they would not make it shake, or tremble, or quake; just so, Lord, when a Bhikkhu has thus become fully emancipated in heart.

27. 'He who has attained to renunciation, to solitude of heart, who has attained to kindness, and to the rooting out of craving,

'He who has attained to the rooting out of thirst, to the absence of delusions from the mind, he sees the source of sensations, his mind is quite set free.

'To such a Bhikkhu, so emancipated, and with calmness in his heart, there is no gathering up of what is done, nothing to be done still remains.

'As a rock, all of one mass, is not shaken by the breezes, just so never can shapes and tastes, and sounds, and smells, and touch—the whole of them

Things wished for, things unwished—make tremble such a one. Firm is his mind, set free. He sees into the end thereof.'

28. And the Blessed One addressed the Bhikkhus, and said: 'Thus, brethren, do young men of worth make their insight known. The truth is spoken, and the self is not obtruded. But herein some foolish ones, may thinks, make known their insight to be a thing ridiculous, and they, thereafter, fall into defeat!'

29. Then the Blessed One said to the venerable Sona, 'You, Sona, have been delicately nurtured. I enjoin upon you, Sona, the use of shoes with one lining.'

I have gone out from the world, Lord, into the houseless state, abandoning eighty cart-loads of gold, and a retinue of seven elephants. It will be said against me for this matter: "Sona Kolivisa went out from the world into the houseless state, abandoning eighty cart-loads of gold, and a retinue of seven elephants; but the very same man now accustoms himself to the use of shoes with a lining to them." If the Blessed One will enjoin their use upon the Order of Bhikkhus, I will also use them. If the Blessed One will not enjoin their use upon the Order of Bhikkhus, neither will I use them.'

Then the Blessed One, on that occasion, having delivered a religious discourse, thus addressed the Bhikkhus:

> *'I enjoin upon you, O Bhikkhus, the use of shoes with one lining to them. Doubly lined shoes, Bhikkhus, are not to be worn, nor trebly lined ones, nor shoes with many linings. Whosoever shall wear such, is guilty of a dukkata offence.'*

2.

1. Now at that time the Khabbaggiya Bhikkhus were in the habit of wearing slippers all of a blue, yellow, red, brown, black, orange, or yellowish colour. People were annoyed, murmured, and became angry, saying, '(These act) like those who still enjoy the pleasures of the world.' The brethren told this thing to the Blessed One.

'Do not wear, O Bhikkhus, shoes that are all of a blue, yellow, red, brown, black, orange, or yellowish colour. Whosoever does so, is guilty of a dukkata offence.'

2. Now at that time the Khabbaggiya Bhikkhus were in the habit of wearing shoes with edges of a blue, yellow, red, brown, black, orange, or yellowish colour.

People were annoyed, murmured, and became angry, saying, 'These act like those who still enjoy the pleasures of the world.' The brethren told this thing to the Blessed One.

'Do not wear, O Bhikkhus, shoes that have edges of a blue, yellow, red, brown, black, orange, or yellowish colour. Whosoever does so, is guilty of a dukkata offence.'

3. Now at that time the Khabbaggiya Bhikkhus were in the habit of wearing shoes with heel-coverings; mocassins; laced boots; boots lined with cotton; boots of various hues, like the wings of partridges; boots pointed with rams' horns, and with goats' horns; ornamented with scorpions' tails; sewn round

with peacocks' feathers; or shoes of all kinds of colours.

People were annoyed (&c., as in § 2, down to:) told this thing to the Blessed One.

'Do not wear, O Bhikkhus, shoes with heel-coverings (&c., as in § 3, down to:) shoes of all kinds of colours. Whosoever does so, is guilty of a dukkata offence.'

4. Now at that time the Khabbaggiya Bhikkhus were in the habit of wearing shoes adorned with lion-skins, tiger-skins, panther-skins, antelope-skins, otter-skins, cat-skins, squirrel-skins, and owl-skins.

People were annoyed (&c., as in § 3, down to the end, substituting 'shoes adorned with lion-skins, &c.,' for 'shoes with heel-coverings, &c.')

3.

1. Now the Blessed One, having dressed early in the morning, went into Ragagaha, duly bowled and robed, for alms, with a certain Bhikkhu as his companion. And that Bhikkhu followed limping step by step behind the Blessed One.

Now a certain lay-disciple who had put on a pair of shoes with many linings, saw the Blessed One approaching from afar. And when he saw him, he took off that pair of shoes and went up to the Blessed One, and saluted him; and went on to that Bhikkhu, and saluted him, and said:

2. 'Why does your reverence limp?'

My feet, friend, are blistered.'

'But here, Sir, are shoes.'

'Enough, good friend! shoes with linings have been forbidden by the Blessed One.'

'Take the shoes, O Bhikkhu!'

Then the Blessed One, on that occasion, having delivered a religious discourse, addressed the Bhikkhus, and said:

I allow you, O Bhikkhus, the use of shoes with linings, when they have been cast off by others. But new shoes with linings are not to be worn. Whosoever does so, is guilty of a dukkata offence.'

4.

1. Now at that time the Blessed One walked up and down in the open air unshod. Noticing that, 'The Master walks unshod,' the Elders (the Thera Bhikkhus) also went unshod when they were walking up and down. But though the Master and the Thera Bhikkhus went unshod, the Khabbaggiya Bhikkhus walked up and down with coverings on their feet.

The temperate Bhikkhus were annoyed, murmured, and became angry, saying, 'How can these Khabbaggiya Bhikkhus walk shod, when the Master and the Thera Bhikkhus walk unshod?'

2. Then those Bhikkhus told this thing to the Blessed One.

'Is it true, what they say, O Bhikkhus, that the Khabbaggiya Bhikkhus walk shod, though the Master and the Elders walk unshod?'

'It is true, Lord.'

The Blessed Buddha rebuked them, saying,

'How, O Bhikkhus, can these foolish persons walk shod, though. For even the lay-men, O Bhikkhus, who are clad in white, for the sake of some handicraft that may procure them a living, will be respectful, affectionate, hospitable to their teachers. Do you, therefore, O Bhikkhus, so let (your light) shine forth, that you having left the world (to enter into) so well taught a doctrine and discipline may be respectful, affectionate, hospitable to your teachers (Akariyas), or those who rank as teachers, and to your superiors (upagghayas), or those who rank as superiors. This will not conduct, O Bhikkhus, to the conversion of the unconverted, and to the augmentation of the number of the converted: but it will result, O Bhikkhus, in the unconverted being repulsed (from the faith), and in many of the converted becoming estranged.' Having thus rebuked them, and having delivered a religious discourse, he thus addressed the Bhikkhus:

None of you, O Bhikkhus, is to walk shod, when your teachers or those who rank as teachers, or your superiors, or those who rank as superiors, are walking unshod. Whosoever does so, is guilty of a dukkata offence.

'And no one of you, O Bhikkhus, is to wear shoes in the open Arama. Whosoever does so, is guilty of a dukkata offence.'

5.

1. Now at that time a certain Bhikkhu had an eruption on his feet. They used to carry that Bhikkhu out when he wanted to ease himself. The Blessed One as he was passing through the sleeping places (of the Bhikkhus) saw them (doing so), and going up to them, he said:

2. 'What is the disease, O Bhikkhus, from which this Bhikkhu suffers?'

This venerable brother has an eruption on his feet, Lord, and we are carrying him out to ease himself.'

Then, on that occasion, the Blessed One, having delivered a religious discourse, addressed the Bhikkhus, and said:

'I enjoin, O Bhikkhus, the use of foot coverings by one whose feet hurt him, or are blistered, or who has an eruption on his feet.'

6.

1. Now at that time the Bhikkhus used to get up on to couches or chairs with unwashen feet; and the robes and seats became soiled.

They told this thing to the Blessed One.

'I enjoin, O Bhikkhus, the use of foot coverings when one of you wishes to get up on to couches or chairs.'

2. Now at that time when the Bhikkhus were going to the Uposatha Hall or to the assembly in the dark, they trod upon stakes or thorns, and their feet were hurt.

They told this thing to the Blessed One.

'I enjoin, O Bhikkhus, the use of foot coverings in the open Arama, and of a torch, or lamp, and a walking stick.'

3. Now at that time the Khabbaggiya Bhikkhus used to rise up in the night towards dawn; and, putting on wooden shoes, walked up and down in the open air talking, in tones high, loud, and harsh, of all kinds of worldly things—such as tales of kings, of robbers, of ministers of state; tales of armies, of terror, of

war; conversation respecting meats, drinks, clothes, couches, garlands, perfumes, relationships, equipages, villages, towns, cities, provinces, women, warriors, and streets; tales about buried treasures, ghost stories; various tales; discussions on the world; disasters by sea; things which are, and things which are not. And so doing they both trod upon and slew all kinds of insects, and disturbed the Bhikkhus in their meditations.

4. The moderate Bhikkhus were annoyed, murmured, and became angry, saying, 'How can the Khabbaggiya Bhikkhus [do so]?'

And those Bhikkhus told this thing to the Blessed One.

'Is it true' ?

'It is true, Lord.'

He rebuked them, and having delivered a religious discourse, he addressed the Bhikkhus, and said: Wooden shoes, O Bhikkhus, are not to be worn. Whosoever wears them, is guilty of a dukkata offence.'

7.

1. Now when the Blessed One had remained at Ragagaha as long as he thought fit, he set out on his journey towards Benares. And wandering from place to place, he came to Benares, and there at Benares the Blessed One stayed in the deer-park Isipatana.

Now at that time the Khabbaggiya Bhikkhus, since the Blessed One had forbidden wooden shoes, used to break off young palmyra palms, and wear shoes made of the talipat leaves. The young palmyra plants withered. People were annoyed, murmured, and became angry, saying, 'How can the Sakyaputtiya Samanas break off young palmyra palms, and wear shoes made of the talipat leaves? The young palmyra plants wither. (By so doing), the Sakyaputtiya Samanas destroy vegetable life.'

2. The Bhikkhus heard those people murmuring in annoyance and indignation; and they told this matter to the Blessed One.

'Is it true'

'It is true, Lord.'

The Blessed Buddha rebuked them, saying, 'How can those foolish persons, O Bhikkhus, [act thus]? For people believe, O Bhikkhus, that life dwells in a tree. Such conduct will not conduct becoming estranged.

Foot coverings made of talipat leaves, O Bhikkhus, are not to be worn. Whosoever wears them, is guilty of a dukkata offence.'

3. Now at that time the Khabbaggiya Bhikkhus, since the Blessed One had forbidden talipat shoes, used to break off young bamboos, and wear shoes made of the bamboo leaves (&c., as in last section down to the end, substituting bamboo for palmyra).

8.

1. Now when the Blessed One had remained at Benares as long as he thought fit, he set out on his journey towards Bhaddiya. And wandering from place to place he came to Bhaddiya: and there, at Bhaddiya, he stayed in the Gatiya Grove.

Now at that time the Bhikkhus at Bhaddiya were accustomed to the use of various kinds of foot coverings for the sake of ornament. They made, or had made for themselves foot coverings of tina-grass, of munga-grass, of babbaga-grass, of the leaves of the date-palm, of kamala-grass, and of wool. And they neglected instruction, enquiry, morality, self-concentration, and wisdom.

2. The moderate Bhikkhus were annoyed, murmured, and became angry, thinking, 'How can they [do so]?' And those Bhikkhus told this thing to the Blessed One.

'Is it true' ?

'It is true, Lord.'

The Blessed Buddha rebuked them, saying, 'How can they [do so]?' This will not conducts (&c., as in chap. 4. 2, down to:) becoming estranged.

3. Having thus rebuked them, and having delivered a religious discourse, he thus addressed the Bhikkhus: 'Shoes, O

Bhikkhus, made of tina-grass are not to be worn, or made of munga-grass, or of babbaga-grass, or of leaves of the date-palm, or of kamala-grass, or of wool, nor [ornamented with] gold, or silver, or pearls, or beryls, or crystal, or copper, or glass, or tin, or lead, or bronze. Whosoever does so, is guilty of a dukkata offence.

'And clogs, O Bhikkhus, that are taken away, are not to be worn. Whosoever does so, is guilty of a dukkata offence.

'I allow you, O Bhikkhus, the use of three kinds of clogs, that are fixed to the ground, and are not taken away, privy-clogs, urinal-clogs, and rinsing-clogs.'

9.

1. Now when the Blessed One had remained at Bhaddiya as long as he thought fit, he set out on a journey towards Savatthi. And walking from place to place he arrived at Savatthi. There the Blessed One dwelt at Savatthi at the Getavana, Anatha-pindika's Grove.

2. Now at that time the Khabbaggiya Bhikkhus used to catch hold of the heifers crossing on the Akiravati River by their horns, or ears, or dewlaps, or tails, or spring up upon their backs, or touch with lustful thoughts their privy parts: and they used to duck the young calves and so kill them. People were annoyed, murmured, and became angry, saying, 'How can the Sakyaputtiya Samanas [act thus]? it is like men still enjoying the pleasures of the world.' And Bhikkhus heard them murmuring in annoyance and indignation: and those Bhikkhus told this thing to the Blessed One.

'Is it true'?

'It is true, Lord.'

He rebuked them, and having delivered a religious discourse, he addressed the Bhikkhus, and said:

'Heifers are not to be caught hold of, O Bhikkhus, by their horns, or their ears, or their dewlaps, or their tails. You are not to get up on their backs. Whosoever gets up on their backs, is guilty of a dukkata offence. And their privy parts, O Bhikkhus, are not to be touched with

lustful thoughts. Whosoever does so, is guilty of a thullakkaya offence. And calves ought not to be killed. Whosoever kills them, let him be dealt with according to law.'

3. Now at that time the Khabbaggiya Bhikkhus used to have themselves carried in vehicles to which cows were yoked with a bull between them, or bulls were yoked with a cow between them. People were annoyed, murmured, and became angry, saying, 'That is as is done at the Feast of the Ganga and the Mahi.'

They told this thing to the Blessed One.

'Do not have yourselves carried in vehicles, O Bhikkhus. Whosoever does so, is guilty of a dukkata offence.'

10 1.

1. Now at that time a certain Bhikkhu, as he was passing through the Kosala country to Savatthi, to visit the Blessed One, was taken ill on the way. And that Bhikkhu went aside out of the road, and sat down at the foot of a certain tree.

When people saw him sitting there, they said: 'Whither is your reverence going?'

'I am going, friends, to Savatthi to visit the Blessed One.'

2. 'Come along, Sir; let us go together.'

'I cannot, friends. I am sick.'

'Well then, Sir, get up into the cart.'

'Enough, friends! The Blessed One has forbidden the use of vehicles.' And fearing to offend, he refused to get up into the cart.

And when that Bhikkhu had come to Savatthi, he told this thing to the Bhikkhus, and they told it to the Blessed One.

'I allow you, O Bhikkhus, if you are sick, to use a cart.'

Now the Bhikkhus thought: 'Should the carts be yoked with cows or bulls?'

They told this thing to the Blessed One.

'I allow you, O Bhikkhus, to use a cart drawn by bullocks, or by hand.'

Now at that time a certain Bhikkhu was exceedingly distressed by the jolting of a cart.

I allow you, O Bhikkhus, the use of a litter or a sedan-chair.'

3. Now at that time the Khabbaggiya Bhikkhus were in the habit of using lofty and large things to recline upon, that is to say: large cushions; divans; coverlets with long fleece; counterpanes of many colours, woollen coverlets, white or marked with thick flowers; mattresses; cotton coverlets, dyed with figures of animals; rugs with long hair on one or both sides; carpets in wrought with gold, or with silk; large woollen carpets such as the nautch girls dance upon; rich elephant housings, horse-rugs, or carriage rugs; panther or antelope skins; couches covered with canopies, or with crimson cushions at both ends.

When people, who went to visit the Viharas, saw these things, they were annoyed, murmured, and became angry, thinking, 'This is as if they were still enjoying the pleasures of the world.'

They told this thing to the Blessed One.

4. 'Lofty and large things to recline upon, such as large cushions (&c., as in § 3, down to:) cushions crimson at both ends, are not, O Bhikkhus, to be used. Whosoever uses them, is guilty of a dukkata offence.'

5. Now at that time the Khabbaggiya Bhikkhus, since the use of lofty and large things to recline upon had been forbidden by the Blessed One, used to use fine skins, such as lion, tiger, and panther skins. These skins were cut to fit the couches, and to fit the chairs; and were spread inside or outside the couches or the chairs.

When people, who went to visit the Viharas, saw these things, they were annoyed, murmured, and became angry, thinking, 'This is as if they were still enjoying the pleasures of the world.' They told this thing to the Blessed One.

6. 'Fine skins, such as lion, tiger, and panther skins, are not, O Bhikkhus, to be used. Whosoever does so, is guilty of a dukkata offence.'

7. Now at that time the Khabbaggiya Bhikkhus, since fine skins had been forbidden by the Blessed

One, began to use the skins of oxen. These skins were cut to fit the couches, or the chairs; and were spread inside or outside the couches, or the chairs.

Now a certain Bhikkhu of bad character was a friend of the family of a certain lay-disciple of a bad character.

And that bad Bhikkhu, early one morning, dressed himself, and with his robe on and his bowl in his hand, went to the dwelling-place of that bad disciple, and sat down on a seat made ready for him.

And the bad disciple went up to the place where the bad Bhikkhu was, and saluted him, and took his seat beside him.

8. Now at that time that bad disciple had a young bull beautiful to behold, quiet, and varied in colour like a panther's cub. And the bad Bhikkhu gazed with longing at the bull.

And that bad disciple said to that bad Bhikkhu: 'Why does your reverence gaze so with longing at that bull?'

'My friend,' said he, 'I want that bull's skin.'

Then that bad disciple slew that bull, and skinned it, and gave it to that bad Bhikkhu. And that bad Bhikkhu, hiding that skin under his robe, went away.

9. Now the cow, greedy for her calf, followed that bad Bhikkhu, keeping behind him. The Bhikkhus said:

'How is it, friend, that this cow keeps following so behind you?'

'I don't know, friends, why it should keep following me.'

But that bad Bhikkhu's robe was soiled with blood; and the Bhikkhus asked him,

'How has this robe of yours got marked with blood?'

Then he told them the whole matter.

'How is that, Sir? You have been causing another to deprive a living thing of life!' 'That is so, friends.'

The modest among the Bhikkhus were annoyed, murmured, and became angry, saying, 'How can this Bhikkhu induce a man to deprive a living thing of life?

Has not the taking of life been censured, and the abstinence therefrom been praised in many a discourse by the Blessed One?'

And the Bhikkhus told this thing to the Blessed One.

Then the Blessed One held because of this, and on that occasion, an assembly of the community of Bhikkhus, and asked that wicked Bhikkhu,

'Is it true, as they say, that you, O Bhikkhu, have been inducing another to deprive a living thing of life?'

'It is true, Lord.'

'But how can you be so foolish as to do so? Have I not censured in many a discourse the taking of life, O foolish one, and praised the abstinence therefrom? Such conduct, thou foolish one, will not conduct to the conversion of the unconverted!'

And having thus rebuked him, and delivered a religious discourse, he addressed the Bhikkhus, and said:

Bhikkhus! No one shall cause a living thing to be deprived of life. Whosoever does so shall be dealt with according to the Laws. Ox-skins are not to be worn, O Bhikkhus. Whosoever does so, is guilty of a dukkata offence. And neither, O Bhikkhus, is any skin to be made use of at all. Whosoever does so, is guilty of a dukkata offence.'

11.

Now at that time men had couches and chairs covered or bound with skins. The Bhikkhus, fearing to offend, would not sit down upon them.

They told this thing to the Blessed One.

'I allow you, O Bhikkhus, to sit down on seats arranged by laymen, but not to lie down upon them.'

Now at that time the Viharas were bound together by thongs made of skin. The Bhikkhus fearing to offend, would not sit down upon them.

They told this thing to the Blessed One.

'I allow you, O Bhikkhus, to sit down upon (skins when they are) only used for binding things together.'

12.

Now at that time the Khabbaggiya Bhikkhus used to go into the villages with their shoes on.

The people were annoyed, murmured, and became angry, saying, That is how those behave who are still enjoying the pleasures of the world!'

They told this thing to the Blessed One.

'You are not to go into the villages, O Bhikkhus, with your shoes on. Whosoever does so, is guilty of a dukkata offence.'

Now at that time a certain Bhikkhu was sick, and unable to go into the village without shoes on. They told this thing to the Blessed One.

'I allow a sick Bhikkhu, O Bhikkhus, to go into the village with his shoes on.'

13 1.

1. Now at that time the venerable Maha Kakkayana was staying in Avanti on the hill called the Precipice, near Kuraraghara. And at that time the lay-disciple named Sona Kutikanna was the personal attendant upon the venerable Maha Kakkayana.

And the disciple Sona Kutikanna went to the place where the venerable Maha Kakkayana was, and saluted him, and took his seat beside him. And when he was thus seated, he said to the venerable Maha Kakkayana:

'As I understand the doctrine laid down by the venerable Maha Kakkayana, it is difficult for the man who dwells at home to live the higher life in all its fullness, in all its purity, in all its bright perfection. I wish therefore to cut off my hair and beard, to clothe myself in the orange-coloured robes, and to go forth from the household life into the houseless state. May the venerable Maha Kakkayana receive me into the Order of those who have renounced the world!'

2. 'Hard is it, Sona, your life long to live the higher life using only one bed, and with but one meal a day.

Do you, therefore, Sona, remain in the state of a householder, and practise only for a time the higher life, the precepts of the Buddhas, using only one bed, and with but one meal a day.'

Then the desire for renunciation which had arisen in the disciple Sona Kutikanna abated in him.

A second time the disciple Sona Kutikanna [made the same request, and received the same reply with the same result].

And a third time Sona Kutikanna made the same request. Then the venerable Maha Kakkayana conferred the pabbagga (ordination) on the disciple Sona Kutikanna.

Now at that time in the Southern country and in Avanti there were but few Bhikkhus.

And it was only after the lapse of three years that the venerable Maha Kakkayana was able, with difficulty, and with trouble, to get together a meeting of the Order in which ten Bhikkhus were present. And then he admitted the venerable Sona into the higher rank of the Order.

3. Now when the venerable Sona had passed the rainy season there sprang up in his mind, when he was meditating alone, this thought:

> *'I have heard indeed that the Blessed One is such and such a one. But I have not as yet seen him face to face. I should like to go and visit the Blessed One, the Arahat Buddha, if my superior would allow me.'*

And in the evening the venerable Sona, leaving his solitude, went to the place where the venerable Maha Kakkayana was, and saluted him, and took his seat beside him. And when he was thus seated, he said to the venerable Maha Kakkayana:

4. 'When I was meditating alone, venerable Sir, the following thought occurred to my mind, "I have heard (&c., as above)." Now I would go and visit the Blessed One, the Arahat Buddha, if you, as my superior, allow it.'

That is good, that is good, Sona! Go then, Sona, to visit the Blessed One, the Arahat Buddha.

You shall see, Sona, how the Blessed One arouses faith, is worthy of faith, calm in his senses, calm in his mind, gifted with the highest self-control and quietude, an elephant among men, subdued, guarded, with his senses in subjection to himself.

Do you therefore, Soma, bow down in my name at the feet of the Blessed One, and say, "Lord! my superior, the venerable Maha Kakkayana, bows down in salutation at the feet of the Blessed One!" and add, "In the Southern country and in Avanti there are, Lord, but few Bhikkhus.

And it was only after the lapse of three years that with difficulty and with trouble an assembly of the Order was got together, in which ten members were present, and I could be received into the higher rank of the Order.

May the Blessed One be pleased, therefore, to allow the higher ordination in the Southern country and in Avanti before a meeting of a lesser number.

In the Southern country and in Avanti, Lord, the soil is black on the surface, rough, and trampled by the feet of cattle. May the Blessed One be pleased, therefore, to allow the use, in the Southern country and in Avanti, of shoes with thick linings.

In the Southern country and in Avanti, Lord, men attach great importance to bathing, and are pure by use of water.

May the Blessed One be pleased to allow, in the Southern country and in Avanti, the constant use of the bath.

In the Southern country and in Avanti, Lord, skins, such as sheep-skins, goat-skins, and deer-skins, are used as coverlets. Just as in the Middle country the eragu, moragu, maggharu, and gantu grasses are used for coverlets, so are sheep-skins, goat-skins, and deer-skins in the Southern country and in Avanti.

May the Blessed One be pleased to allow the use of such coverlets there. At present, Lord, people are in the habit of giving a set of robes to Bhikkhus, who have left the district, saying, 'We give this set of robes to (a Bhikkhu) of such and such a name.'

When they return, the Bhikkhus tell them, 'A set of robes has been given to you by a person of such and such a name.' But they, fearing to offend, do not accept it, saying, 'Let us not be guilty of a Nissaggiya.' May the Blessed One be pleased to make a detailed statement in the matter of robes."

'Even so, Lord,' said the venerable Sona in assent to the venerable Maha Kakkayana, and, rising from his seat, he departed thence, keeping his right side towards him. And taking up his bed, he went on with his robe on, and his bowl in his hand to Savatthi.

8. And wandering from place to place he arrived at the place where the Blessed One was, at Savatthi in the Getavana, Anatha-pindika's park. And when he had come there he saluted the Blessed One, and took his seat beside him.

Then the Blessed One said to the venerable Ananda: 'Make ready a sleeping-place, Ananda, for this Bhikkhu who has just arrived.' And the venerable Ananda thought:

> *'Inasmuch as the Blessed One commands me to make ready a sleeping-place for the Bhikkhu who has just arrived, the Blessed One evidently desires to dwell in the same Vihara with that Bhikkhu, he desires to dwell in the same Vihara with the venerable Sona.' And he made ready a sleeping-place for the venerable Sona at the place where the Blessed One was staying.*

9. Then the Blessed One, after spending the greater part of the night in the open air, entered the Vihara. And also the venerable Sona, having spent the greater part of the night in the open air, entered the Vihara. And the Blessed One rose up, early in the morning, towards dawn, and requested the venerable Sona, saying,

'May the Dhamma so become clear to you that you may speak.' Even so, Lord!' said the venerable Sona in assent to the Blessed One; and he intoned all the verses in the Book of the Eights (Atthaka-vaggikani).

And the Blessed One, at the conclusion of the venerable Sona's recitation, expressed his pleasure, saying,

'Excellent, most excellent, O Bhikkhu! Well have the Eights been grasped by thee, well thought over, well learnt by heart: and with a fine voice art thou gifted, distinct, pleasant, able to make things understood. How many years is it since thou has been ordained?'

'One year, my Lord!'

10. 'But why have you postponed it so long?'

"This long, Lord, since I saw into the danger of the passions, but life in a household is crowded with business and with cares.'

And the Blessed One, when he heard that matter, gave utterance at that time to the expression of emotion:

> *'When he has seen the danger of the world, when he has understood the Truth, when he has become free from Upadhi, 'The pilgrim finds in sin no pleasure, his delight is in the word, the pure.'*

11. Then thought the venerable Sona: 'The Blessed One is pleased with me. This then is the time which my superior spoke of.' And rising from his seat, and arranging his robe on one shoulder, he bowed down with his head at the feet of the Blessed One, and said:

> *'Lord! my superior Maha Kakkayana bows down in salutation at the feet of the Blessed One. In the Southern country and in Avanti there are (&c., as in §§ 4-7, down to the end of the message).'*

Then the Blessed One on that occasion and in that connection, having delivered a religious discourse, addressed the Bhikkhus and said:

> *'The Southern country and Avanti has but few Bhikkhus. I allow the Upasampada (ordination) in border countries to be held in a meeting of only four Bhikkhus, beside the chairman, who must be a Vinayadhara.'*

12. 'In this passage the following are the border countries referred to. To the East is the town Kagangala, and beyond it MahasAlA. Beyond that is border country; this side of it is the Middle country. To the southeast is the river Salalavati. Beyond that is border country; this side of it is the Middle country. To

the South is the town Setakannika. Beyond that is border country; this side of it is the Middle country. To the West is the Brahman district of Thuna. Beyond that is border country; this side of it is the Middle country. To the North is the mountain range called Usiradhaga. Beyond that is border country; this side of it is the Middle country. In such border countries, I allow, O Bhikkhus, the Upasampada (ordination) to be held in a meeting of only four Bhikkhus, beside the chairman, who must be a Vinayadhara.

13. 'In the Southern country and in Avanti, O Bhikkhus, the soil is black on the surface and rough, and trampled by the feet of cattle. I allow the use, in all the border countries, O Bhikkhus, of shoes with thick linings.

'In the Southern country and in Avanti, O Bhikkhus, men attach great importance to bathing, and are pure by use of water. I allow the constant use of the bath, O Bhikkhus, in all the border countries.

'In the Southern country and in Avanti, O Bhikkhus, skins, such as sheep-skins, goat-skins, and deer-skins, are used as coverlets. Just as in the Middle country, Bhikkhus, the eragu, moragu, maggharu, and gantu grasses are used for coverlets, so in the Southern country and in Avanti are used skins, such as sheep-skins, goat-skins, and deer-skins. I allow, O Bhikkhus, the use of skins, such as sheep-skins, goat-skins, and deer-skins, as coverlets, in all the border countries.

'There also, O Bhikkhus, people are in the habit of giving a set of robes to Bhikkhus who have left the district, saying, "We give this set of robes to (a Bhikkhu) with such and such a name." I allow you, O Bhikkhus, to accept such robes. The set of robes does not become subject to the ten-days' rule, before it reaches the hand (of the person for whom it was intended).'

7

The Patimokkha Rules

INTRODUCTION

Having established a background, we will now turn to the rules themselves. Rather than following the traditional listing, we will group rules (of varying seriousness) together under four headings, which might pertain to, or be of interest to, lay people:

HARMLESSNESS

Throughout its history Buddhism has been renowned for its tolerance and compassion towards all living beings and this is reflected in the Buddhist monks' Vinaya. Their rules cover situations of causing harm ranging from murder-which is universally accepted as a crime-to such things as destroying plant life.

Murder: The third Defeater (Paaraajika) Offence deals with murder. The original story describes how some bhikkhus wrongly grasped the Buddha's meditation teaching on the loathsome aspects of the body and, falling into wrong view, committed suicide or asked someone to end their lives for them. The rule can be summarized like this:

> *"Intentionally bringing about the untimely death of a human being, even if it is still a foetus, is [an offence of Defeat.]" (Summary Paar. 3; BMC p.78)*

A bhikkhu must not recommend killing, suicide or help

arrange a murder. Also, because in this rule a human being is defined as beginning with the human foetus, counting "from the time consciousness first arises in the womb," he must not advise or arrange an abortion.

There is no offence if death is caused accidentally or without intention.

Killing: The previous offence was one of Defeat for murder whereas this rule is one of Confession (paacittiya) for killing animals. It originally arose because Venerable Udaayin, a frequent delinquent, detested crows so much that he shot them with arrows and then displayed their cutoff heads.

"Deliberately killing an animal-or having it killed-is [an offence of Confession]. "(Summary Paac. 61; BMC p.423)

'Animal' here is paano, literally 'having breath.' The Commentary explains that it includes living beings down to the size of a bedbug. Elsewhere the texts forbid the killing of "even an ant."

One of the bhikkhu's requisites is a water filter. This is employed to prevent the killing of (visible) waterborne creatures when making use of water from a well or stream. Practically, this also leads bhikkhus to take extra care that they cover water jars or regularly change water so that mosquito larvae do not have opportunity to breed. This shows how the Vinaya Rule emphasizes care and forethought as 'preventive medicine.'

There are two rules concerned with bhikkhus and their use of water:

> *One of these offences was originally perpetrated by the notorious 'group-of-six' monks who used water that contained living beings. It can be summarized:*
>
> *"Using water, knowing that it contains living beings that will die from one's use, is [an offence of Confession.]" (Paac. 62; BMC p.424)*
>
> *In the second offence the monks of AA.lavii were doing repairs and 'sprinkled grass and clay' with water that they knew contained life. It is summarized:*
>
> *"If a bhikkhu knows that water contains living beings*

but still pours it out onto grass or earth it is [an offence of Confession.] Also pouring-or having it poured-into such water anything that would kill the beings therein is [an offence of Confession.]"

Intention is an essential factor here. For example, if a bhikkhu only intends to sweep a path but accidentally kills ants in the process, there is no offence because it is not deliberate. However, ordering an animal to be killed (and it is) is an offence.

Destroying Vegetation: The common belief at the time of the Buddha was that plants (and even soil) were 'one-facultied life.' Today we have ecologically 'green' beliefs that are often equivalent-at least they seem to lead to much the same attitudes. (In Thailand, forest monks are well known as the best protectors of the jungle.)

The eleventh Confession offence concerns destroying plant life. It originated because a bhikkhu harmed 'one-facultied life' by cutting down trees. He continued to cut down a tree even when the tree-deva asked him to stop, so she went and complained to the Buddha. This led to lay criticism of such behaviour and a rule was set down:

"Intentionally damaging or destroying a living plant is [an offence of Confession]. "

Therefore destroying a living plant-for instance, felling a tree, uprooting a flower, burning grass-is a Confession offence; as is picking fruit from a tree, a flower from a bush, etc. It is an offence of wrongdoing (dukkata) to damage or destroy fertile seeds or pips, or viable seedlings.

Bhikkhus who live in tropical forest monasteries constantly have to protect both the jungle and themselves. When paths are overgrown, snakes and other dangerous 'creepy-crawlies' can be trodden on-and bite back! There also may be a need for firebreaks. One way that forest monks cope with this is a daily routine of sweeping the paths. However they are not allowed to dig or clear the land.

The tenth Confession offence arose when bhikkhus dug the ground and got others to dig, and the local people criticized them because they considered the earth to be 'one-facultied life.' The rule is phrased like this:

> *"Should any bhikkhu dig soil or have it dug, it is [an offence of Confession.]" (Paac. 10; BMC p.292)*

Digging, breaking the surface of the earth, lighting a fire on it, pounding a stake into it are all disallowed. (If such 'earth' is more gravel or sand than 'soil'-and has no living creatures in it-it may then be dug.)

It is, however, allowable for monks to hint to laypeople or novices about what needs doing as long as the words or gestures fall short of a command. When bhikkhus need paths to be cleared, necessary work done on the ground, firebreaks made, etc., any lay attendant wanting to help should listen out for hints and indications: 'A post hole dug over there would be useful'; 'make this ground allowable,' etc. What is needed can then be clarified.

One practical and long term effect of these rules is that they have steered bhikkhus away from involvement in agriculture and land ownership. Such a development would also have isolated bhikkhus from the lay community because they would no longer have needed to depend on alms food.

RELATIONSHIPS

Bhikkhus cannot live in complete isolation from lay people, for the mutual support relationship is intrinsic to their way of life. However, it should never become an intimate relationship for this goes against the whole purpose of leaving the 'family life' with its endless 'enclosed' complications.

The 'Holy Life' or Brahmachariya is one that checks the display of any form of sexual desire through the actions and speech of the bhikkhu. (In fact restraint from gross sexual misconduct is already part of the Five Precepts. The Eight and Ten Precepts immediately refine this and then the Vinaya manages it with even greater subtlety.) One's Dhamma life can then advance towards the ending of all desire through mind development and meditation. The most potent object for such sexual desire, that which the mind is most tenaciously grasping after, is usually associated with the opposite sex, so many rules involve this relationship.

Sexual Intercourse: The first offence of all the 227 listed rules of the Paatimokkha concerns a bhikkhu engaging in sexual intercourse. It remains a hot issue, perhaps even more so today, going by the number of sexual scandals that rock the Buddhist religious world in both the East and the West. As Venerable Thiradhammo writes:

> *"While some of the guidelines may seem somewhat rigid or prudish, it is important to reflect upon the volatility and durability of rumour, even if untrue. The incessant sex-scandals in religious circles may provide a sufficient incentive to encourage the greatest measure of prevention and discretion." (HS ch.13)*

The rule was originally laid down because of Venerable Sudinna. He was the son of a rich merchant, who left home to become a bhikkhu only after great opposition from his family. He went away to practice Dhamma and when he came back to visit sometime later, his parents were overjoyed to see him and plotted to lure him back into the lay life again.

They invited him for a meal and then laid out their wealth in front of him, piled up in two huge heaps of gold, while the wife he had left behind dressed herself in her most irresistibly alluring way. Venerable Sudinna remained unmoved by all of this. After telling them to throw the gold away in the river, he called his former wife, "Sister." Nevertheless, when his elderly mother pleaded with him at least to give them an heir, he foolishly gave in and had sexual intercourse with his former wife.

This First Defeater Offence is summarized:

> *"A bhikkhu who engages in any form of sexual intercourse is Defeated."*

Every form and variety of sexual intercourse with sexual penetration-whether genital, oral or anal, whether with woman, man or animal-is forbidden. The penalty is the heaviest one of Paaraajika or Defeat.

Intimacy-Touching: The modern West has stories of sexual harassment, so the ways that the Buddha dealt with such matters should not seem so very strange.

If a bhikkhu touches a woman in a sexual way, he commits a very serious offence requiring formal meetings of the Community and probation (Sanghaadisesa). The scrupulous bhikkhu wants to remain above suspicion so, if he can, he will avoid all physical contact. (Hence his attitude to shaking hands. This also explains why in Thailand a receiving cloth is used to receive offerings from women.

The rule was first set down by the Buddha after a Brahman and his wife had gone to inspect Ven. Udaayin's fine dwelling. As Ven. Udaayin was showing them around, he came up behind the lady and "rubbed up against her limb by limb." After they had left, the husband praised Ven. Udaayin but the wife was critical and explained what had happened. The Brahman then complained, "Isn't it even possible to take one's wife to a monastery without her being molested?" This rule was then set down:

> *"Should any bhikkhu, overcome by lust, with altered mind, engage in bodily contact with a woman, or in holding her hand, holding a lock of her hair, or caressing any of her limbs, it entails initial and subsequent meetings of the Community. "(Sangh. 2; BMC p.100)*

To be at fault, the bhikkhu must usually do some action to bring contact with a woman while lust overcomes his mind. If he accidentally stumbles and bumps into a woman or vice-versa, or if he is accosted by a woman, as long as there is no intention to come into lustful contact there is no offence. However, the average bhikkhu's mind tends to be so quick and unruly-he is, after all, still in training and therefore unenlightened-that he may prefer to be super-cautious about such situations.

If a bhikkhu touches his mother out of affection, then this is still an offence but the lesser one of wrongdoing (dukkata). 46 While gratitude to parents was strongly emphasized by the Buddha, the bhikkhu having left the home-life and his family should not cling to worldly relationships. The only true way for him to fulfil his filial obligations is by gaining insight into Dhamma and then teaching his parents.

If a bhikkhu is acting with lustful intentions, he incurs a grave (thullaccaaya) offence for making bodily contact with a pandaka ('sex-aberrant') and an offence of wrongdoing for contact with a male.

The previous rules dealt with the bhikkhu's physical actions, the next two rules are offences-again of the very serious category-that concern his wrong speech towards women.

Flirting: This rule came into being when many women visitors came together to look over Ven. Udaayin's dwelling. He spoke to them in a lewd, flirtatious way so that some of them said, "It is improper. Even from our husbands we wouldn't like to hear this sort of thing." Therefore, the Buddha laid down this rule:

> *"Should any bhikkhu, overcome by lust, with altered mind, address lewd words to a woman in the manner of young men to a young woman alluding to sexual intercourse, it entails initial and subsequent meetings of the Community." (Sangh. 3; BMC p.110)*

Propositioning: The following rule is very relevant today when some misguidedly believe that submitting to sex with spiritual teachers can help in their spiritual development.

Again, it was originally a lustful Ven. Udaayin who was the cause of this offence. This time, he suggested to a beautiful and devout woman follower that she make a 'special offering' to him, that of sexual intercourse. The Buddha then set forth this rule:

> *"Telling a woman that she would benefit from having sexual intercourse with oneself is [an offence requiring initial and subsequent meetings of the Community.]" (Summary Sangh. 4; BMC p.117)*

Matchmaking: The major issue today seems more to centre around divorce and the breakdown of marriage rather than arranging marriages. However one should note how these affairs can involve the bhikkhu and how he should guard against becoming too drawn in. (It is also noteworthy that this is considered one of the most serious offences.)

Ven. Udaayin caused this rule to be set down because he involved himself in arranging many marriages and liaisons. When some of these failed, they blamed him for the failure. The offence is summarized:

> *"Should any bhikkhu engage in conveying a man's intentions to a woman or a woman's intentions to a man, proposing marriage or paramourage-even if only for a momentary liaison-it entails initial and subsequent meetings of the Community. "(Sangh. 5; BMC p.117)*

A bhikkhu should not officiate at weddings, except perhaps to chant a blessing afterwards and encourage the newly married couple to lead virtuous and faithful lives together based in generosity, virtue and meditation. He also has to be circumspect when counselling couples. (There is no offence in reconciling a married but estranged couple as long as they are not yet divorced.)

Alone with a Woman: A bhikkhu not only has to be impeccable but also must be seen to be so. He sets an example for everyone and therefore must be beyond reproach. Any doubtful situations have to be clarified, which is how the next rules came about. Some knowledge of these rules may also help to explain the sometimes seemingly antisocial attitude of some bhikkhus. (When bhikkhus are reluctant to enter into too private a conversation, it may reflect the unsuitability of the time and place for such a meeting.)

There are two aspects to these particular rules: physical closeness and private conversation. If a woman sees a monk who is sitting alone and she wants to sit close to him, or she wants to have a one-to-one conversation with him, the following rules have to be taken into account.

First, the rules dealing with intimate proximity:

The Two Aniyata, Indefinite or Undetermined Cases, were formulated after Ven. Udaayin went to visit a recently married young woman. He sat privately with her, in a secluded place, just the two of them, talking about worldly affairs. The respected female lay-follower, Visaakhaa, saw them sitting there and said to Ven. Udaayin, "This is improper, Ven. Sir, and unsuitable, that the master should sit in private like this. Although, Ven. Sir, the master may have no desire for sexual intercourse, there are unbelieving people who are difficult to convince."

The Buddha therefore set this down:

"Should any bhikkhu sit in private, alone with a woman in a seat secluded enough to lend itself (to the sexual act), so that a female lay follower whose word can be trusted, having seen (them), might describe it as constituting any of the three cases-involving either Defeat, [Community Meetings], or [Confession]-then the bhikkhu, acknowledging having sat (there), may be dealt with for any of the three cases... or he may be dealt with for whichever case the female lay follower described. This case is undetermined."(Aniyata 1; BMC p.157)

The Second Indefinite Offence is similar to the first, except that the place is less secluded and therefore not suitable for sexual intercourse although it could still be grounds for the other sexual offences, such as "addressing a woman with lewd words."

When a bhikkhu intentionally sits alone with a woman in a secluded or private place (as in the above two rules) it can lead on to more intimate behaviour or at least to misunderstandings from unexpected onlookers. To preclude such problems a bhikkhu needs a companion or 'chaperone.'

A 'secluded place' is where a monk and women can sit (or lie down) on a seat together in a place that is hidden from view and out of earshot, for example, a private room or behind a wall or hedge. In such circumstances, a man or boy old enough to understand what is inappropriate conduct must be also present as chaperone. Therefore, if a woman-or women, for according to this particular rule (Aniyata 1) it does not matter how many there are-sees a bhikkhu sitting alone in such a very secluded place, she should remember about this rule and not go and sit with him but await a more suitable time or find a male to act as chaperone.

A less secluded but still 'private place' (Aniyata 2) would be, for example, a bench in a deserted park or a glassed-in porch or any other place that is private but not secluded enough for sexual intercourse. (BMC p.389) In this case, the Commentary allows the chaperone to be either male or female but they must be someone who knows 'what is and what is not lewd' and they must be 'within sight.' However if the monk and woman talk together the chaperone must be male because of the relevant rule about that.

The following 'Confession Rules' connect with the above 'Indefinite Rules.'

The forty-fourth Confession Offence originated when the husband of a woman denounced Ven. Upananda for sitting alone in a 'secluded place' with his wife. The ruling:

> *"Sitting or lying down with a woman or women in a private, secluded place with no other man present is [an offence of Confession.] "(Summarized Paac. 44; BMC p.385)*

The next Confession Offence follows on with Ven. Upananda, this time, being caught sitting alone with the man's wife in a 'private place.' This time the ruling is:

> *"Should any bhikkhu sit in private, alone with a woman, it is [an offence of Confession.] "(Paac. 45; BMC p.389)*

Therefore as with the Indefinite Offences above there needs to be a chaperone present.

Talking Privately: The previous rules dealt with physical proximity whereas this next rule concerns a bhikkhu and woman talking alone. It might appear strange that a rule should completely forbid confidential interviews with a bhikkhu alone. Yet if one reflects on how things have regularly gone wrong with such private spiritual counselling, it is easier to see that being safe is better than sorry-for the sake of everyone involved. Even if their conduct is completely pure, it still may lead to rumour and criticism.

The seventh Confession offence arose when Ven. Udaayin went to visit lay supporters. He sat close to the mother of the family at the front door, teaching her Dhamma in a quiet, confidential manner, and then approached the daughter-in-law who was by the side door and spoke to her in the same way. Both women mistakenly thought that he was flirting with the other, and criticized him, saying that Dhamma should be given in a clear and open way. As a result the Buddha eventually laid down that:

> *"Teaching more than six sentences [vaacaa] of Dhamma to a woman, except in response to a question, is [an offence of Confession] unless a knowledgeable man is present." (Summarized Paac. 7; BMC p.285)*

There are different interpretations as to exactly what is meant by 'six sentences,' for the Pali word vaacaa can mean 'word,' 'saying' or 'speech.' Even if there are many women, but no other man, it is still considered an offence.

One can see from the origin of this rule that the point (again) is not that women cannot be taught Dhamma but that it should be done in a way that is completely open and above misinterpretation.

Staying Together: The next rule deals with the proximity of bhikkhus and women at night. There are different interpretations of this rule and as it is a frequently asked question extra translations with some discussion will be included.

This rule originally arose when Ven. Anuruddha-one of the most highly accomplished disciples of the Buddha-was travelling and asked the woman who owned a travellers' rest house if he could stay the night. She readily agreed and when more travellers arrived and Ven. Anuruddha let them share the room, she invited him to come and sleep inside instead. She had, however, become infatuated with him and tried to seduce him. When she saw that Ven. Anuruddha was completely unmoved, she came to her senses and asked his forgiveness. Ven. Anuruddha then gave her a Dhamma talk which so delighted her that she took refuge in the Triple Gem.

Here are several translations:

"If a bhikkhu sleeps in a place where there is a surrounding wall and under the same roof with a woman, even for one night, it is [an offence of Confession.]" (Paac. 6; Nv p.14)

"A monk who lies down with a female in the same building under the same roof and within walls, which are complete or almost complete, commits [a Confession Offence.]" (Paac. 6; BBC p.120)

"Lying down at the same time in the same lodging with a woman is [an offence of Confession.]" (Paac. 6; BMC p.280)

There are complications concerning how this rule should be applied to modern conditions, for example:

"Houses in tropical climates are often constructed without the system of doors and rooms found in colder climates, hence the importance of this rule. Bhikkhus obliged to stay in a Western-type house with lockable rooms in places where no [monastery] exists, as must sometimes happen during Dhammaduta [Spreading-Dhamma] work, will hardly be included here." (Paat. 1966 Ed.; p106)

"The Commentary (Samantapaasaadika) further explains that when there are many rooms in a single building-such as in a block of flats or apartments-the 'same sleeping place' is only those rooms which have a common 'entrance' (upacaara). It continues by explaining that an 'entrance' is where one washes one's feet before entering a set of rooms. Now each flat/ apartment usually has a doormat on which one wipes one's feet before entering the flat/apartment and therefore, following the Commentary, the doormat marks the 'entrance' (upacaara) of a single 'same-sleeping-place.' In other words, separate flats/ apartments become separate sleeping places for the purposes of this rule."(AB)

So there are different interpretations as to exactly what is meant by 'same place.' For example, does a locked door make a room a separate place? The Commentary suggests that if a building is divided into units that are not connected and each has a separate entrance, then each unit counts as a 'place.' Therefore apartment blocks would be allowable. And hospitals?

In the West, where there are few monasteries, visiting bhikkhus have to decide how to follow these rules. It is not just a question of being strict but also about how it looks to lay people. Will they be suspicious about a bhikkhu staying too close to women? How will they feel if he stays in an expensive hotel room? A good standard is probably:

> *"...since the Canon gives no clear guidance on this point, the wise policy for an individual bhikkhu is to follow the views of the Community to which he belongs." (BMC p.274)*

Travelling Together: The next point to deal with is that of a bhikkhu travelling with a woman. This is also a very practical question and is often asked about.

In the Buddha's time, a bhikkhu was about to set out on a journey when he met a woman who has just quarrelled with her husband. She asked where he was going and if she could accompany him. He agreed. The husband then appeared, searching for his wife. He heard that she had gone off with a monk and assumed that they were lovers, so when he caught up with the pair he thrashed the bhikkhu before explanations could be made. When the husband realized his mistake, he apologized to the bhikkhu. Therefore this rule was set down:

"Travelling by arrangement with a woman from one village to another is [an offence of Confession.]" (Summarised Paac. 67; BMC p.434)

Modern practice differs according to the Community so lay women should bear this rule in mind when arranging transport for bhikkhus, or going to the same place as them. Reluctance by a bhikkhu to arrange such journeys might also be explained by this rule.

"...it seems reasonable, as there is some uncertainty [as to whether it applies to more than just one monk and one woman,] to be more lenient allowing a journey with one or more women as long as there is at least one male accompanying the monk and the journey is not long. For example, a woman driving two monks in her car to an invitation in the next village seems no more reprehensible than two monks sitting down talking Dhamma to the women, but two women driving across Australia with two monks could be a cause for concern." (AB)

Possessions and Offerings

The term 'bhikkhu' is defined as 'almsman,' or 'mendicant.' He is one who depends on others for his material needs. This relationship of 'right livelihood' incurs responsibilities: the bhikkhu must receive and use offerings in the right way, whereas the lay devotee should make material offerings in the right way and receive Dhamma teachings in the right way. The lay person gives material support, which the bhikkhu properly receives and uses in his Dhamma-practice so he can eventually reciprocate with the 'highest of gifts'-Dhamma.

The proper needs of a bhikkhu and how they are supplied is extensively covered in the Vinaya Rule. If all bhikkhus were enlightened, we obviously would need few guidelines. However, most monks are still in the process of learning how to completely to eradicate greed, anger and delusion, so 'possessions' misused can easily lead to unskilful states of mind.

The Four Requisites: What Does a Bhikkhu Need?: The Buddha said that there were four necessities of life-clothing, food, lodging and medicine-and that they have to be treated properly:

"Properly considering the robe, I use it: simply to ward off cold, to ward off heat, to ward off the touch of flies, mosquitoes, simply for the purpose of covering the parts of the body that cause shame.

"Properly considering almsfood, I use it: not playfully, nor for intoxication, nor for putting on weight, nor for beautification; but simply for the survival and continuance of this body, for ending its afflictions, for the support of the chaste life, (thinking) I will destroy old feelings (of hunger) and not create new feelings (from overeating). Thus I will maintain myself, be blameless, and live in comfort.

"Properly considering the lodging, I use it: simply to ward off cold, to ward off heat, to ward off the touch of flies, mosquitoes, wind, sun and reptiles; simply for protection from the inclemencies of weather and for the enjoyment of seclusion.

"Properly considering medicinal requisites for curing the sick, I use them: simply to ward off any pains of illness that have arisen and for the maximum freedom from disease."

Clothing, food, shelter and medicine are necessary whether one is a lay person or a bhikkhu. The bhikkhu, however, should take a completely balanced stance towards these fundamentals. Advertising and the latest fashion should not draw him, for he should be solely concerned with simplicity and lack of attachment towards things. It seems that the original requisites were 'basics' that wandering bhikkhus could conveniently carry around, for example, an alms bowl, three robes, a sitting cloth, a needle-case, and a waist band. However, extra allowances were gradually given as the need arose, for instance, a water filter, a razor and its sheath, the stone and strop for sharpening it and then articles such as an umbrella and sandals. Later the commentaries allowed other similar items.

Does a Bhikkhu Beg?: The Buddha made it clear that bhikkhus should avoid begging if possible. (In times of great need a bhikkhu is allowed to ask for his basic requisites, for example, if his robes are stolen he may ask any lay person for one replacement robe.) He gave this story about 'begging':

> *A bhikkhu came to the Lord Buddha and complained about a great flock of noisy birds that came to roost at night in the forest surrounding his abode. The Buddha suggested that if he wanted them to go away he should go, many times throughout the night, and beg a feather from each bird. The birds, thinking, 'that monk wants*

a feather, and another, and another...,' left the forest and never returned. The Buddha then explained that begging and hinting were unpleasant even to common animals, how much more so to human beings.

A bhikkhu who is constantly begging for things displays his greedy state of mind. No one likes to see this, and lay supporters may start by criticizing him and then turn to blaming his Community or even the Buddha's Teaching. The Buddha, therefore, set down many rules to guide the bhikkhus about what is proper conduct.

How to Help a Bhikkhu-Invitation: Normally a bhikkhu will not ask for things. Instead, he will wait for something to be offered. This is exemplified in the alms round where the bhikkhu makes no request, does not even look at people, although he may quietly wait to see if an offering is to be made before moving on. One way that lay people enable a bhikkhu to ask them for help is by making an invitation or pavaaranaa.

The Buddha allowed a bhikkhu to accept pavaaranaa or 'invitation.' Such an invitation is made when lay people decide to commit themselves to supplying medicines if a particular bhikkhu should ever become ill, or it can be a broader offer of help. (Although a sick monk is allowed to ask anyone for medicine, asking somebody who has already invited him with a pavaaranaa invitation is obviously preferable.) Therefore if lay people meet a bhikkhu who seems worthy of help and support, they may make such an invitation. Quite a number of the rules deal with what and how much may be asked for when a donor makes this formal invitation.

An invitation can therefore be quite specific about what is being offered and how long that invitation will last. (Obviously, if circumstances change or the request is unreasonable, the donor has no obligations-and a conscientious bhikkhu is always sensitive about this.)

A clear invitation will also help prevent misunderstandings. For instance, the bhikkhu will know exactly what has been offered and so will not ask for more than that; and the lay person will not be overwhelmed by extravagant requests.

The original circumstances of the forty-seventh Confession Offence were as follows:

> *A lay supporter possessed much 'medicinal ghee' so he invited the monks to make use of it during the following four months. Much of the medicine was still left, so he extended his invitation for another four months and then extended it for life. The Buddha allowed this. However, that same lay donor had once criticized the 'group-of-six' monks because of their previous improper conduct so they decided to take their revenge by asking him for an impossibly large amount of medicine (ghee) and then criticized him when he could not immediately produce what he had promised. This rule was set down:*
>
> *"A bhikkhu who is not ill may accept (make use of) a four-month invitation [pavaaranaa] to ask for requisites. If he should accept (make use of) it for longer than that-unless the invitation is renewed or is permanent-it is [an offence of Confession.]" (Paac. 47; BMC p.393)*

When the invitation is more vague-for example, a lay person may just say, "If you need anything, Bhante, let me know"-the bhikkhu should not exceed the spirit of the invitation. In fact some communities consider that an invitation in which the lay person does not mention any time limit is valid only for four months and that taking up the invitation beyond that time is an offence.

A bhikkhu is always allowed to ask for requisites from his relatives without having formal invitation first. (Whether they actually supply anything is, of course, up to them.) 'Relatives' are considered to be those with whom the bhikkhu has common ancestors back through seven generations, on both the mother's and father's side. Here 'in-laws' are not counted as relatives.

"Thus all descendants of one's great-great-great-great-great-great-great-grandfather are counted as one's relatives... [although] a bhikkhu at present would be well-advised to regard as his relatives only those blood-relations with whom ties of kinship are actually felt." (BMC p.183)

What does a Bhikkhu Possess?: The ideal possessions of the bhikkhu are just his basic requisites: three main robes (described in the following section); alms bowl; waistband; needle and thread; razor and water filter.

The alms bowl can be made from clay or iron but must be properly fired to harden it (if clay) and rustproof it (if iron). Three bowl-sizes are mentioned: small, medium and large. There are also several rules about begging for a new bowl before one's old one is worn out, which entails forfeiture of the wrongly acquired bowl. (Nis. Paac. 22; 23)

The waistband became necessary when a monk's 'skirt-robe' fell down while he was in a village. The needle and thread are needed for patching and repairing the robes-and many teachers instruct that it is a wrongdoing for a monk not to repair them the same day. While the razor became necessary when:

> *"At one time, bhikkhus' hair was long. The Buddha asked the bhikkhus:" ''Bhikkhus, are the bhikkhus able to cut one another's hair?" "When they answered in the affirmative, he allowed a razor, whetstone, razor-case, felt wrapping and barbers' equipment... "Lay people criticized the group of six bhikkhus for wearing long hair. The Buddha made this a Wrongdoing, allowing only two finger-breadths in length or two months growth, whichever came first... Hair and beards should not be styled, combed or smoothed, or gray hairs plucked out-all considered to be 'like pleasure-enjoying householders.'" (HS ch.12)*

The water filter is needed to avoid killing small creatures in drinking water.

However, most bhikkhus will have more than this-ranging from everyday items like soap and toothpaste, candles and matches, pen and books, a watch or clock, a flashlight or torch, to more sophisticated things appropriate to their environment. The principle is that such things should not be luxurious or expensive. Anything that is given to him (that is allowable) is his to keep, and he is allowed to give his things away if it is done in the right way and does not cause the donor's faith to decline.

Disposal or appropriation of anything owned by the Community, or belonging to the monastery, is strictly controlled and is covered by the rules that follow in the next section.

After a bhikkhu dies, his possessions will normally revert to the Sangha:

> *"Articles belonging to bhikkhus and novices who have died have the Sangha [Community] as owner, that is they are the inheritance of the Sangha." (EV,II,p.151)*

Wrongly Receiving Gifts: When a bhikkhu receives a general (*i.e.*, non-personal) gift, there are two rules to guard against his misdirecting it.

The first of these rules arose when a guild was preparing to make an offering of a meal and some cloth to the whole Community whereupon the 'group-of-six' bhikkhus arrived and pressured the donors into giving the cloth to them instead:

> *"Should any bhikkhu knowingly divert to himself gains that had been intended for a Community, it is [an offence of Confession with Forfeiture.]" (Nis. Paac. 30; BMC p.256)*

> *"'Gains' here refers to robes, alms food, abodes and medicines... and other allowable things. [They are] gifts dedicated as offerings to the Sangha but not yet offered. A bhikkhu diverts such gifts to himself by asking directly for them or by roundabout speech so that the donor will give them to him." (Nis. Paac. 30; Paat. 1969 Ed.; p159)*

In the above rule the wrongly obtained 'gift' must be forfeited to another bhikkhu(s). (However, money is a special case. See Valuables and Money.) The following rule complements the one above but is an offence of Confession:

> *"Persuading a donor to give to another individual a gift that he or she had planned to give to a Community- when one knows that it was intended for the Community- is [an offence of Confession.] "(Paac. 82; BMC p.461)*

What can be Offered?: As has been mentioned above, the Buddha said that there were four necessities for life-Clothing, Food or 'edibles,' Shelter or lodging and Medicine-so we will use those divisions in the following sections.

There is also a Sutta where it is mentioned that bhikkhus do not accept gifts of gardens, paddy-fields and other sorts of land, or draught animals, and other sorts of animals, etc. (EV, II, p.150)

Clothing: The Robe: The basic clothing that the Buddha originally suggested for a bhikkhu was made from discarded cloth ('rags') sewn together and dyed. After sewing the pieces together, they were just large rectangular pieces of cloth worn wraparound style.

In the beginning, it seems that there were two robes: a sarong skirt-like robe (antaravaasaka) tied with a belt, and a robe to cover the upper part of the body (uttaraasanga). When the cold weather required more protection, the Buddha allowed a third robe, which was a double-thickness outer robe (sanghaati).

Some rules limit the size of robes because cloth in India in those days was expensive due to the simple methods of spinning and weaving. Also, so that the robe would not be worth stealing, the cloth always had to be cut into panels that were then sewn together based on the design of paddy fields seen from a mountain:

> *After having received an offering of white cloth and having properly cut and sewn the panels together, the bhikkhu must dye it to produce the 'yellow robe.' Traditionally, vegetable dyes were used in this process. Different plants and woods when boiled up will produce slightly different shades of dye colour-the Pali text calls the standard colour kaasaaya or kaasaava, translated as 'dun-coloured dye-water' so there is some variety. When bhikkhus from different communities come together, their different shades of 'yellow'-dyed robes makes this very noticeable. (The destruction of the South East Asian forests has led to chemical dyes being used*

more frequently, so that cloth offered nowadays is often pre-dyed and brighter in colour.)

Slightly varied styles of wearing the traditional set of three robes have developed over the years in different countries. But basically, the rectangular shaped robe is put around the body and the two vertical edges are folded or rolled together. Then either it is tucked in and secured with a belt (for the skirt-robe) or, for the larger outer robes, the edge is 'thrown' or flicked over the left shoulder and pinched under the left arm so that it will not slip off. There are various techniques for this. (It needs some practice!)

In the Lord Buddha's time, it was a sign of respect to bare one's right shoulder. Therefore when in the monastery the bhikkhu will normally wear his outer robe with the right shoulder visible. On leaving the monastery for inhabited areas he must cover both shoulders.

In addition to this required set of the 'triple robe,' which every bhikkhu must have and look after, there are extra cloths that can be used occasionally.

The Robe Offering Time: The month following the three months of the Rains Retreat-sometime in the October-November period-is the traditional Kathina time for renewing bhikkhus' robes. In ancient times, this was when bhikkhus would help one another in hand-sewing cloth into new robes-using the special wooden kathina frame.

This is the time when lay supporters often make a special offering of cloth and other requisites to all the monks at a particular monastery. A sewing machine is normally used but all the monks still try to help in the marking out, cutting, sewing, or dying process. The cloth has to be offered, sewn and dyed, so that it is a finished robe and ready to wear within the same day. (Often the robe nowadays is already sewn and pre-dyed.) If this procedure is carried through correctly, the bhikkhus are then entitled to special allowances for the next few months.

The Kathina Ceremony is optional (unlike some other observances that are mandatory) and requires a quorum of five (eligible) bhikkhus. It has, however, generally become an important festival and almsgiving occasion.

Alms Food: As has been mentioned above, the Buddha said that there were four necessities of life: clothing, food, shelter and medicine.

The Buddha suggested that the basic source of food for bhikkhus was that received on the morning alms round (pindapaata). This daily dependence on alms food reminds both the bhikkhus and the lay devotees of their interdependence and prevents the bhikkhu from becoming too isolated from the lay community. He 'meets' them every day and eats the food that they share with him. Several important rules are concerned with this as well as a major section of the Sekhiya Training rules.

An alms round is not considered begging, for the bhikkhu does not solicit anything but is ready mindfully to receive any alms that lay people may wish to give. Although alms food may sometimes be meager, the bhikkhu is always expected to be grateful for whatever he is given.

It is surprising how particular we can be about what food we like to eat; and what complications that can cause. This is reflected in the way rules concerning 'edibles' are arranged, which may seem very complex especially when the bhikkhu's life is supposed to be so simple. It should be borne in mind that the rules often deal with extraordinary circumstances and try to prevent them from becoming the norm.

Begging for Food: When the 'group-of-six' monks in the Buddha's time solicited 'special foods' and ate them themselves, the lay people criticized this saying, "Who isn't fond of good food and sweets?" The Buddha therefore laid down this rule:

> *"There are these finer staple foods,* i.e., *ghee, fresh butter, oil, honey, sugar/molasses, fish, meat, fresh milk, and curds. Should any bhikkhu who is not ill, having asked for finer staple foods such as these for his own sake, then eat them, it is [an offence of Confession.]" (Paac. 39; BMC p.367)*

"There are sumptuous foods, namely foods mixed with ghee, butter, oil, honey, molasses, fish, meat, milk and curd; and a monk who, though not sick, asks for such sumptuous foods for himself and eats them commits [an offence of Confession.]" (Paac. 39; BBC p.127)

The ancient commentators suggest that these 'finer foods' are actually made when one mixes rice, for example, with butter or fish, etc.

An exception is made for a monk who is ill, and a bhikkhu can ask for special food for the sake of a fellow monk who is sick. (He is always allowed to ask a relative or someone who has offered a Pavaaranaa Invitation).

Receiving and Eating Food: A whole section of the seventy-five Sekhiya Training guidelines is concerned with how a bhikkhu receives and eats his alms food. Although 'table manners' may differ from country to country, and from age to age, these Sekhiya rules still largely conform to what is considered good manners:

"I will receive alms food appreciatively." (Sekhiya 27)

"When receiving alms food, I will focus my attention on the bowl." (Sekhiya 28)

This explains why the bhikkhu may not look at the donor when accepting food-he is concentrating on properly receiving it.

"I will receive/eat (bean-)curries in the right proportion to the rice." (Sekhiya 29/34)

It is suggested that this was laid down so that bhikkhus on alms round would not pass by people offering plain rice in favour of better quality food.

"I will receive alms food only until it reaches the rim of the bowl." (Sekhiya 30)

However, on festival or special occasions the bhikkhu's bowl may be emptied so that everyone who wants to join in offering has the opportunity.

"I will eat alms food attentively." (Sekhiya 31) "When eating alms food, I will look only into the bowl." (Sekhiya 32)

This is also why the bhikkhu should not be expected to talk while he is eating, for this will distract his attention.

"I will not cover up curries or other food with rice out of a desire to get more." (Sekhiya 36)

If donors think that the monk has only plain rice in his bowl, they may give him some 'better' food.

"When I am not sick, I will not ask for curries or rice for my own benefit." (Sekhiya 37)

Other Sekhiya rules seem aimed at bhikkhus eating from their bowl using their fingers in the traditional way of India:

"I will not make up an overlarge mouthful of food; nor open my mouth until the portion of food has been brought to it; nor put my fingers into my mouth; nor speak with my mouth full.

"I will not eat: stuffing out my cheeks; shaking my hand about; scattering grains of rice about; putting out my tongue; making a champing sound; (or drink) making a sucking sound; licking my hands; scraping the bowl; licking my lips. I will not take hold of a vessel of water with my hand soiled with food."

Meal Time: In the West the first meal of the day is 'breakfast.' For the bhikkhu this is literally true, for he will not have taken any food since the previous morning. Food intake is limited to the hours between dawn and noon. The practice of not eating in the afternoon is a very old tradition mentioned in the earliest Suttas. It is also included in the Ten Precepts of the novice (saamanera) and dasasiila mata nun; and the Eight Precepts of the lay devotee.

'Food' here refers to things like cooked grains; sweets made from flour, beans, etc.; fish; meat; fresh milk and sour milk;... fruits, tubers and all 'main course' foods.

When these staple foods go beyond their time limit (*i.e.*, after noon) a bhikkhu will incur an offence if he consumes them. The original story shows the complications that can arise from leaving the monastery at the wrong time:

The 'group-of-seventeen' bhikkhus-another set of frequent misdoers-went out one afternoon to enjoy themselves at a festival outside the city. When lay people saw them they gave them a meal and food to take back to the monastery. The Buddha therefore laid down this rule:

"Should any bhikkhu chew or consume staple or non-staple food at the wrong time, it is [an offence of Confession.]" (Paac. 37; BMC p.362)

This 'wrong time' is defined to be from noon until dawn the following day. A bhikkhu is still at fault even if he genuinely miscalculates the time or mistakes an item of 'food' for a 'medicine.' Therefore if donors are preparing food for a bhikkhu they should be careful that they are not late in offering it so that the meal can be finished before noon. It is also noteworthy that an ill bhikkhu has no exemption from this rule so he likewise should not take food in the afternoon.

The Four Sorts of Edibles: Any nutriment that a bhikkhu puts into his mouth is classified in four groups, which specify the time limits during which he can consume or store them:

(i) Food-Limited from Dawn to Noon (Yaavakaalika)

(ii) Fruit juices-Limited to One Day (Yaamakaalika)

(iii) Medicinal-tonics-Limited to Seven Days (Sattaaha-kaalika)

(iv) Other Medicines-For All One's Life (Yaavajiivika)

Mixing Edibles: When different kinds of 'edibles' are mixed, their category will usually change to that with the shortest life span. For example, ginger can be used as a herbal 'lifetime' medicine for stomach ailments. However, grated-ginger that has been used for food preparation is classed as 'food' and therefore should not be kept overnight or used as a medicine. Likewise, if honey is used as a solvent or base for herbal medicines, because the honey has a seven-day limit, that lifetime (herbal) medicine becomes a seven-day medicine.

This is another reason that bhikkhus may be careful about the ingredients of medicines that are offered. When offering 'medicines' the donor should try to be aware of what the bhikkhu considers allowable and what will cause him to fall into offence.

Offering 'Edibles': We have already mentioned the bhikkhu's alms round and his dependence on receiving food from lay supporters. But how is the gift made and how is it properly received? This is accomplished in quite a formal way yet it can still be confusing to lay devotees for different monks receive an offering in slightly different ways.

The rule that explains about formally having to make an offering to bhikkhus arose when a certain bhikkhu lived in a charnel ground, wearing robes made from rags collected from there. He also subsisted on the food left for 'departed spirits' by relatives of the dead person. The lay people criticized him, wrongly suspecting he might also be feeding on human flesh so the Buddha set down this rule.

"Should a bhikkhu take into his mouth an edible that has not been given-except for water and tooth-cleaning sticks-it is [an offence of Confession.] "(Paac. 40; BMC p.370)

"A monk who puts in his mouth, any nutriment, which has not been proffered to him, commits [a Confession offence.]" (Paac. 40; BBC p.127)

How to Make an Offering: Present day practice regarding this rule (Paac. 40 above) varies so much because of the intricacy of interpretation. However, usually, anything that goes into the mouth-food or 'medicines'-should be properly given. That means it should be:

(a) given by means of the body, (*e.g.*, given by hand), or by something attached to the body, (*e.g.*, a spoon), or by throwing, (*e.g.*, tossing a lump of sticky rice into the bowl).

(b) given so that the donor and the bhikkhu are (literally) within arms reach (1.25 metres) of each other.

(c) received by means of the body, (*e.g.*, received in the hand) or by something attached to the body, (*e.g.*, the monk's bowl or, in Thailand, the monk's receiving cloth).

The Commentaries then further expand the details of the correct way that food should be given:

(d) the offered food should not be so heavy that an average size man cannot lift it.

In many communities this has led to the food having to be literally lifted into the monk's hands or onto his receiving cloth. The Commentary allows it to be slid along the floor or table into the monk's hands.

(e) the donor must actually move the food (on a tray, for example) towards the bhikkhu, (*i.e.*, the bhikkhu does not reach out for it first).

This has also been understood as meaning that the donor makes a gesture (of respect) when making the offering. (This has to be balanced with the Sekhiya Training rule where it is the monk who should "be appreciative and attentive when receiving food.") However, in the West, this gesture of respect may be taken according to local custom.

In some monasteries food is not considered properly given if the lay person wears shoes or sandals when offering to a barefooted bhikkhu. Also, in some communities, when properly offered food is touched again or moved by lay people, even accidentally, it has to be re-offered.

The major point to remember is that in offering food (or anything edible) to a monk there is a formal way of doing so-otherwise the bhikkhu may not be able to eat it. Once one gets used to this interaction with the monk, it becomes quite a meaningful gesture.

Storing Food: After formally receiving food, a bhikkhu is not allowed to store it away for another day. This is another rule that supports the mendicant ideal and the interdependence of monk and lay person, and stops the bhikkhu from becoming attached to his favourite tastes.

The case originally arose when a monk coming back from alms round would eat some food and then dry any remaining rice in the sun to store for the next days' meals. In this way he did not have to go on an alms round every day. It can be summarized:

"Eating food that a bhikkhu-oneself or another-formally received on a previous day is [an offence of Confession.]" (Paac. 38; BMC p.367)

After the daily meal-often the monks of the community will gather to share this-all that day's excess food may be distributed among whoever is present so that nothing is wasted or left over.

Lay people themselves are also allowed to deposit food in the properly approved storeroom so that it can be offered to the monks on another day. If the lay people store it there, the monks will not be counted as having formally received it. (So the formal act of offering also serves the purpose of determining whether food can be stored or not.)

Meal Invitations: It is traditional for lay devotees on special occasions to invite bhikkhus to go and have a meal at their house. This is normally a very straightforward matter and the bhikkhu(s) will explain if they are able to go on that particular day. To show some aspects from the Buddha's time, there are these rules:

The origin of this first rule displays the care that a bhikkhu should take when accepting such an invitation.

A poor workman was inspired to invite the Buddha and all the bhikkhus of the town for a meal, and he insisted they still come even when the Buddha cautioned him about the large number of monks involved. Some bhikkhus assumed that he would not be able to afford very much food so they first went on an alms round and ate beforehand. Therefore when they came to go for the poor man's meal they could not eat very much-even though there was in fact plenty of food because other people had helped to support the poor workman's faith by sending round donations of food. The poor workman became upset saying, "How can you eat elsewhere... am I not competent to give sufficient?"

The rule is summarized:

"Eating a meal before going to another meal to which one was invited, or accepting an invitation to one meal and eating elsewhere instead, is [an offence of Confession] except when one is ill or at the time of giving cloth or making robes." (Paac. 33; BMC p.352)

Should a bhikkhu seem somewhat reluctant to accept your invitation, be aware that he may not be able to change his acceptance of a previous invitation. There is, however, an allowance for the bhikkhu to 'share' or transfer his invitation to another bhikkhu or novice so that he can accept a new one. Even so, it is considered good manners first to contact the original donors about this.

Another, rather obscure, rule about meal invitations originated like this:

> *Ven. Devadatta attempted to take over the Sangha and then tried to kill the Buddha. The Sangha informed the local inhabitants about Ven. Devadatta's behaviour so that it would not reflect on the Sangha as a whole. Ven. Devadatta then found alms so difficult to obtain that he solicited alms-"having asked and asked"-(for all his group) and the lay people criticized them for such unseemly conduct.*

It seems that this rather enigmatic rule may forbid bhikkhus from accepting an invitation to a 'group meal' of four or more specified monks at a donor's house when the whole local community is not invited-as would have been more normal in the Buddha's days. This would then have avoided the forming of cliques inside a community.

The Buddha therefore laid down that:

> *"Eating a meal to which four or more individual bhikkhus have been specifically invited-except on special occasions-is [an offence of Confession.]" (Summary Paac. 32; BMC p.348)*

Another interpretation of this obscure rule requires that bhikkhus:

> *"... do not accept the invitations of those who mention the names of the foods to be offered. The inviter who understands this, makes invitation just in this way: "I invite you to receive alms-food," or, "I invite you to take breakfast... or lunch." By speaking in this way it is possible for bhikkhus to accept." (Paat. 1969 Ed.; p161)*

If the community lives by this second interpretation, one should be careful when inviting bhikkhus for a meal not to mention the specific food that one intends to offer.

Meat-eating: In western countries vegetarianism has recently increased in popularity and this has led to some questioning about bhikkhus and meat-eating. (In less materially developed countries the question is more about 'what, if anything, is there to eat?')

The question of monks' eating meat is an old one that was originally raised by the 'renegade monk' Ven. Devadatta. He asked the Buddha to prohibit bhikkhus from eating fish and flesh in what seems was a ploy to take over the leadership of the Sangha. (The 'stricter ascetic' tactic.) The Buddha had already made a strict rule for both bhikkhus and lay people about not taking life so He did not agree to Ven. Devadatta's new formulation.

The Buddha did allow bhikkhus to eat meat and fish except under the following circumstances:

> *If a bhikkhu sees, hears or suspects that it has been killed for him, he may not eat it. (M.I,369)*

If a bhikkhu is given meat on alms round and he has no knowledge about how the animal died he has to 'receive it with attentiveness.' He should be grateful and recollect that the food he is given is what enables him to continue to live the bhikkhu life, and that as a mendicant he is not in a position to choose what he gets. If he later comes to know the family and they ask him about Dhamma, he will be able to explain the precept about not killing. This may cause them to reflect on their attitude to meat eating.

An individual lay person can choose whether to be a vegetarian. Problems usually arise only when vegetarians want to impose their choice on others, and as meal times are normally a family or shared affair this can create tensions and misunderstandings.

An individual bhikkhu who lives on alms food cannot make such choices. Often the donors are unknown-perhaps not even Buddhist, or just starting to find out about Dhamma-and to refuse their generosity may so offend them that they never have anything to do with Dhamma again.

Finally it comes down to the lay people who go to the market to buy food to give to the bhikkhus. If they are vegetarian themselves or like to give vegetarian food, then the bhikkhu should receive that food with 'appreciation'-especially if it means that fewer animals are being slaughtered. Nevertheless, it should not become a political issue where other people are attacked for their behaviour.

Offering Fruit: Kappiya: At the time of the Buddha, some lay people complained that the monks had destroyed the 'life' in seeds. Destroying seeds therefore became a minor (dukkata) offence, and the monk had to ask the lay people whether they found it 'allowable' for him to eat certain fruits.

Fruits with seeds that can germinate and roots (bulbs, tubers) that can be planted again should be made 'allowable' or kappiya for bhikkhus. An unordained person can do this by touching it with fire, by drawing a knife over it, or by marking it with a finger nail.

In some monasteries, there is a ceremony-briefly mentioned in the actual Vinaya but given in detail in the Commentaries-where the lay person offering the fruit, makes it 'allowable' for the bhikkhu to eat. For example, this may be done with an orange by slightly cutting the peel when the monk says, "Kappiya.m karohi" ("Make this allowable") and answering him with, "Kappiyam Bhante" ("It is allowable, Ven. Sir."). If there are many oranges, and if they are all together and touching, making one fruit allowable makes them all allowable. (In other communities, if the donor offers fruit already 'damaged' (*e.g.*, peeled or cut) it is considered already allowable.)

There is no need for this ceremony with seedless fruit, with fruit if the seeds are unripe so that they cannot regenerate, and with fruit offered already cut with all the seeds removed. Also, if the bhikkhu carefully eats certain sorts of fruits-for instance, mangoes, jackfruit, plums, peaches, prunes, etc.-without damaging the seed, stone, pit or pips, there is no offence.

Food in the Wilderness: The following rule again shows the interdependence and care which must be cultivated between bhikkhus and those who support them.

In the Buddha's time some ladies were ambushed and raped on their way to give food to bhikkhus living in a dangerous jungle area. Their family criticized the bhikkhus for not warning them of the hazards. If lay people intend to give food to a bhikkhu(s) in such a danger zone then they must announce that to the bhikkhu(s) beforehand so that the bhikkhu(s) has a chance to warn them or reduce the threat. The rule can be summarized:

> *"Eating an unannounced gift of staple or non-staple food, after accepting it in a dangerous wilderness abode when one is not ill is [an offence of Acknowledgement.]" (Paatidesaniya 4; BMC p.488)*

Fruit Juices: The above sections have dealt with food (yaavakaalika) but as has been already mentioned fruit juices are considered under a different category. Although bhikkhus should not eat fruit-which is food-after midday, they can drink the 'fruit juice' any time throughout the day. However, they cannot store fruit juice beyond that single day. This is called yaamakaalika and is a juice-drink made from crushed fruit, which is then carefully strained of any pulp or particles. (The Vinayamukha (EV) Commentary suggests that it could not be stored beyond the next dawn because sugar mixed in with the fruit juice might lead to slight fermentation.)

When offering fruit juice it is important that it is well strained so that no pulp or fruit particles remain, for the fruit itself counts as food and so cannot be consumed in the afternoon. Some places in Thailand will strain the juice in a cloth filter seven times to make sure, but the main point is that the filter is fine enough.

"Juice drinks include the freshly squeezed juice of sugar cane, lotus root, all fruits except grain, all leaves except cooked vegetables, and all flowers except the [bassia latifolia] (Mahaavagga.VI.35.6). According to the Commentary, the juice must be strained, and may be warmed by sunlight but not heated over a fire."(BMC p.339)

Some communities will not accept fruit juice made from 'large fruits':

"In discussing the Great Standards, the Commentary says that grain is a "great fruit," and thus the juice of any one of nine large fruits-palmyra fruit, coconut, jack fruit, breadfruit, bottle gourd, white gourd, musk melon, water melon, and squash-would fall under the same class as the juice of grain... From this judgment, many Communities [in Thailand] infer that the juice of any large fruit, such as pineapple or grapefruit, would also be classed as a non-staple food [and therefore could not be consumed in the afternoon.]" (BMC p.339)

Medicines or Tonics: We have dealt above with food and fruit juice. There is now the category of 'tonic-medicines' (sattaahakaalika). These can be consumed at any time but cannot be stored longer than seven days (after they are offered).

These tonic-medicines were originally regulated when Venerable Pilindavaccha's great feats of psychic power made him so famous that he received many offerings of the five 'tonics.' Even though he distributed these among other monks there was so much that the excess had to be stored away and their dwellings were overrun by rats. Visiting lay people criticized the monks for "storing up goods in abundance like a king." The Buddha therefore set down this rule:

"Keeping any of the five tonics-ghee, fresh butter, oil, honey, or sugar/molasses-for more than seven days is [an offence of Confession with Forfeiture.] (Summarized Nis. Paac. 23; BMC p.242)

There are various translations and interpretations about these 'tonic-medicines'-according to different Communities and different countries. Some places consider only liquids allowable while a few communities will drink only plain water in the afternoon. Some communities will not accept re-offered tonic-medicines (after the seven days period is over), some will under certain circumstances. Therefore lay devotees need to enquire about the practice of their local Community and follow that way.

Some contemporary observations:

"The five medicines-ghee, navaniitam, oil, honey, and suga-were allowed by the Buddha to be consumed by 'sick' monks at any time of the day or night. According to the Mahaavagga, these five were 'agreed upon as medicines and, although they served as nutriment for people, were not considered as substantial food.' The degree of infirmity required before a monk is allowed to consume these [tonic-]medicines is a controversial point... It seems that feeling rundown or feeling tired after physical exertion would be sufficient cause to be able to make use of the Five Medicines."(AB)

"The main effectiveness of these medicines seems to be in their nutritional value. They do not have medicinal value as commonly understood today, for example, relieving pain or as an antiseptic. However, as nutriment they would help to maintain bodily strength and assist in recuperation while, since they are so rich, would not be a substitute for normal food." (HS ch.10)

Also, if the tonic-medicine is mixed with a tiny amount of food then it would be acceptable according to this allowance:

"...if sugar has a little flour mixed with it simply to make it firmer-as sometimes happens in sugar cubes and blocks of palm sugar-it is still classed as a tonic as it is still regarded simply as 'sugar.'" (BMC p.238-9)

If the flour is for more food-like reasons then it would be counted as food.

Lifetime Medicines: The fourth category of edibles is that of Lifetime Medicines (yaavajiivika), which includes what we generally think of as medicines.

The basic principle set down by the Buddha about all medicines is in this reflection:

"Properly considering medicinal requisites for curing the sick, I use them: simply to ward off any pains of illness that have arisen, and for the maximum freedom from disease." [OP p. 47; (Pali: M. I, 10; A. III, 387)]

In the beginning, the basic (herbal) medicines allowed by

the Buddha were those pickled in urine. Later, nearly all other types came to be considered allowable.

Medicines that may be consumed without time limitation are called yaavajiivika. The Texts mention different sorts of herbal medicines such as: plant roots, *e.g.*, ginger, turmeric, sweet flag, etc.; decoctions, such as of the neem or nux-vomica; tree-leaves, such as neem-leaves, tulsi or holy basil; fruits, such as long peppers, myrobalan, wormwood; resins, such as asafoetida; salts, such as sea-salt, rock salt, etc. Any other medicine or herbs similar to these that is not reckoned to be food is included under this 'lifetime' category.

Modern western medicines are usually included-using the Great Standards-under this category and therefore can be taken at any time of the day and kept as long as necessary.

Drugs and Alcohol: Finally, we turn to those 'substances of abuse' that are entirely prohibited. The fifth of the Five Precepts for all Buddhists is restraint from drinking alcohol and similar substances that destroy mindfulness, and are thereby a frequent cause of unskilful actions and speech. The equivalent rule for bhikkhus is the fifty-first Confession Rule:

> *"The drinking of alcohol or fermented liquors is [an offence of Confession.]" (Paac. 51; BMC p.402)*

The origin-story concerns Ven. Saagata who conquered a fierce naaga-a type of serpent with magical powers-by his meditation-developed psychic powers. The townspeople heard about this feat and wanted to make some sort of offering to him, upon which the 'group-of-six' bhikkhus impudently suggested that they all should give him alcohol. When he arrived on his almsround every household offered alcohol and he finally collapsed, drunk, at the town gate and had to be carried back to the monastery. He was laid down in a stupor with his head towards the Buddha but in his drunkenness he turned around so that his feet pointed at the Buddha. The Buddha called attention to his changed behaviour, remarking that he certainly could not oppose "even a salamander" in such a state.

The Buddha also said:

> *"Bhikkhus,... there are these four stains because of which samanas and brahmans glow not, shine not, blaze not. What are these four? Drinking alcoholic beverages... indulging in sexual intercourse... accepting gold and money... obtaining requisites through a wrong mode of livelihood." (A.II,53) (AB)*

The Four Great Standards may be further used to argue that using narcotics-which also destroy mindfulness and lead to heedlessness-would also be an offence of Confession. Then there is the general principle of respecting the 'law of the land' (when it accords with Dhamma) so such illegal drugs would be disallowed anyway.

8

Kamma or the Law of Moral Causation

We are faced with a totally ill-balanced world. We perceive the inequalities and manifold destinies of men and the numerous grades of beings that exist in the universe. We see one born into a condition of affluence, endowed with fine mental, moral and physical qualities and another into a condition of abject poverty and wretchedness. Here is a man virtuous and holy, but, contrary to his expectation, ill-luck is ever ready to greet him. The wicked world runs counter to his ambitions and desires. He is poor and miserable in spite of his honest dealings and piety. There is another vicious and foolish, but accounted to be fortune's darling. He is rewarded with all forms of favours, despite his shortcomings and evil modes of life.

Why, it may be questioned, should one be an inferior and another a superior? Why should one be wrested from the hands of a fond mother when he has scarcely seen a few summers, and another should perish in the flower or manhood, or at the ripe age of eighty or hundred? Why should one be sick and infirm, and another strong and healthy? Why should one be handsome, and another ugly and hideous, repulsive to all? Why should one be brought up in the lap of luxury, and another in absolute poverty, steeped in misery? Why should one be born a millionaire and another a pauper? Why should one be born with saintly characteristics, and another with criminal tendencies? Why should some be linguists, artists, mathematicians or musicians from the very cradle? Why should some be congenitally blind, deaf and deformed? Why should some be blessed and others cursed from their birth?

These are some problems that perplex the minds of all thinking men. How are we to account for all this unevenness of the world, this inequality of mankind?

Is it due to the work of blind chance or accident?

There is nothing in this world that happens by blind chance or accident. To say that anything happens by chance, is no more true than that this book has come here of itself. Strictly speaking, nothing happens to man that he does not deserve for some reason or another.

Could this be the fiat of an irresponsible Creator?

Huxley writes:

"If we are to assume that anybody has designedly set this wonderful universe going, it is perfectly clear to me that he is no more entirely benevolent and just in any intelligible sense of the words, than that he is malevolent and unjust."

According to Einstein:

"If this being (God) is omnipotent, then every occurrence, including every human action, every human thought, and every human feeling and aspiration is also his work; how is it possible to think of holding men responsible for their deeds and thoughts before such an Almighty Being.

"In giving out punishments and rewards, he would to a certain extent be passing judgment on himself. How can this be combined with the goodness and righteousness ascribed to him."

"According to the theological principles man is created arbitrarily and without his desire and at the moment of his creation is either blessed or damned eternally. Hence man is either good or evil, fortunate or unfortunate, noble or depraved, from the first step in the process of his physical creation to the moment of his last

breath, regardless of his individual desires, hopes, ambitions, struggles or devoted prayers. Such is theological fatalism." — Spencer Lewis

As Charles Bradlaugh says:

"The existence of evil is a terrible stumbling block to the Theist. Pain, misery, crime, poverty confront the advocate of eternal goodness and challenge with unanswerable potency his declaration of Deity as all-good, all-wise, and all-powerful."

In the words of Schopenhauer:

"Whoever regards himself as having become out of nothing must also think that he will again become nothing; for an eternity has passed before he was, and then a second eternity had begun, through which he will never cease to be, is a monstrous thought.

"If birth is the absolute beginning, then death must be his absolute end; and the assumption that man is made out of nothing leads necessarily to the assumption that death is his absolute end."

Commenting on human sufferings and God, Prof. J.B.S. Haldane writes:

"Either suffering is needed to perfect human character, or God is not Almighty. The former theory is disproved by the fact that some people who have suffered very little but have been fortunate in their ancestry and education have very fine characters. The objection to the second is that it is only in connection with the universe as a whole that there is any intellectual gap to be filled by the postulation of a deity. And a creator could presumably create whatever he or it wanted."

Lord Russell states:

"The world, we are told, was created by a God who is both good and omnipotent. Before He created the world he foresaw all the pain and misery that it would contain. He is therefore responsible for all of it. It is useless to argue that the pain in the world is due to sin. If God knew in advance the sins of which man would be guilty,

> *He was clearly responsible for all the consequences of those sins when He decided to create man."*
>
> *In "Despair," a poem of his old age, Lord Tennyson thus boldly attacks God, who, as recorded in Isaiah, says, "I make peace and create evil." (Isaiah, xiv. 7.)*
>
> *"What! I should call on that infinite love that has served us so well? Infinite cruelty, rather that made everlasting hell, Made us, foreknew us, foredoomed us, and does what he will with his own. Better our dead brute mother who never has heard us groan."*

Surely "the doctrine that all men are sinners and have the essential sin of Adam is a challenge to justice, mercy, love and omnipotent fairness."

Some writers of old authoritatively declared that God created man in his own image. Some modern thinkers state, on the contrary, that man created God in his own image. With the growth of civilization man's concept of God also became more and more refined.

It is however, impossible to conceive of such a being either in or outside the universe.

Could this variation be due to heredity and environment? One must admit that all such chemico-physical phenomena revealed by scientists, are partly instrumental, but they cannot be solely responsible for the subtle distinctions and vast differences that exist amongst individuals. Yet why should identical twins who are physically alike, inheriting like genes, enjoying the same privilege of upbringing, be very often temperamentally, morally and intellectually totally different?

Heredity alone cannot account for these vast differences. Strictly speaking, it accounts more plausibly for their similarities than for most of the differences. The infinitesimally minute chemico-physical germ, which is about 30 millionth part of an inch across, inherited from parents, explains only a portion of man, his physical foundation. With regard to the more complex and subtle mental, intellectual and moral differences we need more enlightenment. The theory of heredity cannot give a satisfactory explanation for the birth of a criminal in a long line of honourable ancestors, the birth of a saint or a noble man in a family of evil repute, for the arising of infant prodigies, men of genius and great religious teachers.

According to Buddhism this variation is due not only to heredity, environment, "nature and nurture," but also to our own kamma, or in other words, to the result of our own inherited past actions and our present deeds. We ourselves are responsible for our own deeds, happiness and misery. We build our own hells. We create our own heavens. We are the architects of our own fate. In short we ourselves are our own kamma.

On one occasion a certain young man named Subha approached the Buddha, and questioned why and wherefore it was that among human beings there are the low and high states.

> *"For," said he, "we find amongst mankind those of brief life and those of long life, the hale and the ailing, the good looking and the ill-looking, the powerful and the powerless, the poor and the rich, the low-born and the high-born, the ignorant and the intelligent."*

The Buddha briefly replied: "Every living being has kamma as its own, its inheritance, its cause, its kinsman, its refuge. Kamma is that which differentiates all living beings into low and high states."

He then explained the cause of such differences in accordance with the law of moral causation.

Thus from a Buddhist standpoint, our present mental, intellectual, moral and temperamental differences are mainly due to our own actions and tendencies, both past the present.

Kamma, literally, means action; but, in its ultimate sense, it means the meritorious and demeritorious volition *(Kusala Akusala Cetana).* Kamma constitutes both good and evil. Good gets good. Evil gets evil. Like attracts like. This is the law of Kamma.

As some Westerners prefer to say Kamma is "action-influence."

We reap what we have sown. What we sow we reap somewhere

or some when. In one sense we are the result of what we were; we will be the result of what we are. In another sense, we are not totally the result of what we were and we will not absolutely be the result of what we are. For instance, a criminal today may be a saint tomorrow.

Buddhism attributes this variation to Kamma, but it does not assert that everything is due to Kamma.

If everything were due to Kamma, a man must ever be bad, for it is his Kamma to be bad. One need not consult a physician to be cured of a disease, for if one's Kamma is such one will be cured.

According to Buddhism, there are five orders or processes *(Niyamas)* which operate in the physical and mental realms:

(i) *Kamma Niyama*, order of act and result, e.g., desirable and undesirable acts produce corresponding good and bad results.

(ii) *Utu Niyama,* physical (inorganic) order, *e.g.*, seasonal phenomena of winds and rains.

(iii) *Bija Niyama,* order of germs or seeds (physical organic order); *e.g.*, rice produced from rice-seed, sugary taste from sugar cane or honey etc. The scientific theory of cells and genes and the physical similarity of twins may be ascribed to this order.

(iv) *Citta Niyama,* order of mind or psychic law, *e.g.*, processes of consciousness *(Citta vithi),* power of mind etc.

(v) *Dhamma Niyama,* order of the norm, *e.g.*, the natural phenomena occurring at the advent of a Bodhisatta in his last birth, gravitation, etc.

Every mental or physical phenomenon could be explained by these all-embracing five orders or processes which are laws in themselves.

Kamma is, therefore, only one of the five orders that prevail in the universe. It is a law in itself, but it does not thereby follow that there should be a law-giver. Ordinary laws of nature, like gravitation, need no law-giver. It operates in its own field without the intervention of an external independent ruling agency.

Nobody, for instance, has decreed that fire should burn. Nobody has commanded that water should seek its own level. No scientist has ordered that water should consist of H_2O, and that coldness should be one of its properties. These are their intrinsic characteristics. Kamma is neither fate nor predestination imposed upon us by some mysterious unknown power to which we must helplessly submit ourselves. It is one's own doing reacting on oneself, and so one has the possibility to divert the course of Kamma to some extent. How far one diverts it depends on oneself.

It must also be said that such phraseology as rewards and punishments should not be allowed to enter into discussions concerning the problem of Kamma.

For Buddhism does not recognize an Almighty Being who rules His subjects and rewards and punishes them accordingly. Buddhists, on the contrary, believe that sorrow and happiness one experiences are the natural outcome of one's own good and bad actions. It should be stated that Kamma has both the continuative and the retributive principle.

Inherent in Kamma is the potentiality of producing its due effect. The cause produces the effect; the effect explains the cause. Seed produces the fruit; the fruit explains the seed as both are inter-related. Even so Kamma and its effect are inter-related; "the effect already blooms in the cause."

A Buddhist who is fully convinced of the doctrine of Kamma does not pray to another to be saved but confidently relies on himself for his purification because it teaches individual responsibility.

It is this doctrine of Kamma that gives him consolation, hope, self reliance and moral courage. It is this belief in Kamma "that validates his effort, kindles his enthusiasm," makes him ever kind, tolerant and considerate. It is also this firm belief in Kamma that prompts him to refrain from evil, do good and be good without being frightened of any punishment or tempted by any reward.

It is this doctrine of Kamma that can explain the problem of suffering, the mystery of so-called fate or predestination of other religions, and above all the inequality of mankind.

Kamma and rebirth are accepted as axiomatic.

REBIRTH

As long as this Kammic force exists there is rebirth, for beings are merely the visible manifestation of this invisible Kammic force. Death is nothing but the temporary end of this temporary phenomenon. It is not the complete annihilation of this so-called being. The organic life has ceased, but the Kammic force which hitherto actuated it has not been destroyed. As the Kammic force remains entirely undisturbed by the disintegration of the fleeting body, the passing away of the present dying thought-moment only conditions a fresh consciousness in another birth.

It is Kamma, rooted in ignorance and craving, that conditions rebirth. Past Kamma conditions the present birth; and present Kamma, in combination with past Kamma, conditions the future. The present is the offspring of the past, and becomes, in turn, the parent of the future.

If we postulate a past, present, and a future life, then we are at once faced with the alleged mysterious problem — "What is the ultimate origin of life?"

Either there must be a beginning or there cannot be a beginning for life.

One school, in attempting to solve the problem, postulates a first cause, God, viewed as a force or as an Almighty Being.

Another school denies a first cause for, in common experience, the cause ever becomes the effect and the effect becomes the cause. In a circle of cause and effect a first cause is inconceivable. According to the former, life has had a beginning, according to the latter, it is beginningless.

From the scientific standpoint, we are the direct products of the sperm and ovum cells provided by our parents. As such life precedes life. With regard to the origin of the first protoplasm of life, or colloid, scientists plead ignorance.

According to Buddhism we are born from the matrix of action (Kammayoni). Parents merely provide an infinitesimally small cell. As such being precedes being. At the moment of conception it is past Kamma that conditions the initial consciousness that vitalizes the fetus. It is this invisible Kammic energy, generated from the past birth that produces mental phenomena and the phenomenon of life in an already extent physical phenomenon, to complete the trio that constitutes man.

For a being to be born here a being must die somewhere. The birth of a being, which strictly means the arising of the five aggregates or psycho-physical phenomena in this present life, corresponds to the death of a being in a past life; just as, in conventional terms, the rising of the sun in one place means the setting of the sun in another place. This enigmatic statement may be better understood by imagining life as a wave and not as a straight line. Birth and death are only two phases of the same process. Birth precedes death, and death, on the other hand, precedes birth. The constant succession of birth and death in connection with each individual life flux constitutes what is technically known as *Samsara* — recurrent wandering.

What is the Ultimate Origin of Life?

The Buddha declares:

"Without cognizable end is this Samsara. A first beginning of beings, who, obstructed by ignorance and fettered by craving, wander and fare on, is not to be perceived."

This life-stream flows *ad infinitum,* as long as it is fed by the muddy waters of ignorance and craving. When these two are completely cut off, then only, if one so wishes, does the stream cease to flow, rebirth ends as in the case of the Buddhas and Arahats. An ultimate beginning of this life-stream cannot be determined, as a stage cannot be perceived when this life-force was not fraught with ignorance and craving.

The Buddha has here referred merely to the beginning of the life-stream of living beings. It is left to scientists to speculate on the origin and the evolution of the universe. The Buddha does not attempt to solve all the ethical and philosophical problems that perplex mankind. Nor does He deal with theories and speculations that tend neither to edification nor to enlightenment. Nor does He demand blind faith from His adherents. He is chiefly concerned with the problem of suffering and its destruction. With but this one practical and specific purpose in view, all irrelevant side issues are completely ignored.

But how are we to believe that there is a past existence?

The most valuable evidence Buddhists cite in favour of rebirth is the Buddha, for He developed a knowledge which enabled Him to read past and future lives.

Following His instructions, His disciples also developed this knowledge and were able to read their past lives to a great extent.

Even some Indian Rishis, before the advent of the Buddha, were distinguished for such psychic powers as clairaudience, clairvoyance, thought-reading, remembering past births, etc.

There are also some persons, who probably in accordance with the laws of association, spontaneously develop the memory of their past birth, and remember fragments of their previous lives. Such cases are very rare, but those few well-attested, respectable cases tend to throw some light on the idea of a past birth. So are the experiences of some modern dependable psychics and strange cases of alternating and multiple personalities.

In hypnotic states some relate experiences of their past lives; while a few others, read the past lives of others and even heal diseases.

Sometimes we get strange experiences which cannot be explained but by rebirth.

How often do we meet persons whom we have never met, and yet instinctively feel that they are quite familiar to us? How often do we visit places, and yet feel impressed that we are perfectly acquainted with those surroundings?

The Buddha tells us:

"Through previous associations or present advantage, that old love springs up again like the lotus in the water."

Experiences of some reliable modern psychics, ghostly phenomena, spirit communications, strange alternating and multiple personalities and so on shed some light upon this problem of rebirth.

Into this world come Perfect Ones like the Buddhas and highly developed personalities. Do they evolve suddenly? Can they be the products of a single existence?

How are we to account for great characters like Buddhaghosa, Panini, Kalidasa, Homer and Plato; men of genius like Shakespeare, infant prodigies like Pascal, Mozart, Beethoven, Raphael, Ramanujan, etc.?

Heredity alone cannot account for them. "Else their ancestry would disclose it, their posterity, even greater than themselves, demonstrate it."

Could they rise to such lofty heights if they had not lived noble lives and gained similar experiences in the past? Is it by mere chance that they are been born or those particular parents and placed under those favourable circumstances?

The few years that we are privileged to spend here or, for the most five score years, must certainly be an inadequate preparation for eternity.

If one believes in the present and in the future, it is quite logical to believe in the past. The present is the offspring of the past, and acts in turn as the parent of the future.

If there are reasons to believe that we have existed in the past, then surely there are no reasons to disbelieve that we shall continue to exist after our present life has apparently ceased.

It is indeed a strong argument in favour of past and future lives that "in this world virtuous persons are very often unfortunate and vicious persons prosperous."

A Western writer says:

> *"Whether we believe in a past existence or not, it forms the only reasonable hypothesis which bridges certain gaps in human knowledge concerning certain facts of every day life. Our reason tells us that this idea of past birth and Kamma alone can explain the degrees of difference that exist between twins, how men like Shakespeare with a very limited experience are able to portray*

with marvelous exactitude the most diverse types of human character, scenes and so forth of which they could have no actual knowledge, why the work of the genius invariably transcends his experience, the existence of infant precocity, the vast diversity in mind and morals, in brain and physique, in conditions, circumstances and environment observable throughout the world, and so forth."

It should be stated that this doctrine of rebirth can neither be proved nor disproved experimentally, but it is accepted as an evidentially verifiable fact.

The cause of this Kamma, continues the Buddha, is *avijja* or ignorance of the Four Noble Truths. Ignorance is, therefore, the cause of birth and death; and its transmutation into knowingness or *vijja* is consequently their cessation.

The result of this analytical method is summed up in the *Paticca Samuppada.*

PATICCA SAMUPPADA

Paticca means because of, or dependent upon: *Samuppada* "arising or origination." *Paticca Samuppada,* therefore, literally means — "Dependent Arising" or "Dependent Origination."

It must be borne in mind that *Paticca Samuppada* is only a discourse on the process of birth and death and not a theory of the ultimate origin of life. It deals with the cause of rebirth and suffering, but it does not in the least attempt to show the evolution of the world from primordial matter.

Ignorance *(Avijja)* is the first link or cause of the wheel of life. It clouds all right understanding. Dependent on ignorance of the Four Noble Truths arise activities *(Sankhara)* — both moral and immoral. The activities whether good or bad rooted in ignorance which must necessarily have their due effects, only tend to prolong life's wandering. Nevertheless, good actions are essential to get rid of the ills of life.

Dependent on activities arise rebirth-consciousness *(Vinnana).* This links the past with the present.

Simultaneous with the arising of rebirth-consciousness there come into being mind and body *(Nama-rupa).*

The six senses *(Salayatana)* are the inevitable consequences of mind and body.

Because of the six senses contact *(Phassa)* sets in. Contact leads to feeling *(Vedana).*

These five — *viz.*, consciousness, mind and matter, six senses, contact and feeling — are the effects of past actions and are called the passive side of life.

Dependent on feeling arises craving *(Tanha).* Craving results in grasping *(Upadana).* Grasping is the cause of Kamma *(Bhava)* which in its turn, conditions future birth *(Jati).* Birth is the inevitable cause of old age and death *(Jara-marana).*

If on account of cause effect comes to be, then if the cause ceases, the effect also must cease.

The reverse order of the *Paticca Samuppada* will make the matter clear.

Old age and death are possible in and with a psychophysical organism. Such an organism must be born; therefore it presupposes birth. But birth is the inevitable result of past deeds or Kamma. Kamma is conditioned by grasping which is due to craving. Such craving can appear only where feeling exists. Feeling is the outcome of contact between the senses and objects. Therefore it presupposes organs of senses which cannot exist without mind and body. Where there is a mind there is consciousness. It is the result of past good and evil. The acquisition of good and evil is due to ignorance of things as they truly are.

The whole formula may be summed up thus:

Dependent on Ignorance arise Activities (Moral and Immoral)

- Activities arises Consciousness (Rebirth Consciousness)
- Consciousness arise Mind and Matter
- Mind and Matter arise the six Spheres of Sense
- the Six Spheres of Sense arises Contact
- Contact arises Feeling
- Feeling arises Craving

- Craving arises Grasping
- Grasping arise Actions (Kamma)
- Actions arises Rebirth
- Birth arise Decay, Death, Sorrow, Lamentation, Pain, Grief, and Despair.

Thus does the entire aggregate of suffering arise. The first two of these twelve pertain to the past, the middle eight to the present, and the last two to the future.

The complete cessation of Ignorance leads to the cessation of Activities.

The cessation of Activities leads to the cessation of Consciousness.

- Consciousness leads to the cessation of mind and matter.
- Mind and Matter leads to the cessation of the six Spheres of Sense.
- The six Spheres of Sense leads to the cessation of Contact,
- Contact leads to the cessation of Feeling.
- Feeling leads to the cessation of Craving.
- Craving leads to the cessation of Grasping.
- Grasping leads to the cessation of Actions.
- Actions leads to the cessation of Rebirth.
- Rebirth leads to the cessation of Decay, Death, Sorrow, Lamentation, Pain, Grief, and Despair.

Thus does the cessation of this entire aggregate of suffering result.

This process of cause and effect continues ad infinitum. The beginning of this process cannot be determined as it is impossible to say whence this life-flux was encompassed by nescience. But when this nescience is turned into knowledge, and the life-flux is diverted into *Nibbanadhatu,* then the end of the life process of *Samsara* comes about.

ANATTA OR SOUL-LESSNESS

This Buddhist doctrine of rebirth should be distinguished from the theory of re-incarnation which implies the transmigration of a soul and its invariable material rebirth. Buddhism denies the existence of an unchanging or eternal soul created by a God or emanating from a Divine Essence *(Paramatma).* If the immortal soul, which is supposed to be the essence of man, is eternal, there cannot be either a rise or a fall. Besides one cannot understand why "different souls are so variously constituted at the outset."

To prove the existence of endless felicity in an eternal heaven and unending torments in an eternal hell, an immortal soul is absolutely necessary. Otherwise, what is it that is punished in hell or rewarded in heaven?

> *"It should be said," writes Bertrand Russell, "that the old distinction between soul and body has evaporated quite as much because 'matter' has lost its solidity as mind has lost its spirituality. Psychology is just beginning to be scientific. In the present state of psychology belief in immortality can at any rate claim no support from science."*

Buddhists do agree with Russell when he says "there is obviously some reason in which I am the same person as I was yesterday, and, to take an even more obvious example if I simultaneously see a man and hear him speaking, there is some sense in which the 'I' that sees is the same as the 'I' that hears."

Till recently scientists believed in an indivisible and indestructible atom. "For sufficient reasons physicists have reduced this atom to a series of events. For equally good reasons psychologists find that mind has not the identity of a single continuing thing but is a series of occurrences bound together by certain intimate relations. The question of immortality, therefore, has become the question whether these intimate relations exist between occurrences connected with a living body and other occurrence which take place after that body is dead."

As C.E.M. Joad says in "The Meaning of Life," matter has since disintegrated under our very eyes. It is no longer solid; it is no longer enduring; it is no longer determined by compulsive causal laws; and more important than all, it is no longer known.

The so-called atoms, it seems, are both "divisible and destructible." The electrons and protons that compose atoms "can meet and annihilate one another while their persistence, such as it is, is rather that of a wave lacking fixed boundaries, and in process of continual change both as regards shape and position than that of a thing."

Bishop Berkeley who showed that this so-called atom is a metaphysical fiction held that there exists a spiritual substance called the soul.

Hume, for instance, looked into consciousness and perceived hat there was nothing except fleeting mental states and concluded that the supposed "permanent ego" is non-existent.

> *"There are some philosophers," he says, "who imagine we are every moment conscious of what we call 'ourself,' that we feel its existence and its continuance in existence and so we are certain, both of its perfect identity and simplicity. For my part, when I enter most intimately into what I call 'myself' I always stumble on some particular perception or other — of heat or cold, light or shade, love or hatred, pain or pleasure. I never catch myself... and never can observe anything but the perception... nor do I conceive what is further requisite to make me a perfect non-entity."*

Bergson says, "All consciousness is time existence; and a conscious state is not a state that endures without changing. It is a change without ceasing, when change ceases it ceases; it is itself nothing but change."

Dealing with this question of soul Prof. James says — "The soul-theory is a complete superfluity, so far as accounting for the actually verified facts of conscious experience goes. So far no one can be compelled to subscribe to it for definite scientific reasons." In concluding his interesting chapter on the soul he says: "And in this book the provisional solution which we have reached must be the final word: the thoughts themselves are the thinkers."

Watson, a distinguished psychologist, states: "No one has

ever touched a soul or has seen one in a test tube or has in any way come into relationship with it as he has with the other objects of his daily experience. Nevertheless to doubt its existence is to become a heretic and once might possibly even had led to the loss of one's head. Even today a man holding a public position dare not question it."

The Buddha anticipated these facts some 2500 years ago.

According to Buddhism mind is nothing but a complex compound of fleeting mental states. One unit of consciousness consists of three phases — arising or genesis *(uppada)* static or development *(thiti),* and cessation or dissolution *(bhanga).* Immediately after the cessation stage of a thought moment there occurs the genesis stage of the subsequent thought-moment. Each momentary consciousness of this ever-changing life-process, on passing away, transmits its whole energy, all the indelibly recorded impressions to its successor. Every fresh consciousness consists of the potentialities of its predecessors together with something more. There is therefore, a continuous flow of consciousness like a stream without any interruption. The subsequent thought moment is neither absolutely the same as its predecessor — since that which goes to make it up is not identical — nor entirely another — being the same continuity of Kamma energy. Here there is no identical being but there is an identity in process.

Every moment there is birth, every moment there is death. The arising of one thought-moment means the passing away of another thought-moment and vice versa. In the course of one lifetime there is momentary rebirth without a soul.

It must not be understood that a consciousness is chopped up in bits and joined together like a train or a chain. But, on the contrary, "it persistently flows on like a river receiving from the tributary streams of sense constant accretions to its flood, and ever dispensing to the world without the thought-stuff it has gathered by the way." It has birth for its source and death for its mouth. The rapidity of the flow is such that hardly is there any standard whereby it can be measured even approximately. However, it pleases the commentators to say that the time duration of one thought-moment is even less than one-billionth part of the time occupied by a flash of lightning.

Here we find a juxtaposition of such fleeting mental states of consciousness opposed to a superposition of such states as some appear to believe. No state once gone ever recurs nor is identical with what goes before. But we worldlings, veiled by the web of illusion, mistake this apparent continuity to be something eternal and go to the extent of introducing an unchanging soul, an Atta, the supposed doer and receptacle of all actions to this ever-changing consciousness.

"The so-called being is like a flash of lightning that is resolved into a succession of sparks that follow upon one another with such rapidity that the human retina cannot perceive them separately, nor can the uninstructed conceive of such succession of separate sparks." As the wheel of a cart rests on the ground at one point, so does the being live only for one thought-moment. It is always in the present, and is ever slipping into the irrevocable past. What we shall become is determined by this present thought-moment.

If there is no soul, what is it that is reborn, one might ask. Well, there is nothing to be re-born. When life ceases the Kammic energy re-materializes itself in another form. As Bhikkhu Silacara says: "Unseen it passes whithersoever the conditions appropriate to its visible manifestation are present. Here showing itself as a tiny gnat or worm, there making its presence known in the dazzling magnificence of a Deva or an Archangel's existence. When one mode of its manifestation ceases it merely passes on, and where suitable circumstances offer, reveals itself afresh in another name or form."

Birth is the arising of the psycho-physical phenomena. Death is merely the temporary end of a temporary phenomenon.

Just as the arising of a physical state is conditioned by a preceding state as its cause, so the appearance of psycho-physical phenomena is conditioned by cause anterior to its birth. As the process of one life-span is possible without a permanent entity passing from one thought-moment to another, so a series of life-processes is possible without an immortal soul to transmigrate from one existence to another.

Buddhism does not totally deny the existence of a personality in an empirical sense. It only attempts to show that it does not exist in an ultimate sense. The Buddhist philosophical term for an individual is *Santana, i.e.,* a flux or a continuity. It includes the mental and physical elements as well. The Kammic force of each individual binds the elements together. This uninterrupted flux or continuity of psycho-physical phenomenon, which is conditioned by Kamma, and not limited only to the present life, but having its source in the beginningless past and its continuation in the future — is the Buddhist substitute for the permanent ego or the immortal soul of other religions.

THE LAW OF KARMA

We have come to a couple of related ideas which are common in Buddhism and they are the ideas of karma and rebirth. These ideas are closely inter-related, but because the subject is a fairly wide one, we will begin to deal with the idea of karma todayand rebirth in another lecture.

We know that what binds us in samsara are the defilements — desire, ill-will and ignorance. We spoke about this when we talked about the Second Noble Truth — the truth of the cause of suffering. These defilements are something which every living being in samsara shares, whether we speak of human beings or animals or beings who live in the other realms which we do not normally perceive. In this, all living beings are alike and yet amongst all the living beings that we can normally perceive, there are many differences. For instance, some of us are wealthy, some are less wealthy, some are strong and healthy, others are disabled and so forth. There are many differences amongst living beings and even more so there are differences between animals and human beings. These differences are due to karma.

What we all share - desire, ill-will and ignorance - are common to all living beings, but the particular condition in which we find ourselves is the result of our particular karma that conditions the situation in which we find ourselves, the situation in which we may be wealthy, strong and so forth. These circumstances are decided by karma. It is in this sense that karma explains the differences amongst living beings. It explains why some beings are fortunate while others are less fortunate, some are happy while others are less happy. The Buddha has specifically stated that karma explains the differences between living beings. You might also recall that the understanding of how karma affects the birth of living beings in happy or unhappy circumstances — the knowledge of how living beings move from happy circumstances to unhappy circumstances, and vice versa, from unhappy to happy circumstances as a result of their karma - was part of the Buddha's experience on the night of His enlightenment. It is karma that explains the circumstances that living beings find themselves in.

Having said this much about the function of karma, let us look more closely at what karma is. Let us define karma. Maybe we can define karma best by first deciding what karma is not. It is quite often the case that we find people misunderstanding the idea of karma. This is particularly true in our daily casual use of the term. We find people saying that one cannot change one's situation because of one's karma. In this sense, karma becomes a sort of escape. It becomes similar to predestination or fatalism. This is emphatically not the correct understanding of karma. It is possible that this misunderstanding of karma has come about because of the popular idea that we have about luck and fate. It may be for this reason that our idea of karma has become overlaid in popular thought with the notion of predestination. Karma is not fate or predestination.

If karma is not fate or predestination, then what is it? Let us look at the term itself. Karma means action, means "to do". Immediately we have an indication that the real meaning of karma is not fate because karma is action. It is dynamic. But it is more than simply action because it is not mechanical action. It is not unconscious or involuntary action. It is intentional, conscious, deliberate, willful action. How is it that this intentional, will action conditions or determines our situation? It is because every action must have a reaction, an effect. This truth has been expressed in regard to the physical universe by the great physicist Newton who formulated the law which states that every action must have an equal and opposite reaction. In the moral sphere of conscious actions, we have a counterpart to the physical law of action and reaction, the law that every intentional, will action must have its effect. This is why we sometimes speak either of Karma-Vipaka, intentional action and its ripened effect, or we speak of Karma-Phala, intentional action and its fruit. It is when we speak of intentional action together with its effect or fruit that we speak of the Law of Karma.

In its most basic sense, the Law of Karma in the moral sphere teaches that similar actions will lead to similar results. Let us take an example. If we plant a mango seed, the plant that springs up will be a mango tree, and eventually it will bear a mango fruit. Alternatively, if we plant a Pong Pong seed, the tree that will spring up will be a Pong Pong tree and the fruit a Pong Pong. As one sows, so shall one reap. According to one's action, so shall be the fruit. Similarly, in the Law of Karma, if we do a wholesome action, eventually we will get a wholesome fruit, and if we do an unwholesome action eventually we will get an unwholesome, painful result. This is what we mean when we say that causes bring about effects that are similar to the causes. This we will see very clearly when we come to specific examples of wholesome and unwholesome actions.

We can understand by means of this general introduction that karma can be of two varieties - wholesome karma or good karma and unwholesome karma or bad karma. In order that we should not misunderstand this description of karma, it is useful for us to look at the original term. In this case, it is kushala or akushala karma, karma that is wholesome or unwholesome. In order that we understand how these terms are being used, it is important that we know the real meaning of kushala and akushala. Kushala means intelligent or skilful, whereas akushala means not intelligent, not skilful. This helps us to understand how these terms are being used, not in terms of good and evil but in terms of skilful and unskilful, in terms of intelligent and unintelligent, in terms of wholesome and unwholesome. Now how wholesome and how unwholesome? Wholesome in the sense that those actions which are beneficial to oneself and others, those actions that spring not out of desire, ill-will and ignorance, but out of renunciation, loving-kindness and compassion, and wisdom.

One may ask how does one know whether an action that is wholesome or unwholesome will produce happiness or unhappiness. The answer is time will tell. The Buddha Himself answered the question. He has explained that so long as an unwholesome action does not bear its fruit of suffering, for so long a foolish person will consider that action good. But when that unwholesome action bears its fruit of suffering then he will realize that the action is unwholesome. Similarly, so long as a wholesome action does not bear its fruit of happiness, a good person may consider that action unwholesome. When it bears its fruit of happiness, then he will realize that the action is good. So one needs to judge wholesome and unwholesome action from the point of view of long-term effect. Very simply, wholesome actions result in eventual happiness for oneself and others, while unwholesome actions have the opposite result, they result in suffering for oneself and others.

Specifically, the unwholesome actions which are to be avoided relate to the three doors or means of action, and these are body, speech and mind. There are three unwholesome actions of the body, four of speech and three of mind that are to be avoided. The three unwholesome actions of body that are to be avoided are killing, stealing and sexual misconduct. The four unwholesome actions of speech that are to be avoided are lying, slander, harsh speech and malicious gossip. The three unwholesome actions of mind that are to be avoided are greed, anger and delusion. By avoiding these ten unwholesome actions we will avoid their consequences. The unwholesome actions have suffering as their fruit. The fruit of these unwholesome actions can take various forms. The fully ripened fruit of the unwholesome actions consists of rebirth in the lower realms, in the realms of suffering — hell, hungry ghosts and animals. If these unwholesome actions are not sufficient to result in rebirth in these lower realms, they will result in unhappiness in this life as a human being. Here we can see at work the principle of a cause resulting in a similar effect. For example, habitual killing which is motivated by ill-will and anger and which results in the taking of the life of other beings will result in rebirth in the hells where one's experience is saturated by anger and ill-will and where one may be repeatedly killed. If killing is not sufficiently habitual or weighty to result in rebirth in the hells, killing will result in shortened life as a human being, separation from loved ones, fear or paranoia. Here too we can see how the effect is similar to the cause. Killing shortens the life of others, deprives others of their loved ones and so forth, and so if we kill we will be liable to experience these effects. Similarly, stealing which is borne of the defilement of desire may lead to rebirth as a hungry ghost where one is totally destitute of desired objects. If it does not result in rebirth as a ghost, it will result in poverty, dependence upon others for one's livelihood and so forth. Sexual misconduct results in martial distress or unhappy marriages.

While unwholesome actions produce unwholesome results - suffering, wholesome actions produce wholesome results - happiness. One can interpret wholesome actions in two ways. One can simply regard wholesome actions as avoiding the unwholesome actions, avoiding killing, stealing, sexual misconduct and the rest. Or one can speak of wholesome actions in positive terms. Here one can refer to the list of wholesome actions that includes generosity, good conduct, meditation, reverence, service, transference of merits, rejoicing in the merit of others, hearing the Dharma, teaching the Dharma and straightening of one's own views. Just as unwholesome actions produce suffering, these wholesome actions produce benefits. Again effects here are similar to the actions. For example, generosity results in wealth. Hearing of the Dharma results in wisdom. The wholesome actions have as their consequences similar wholesome effects just as unwholesome actions have similar unwholesome effects.

Karma, be it wholesome or unwholesome, is modified by the conditions under which the actions are performed. In other words, a wholesome or unwholesome action may be more or less strong depending upon the conditions under which it is done. The conditions which determine the weight or strength of karma may be divided into those which refer to the subject — the doer of the action — and those which refer to the object — the being to whom the action is done. So the conditions that determine the weight of karma apply to the subject and object of the action. Specifically, if we take the example of killing, in order for the act of killing to have its complete and unmitigated power, five conditions must be present — a living being, the awareness of the existence of a living being, the intention to kill the living being, the effort or action of killing the living being, and the consequent death of the living being. Here too, we can see the subjective and the objective conditions. The subjective conditions are the awareness of the living being, the intention to kill and the action of killing. The objective conditions are the presence of the living being and the consequent death of the living being.

Similarly, there are five conditions that modify the weight of karma and they are persistent, repeated action; action done with great intention and determination; action done without regret; action done towards those who possess extraordinary qualities; and action done towards those who have benefited one in the past. Here too there are subjective and objective conditions. The subjective conditions are persistent action; action done with intention; and action done without regret. If one does an unwholesome action again and again with great intention and without regret, the weight of the action will be enhanced. The objective conditions are the quality of the object to whom actions are done and the nature of the relationship. In other words, if one does a wholesome or unwholesome action towards living beings who possess extraordinary qualities such as the arhats, or the Buddha, the wholesome or unwholesome action done will have greater weight. Finally the power of wholesome or unwholesome action done towards those who have benefited one in the past, such as one's parents, teachers and friends, will be greater.

The objective and subjective conditions together determine the weight of karma. This is important because understanding this will help us to understand that karma is not simply a matter of black and white, or good and bad. Karma is moral action and moral responsibility. But the working of the Law of Karma is very finely tuned and balanced so as to match effect with cause, so as to take into account the subjective and objective conditions that determine the nature of an action. This ensures that the effects of actions are equal to and similar to the nature of the causes.

The effects of karma may be evident either in the short term or in the long term. Traditionally we divide karma into three varieties related to the amount of time that is required for the effects of these actions to manifest themselves. Karma can either manifest its effects in this very life or in the next life or only after several lives. When karma manifests its effects in this life, we can see the fruit of karma within a relatively short length of time. This variety of karma is easily verifiable by any of us. For instance, when someone refuses to study, when someone indulges in harmful distractions like alcohol and drugs, when someone begins to steal to support his harmful habits; the effects will be evident within a short time. They will be evident in loss of livelihood and friendship, health and so forth. We cannot see the long-term effect of karma, but the Buddha and His prominent disciples who have developed their minds are able to perceive directly the long-term effects. For instance, when Maudgalyayana was beaten to death by bandits, the Buddha was able to tell that this event was the effect of something Maudgalyayana had done in a previous life when he had taken his aged parents to the forest and having beaten them to death, had then reported that they had been killed by bandits. The effect of this unwholesome action done many lives before was manifested only in his last life. At death we have to leave everything behind — our property and our loved ones, but our karma will accompany us like a shadow. The Buddha has said that nowhere on earth or in heaven can one escape one's karma. So when the conditions are correct, dependent upon mind and body, the effects of karma will manifest themselves just as dependent on certain conditions a mango will appear on a mango tree. We can see that even in the world of nature certain effects take longer to appear than others. If for instance, we plant the seed of a papaya, we will obtain the fruit in shorter period than if we plant the seed of a durian. Similarly, the effects of karma manifest either in the short term or in the long term.

Besides the two varieties of karma, wholesome and unwholesome karma, we should mention neutral or ineffective karma. Neutral karma is karma that has no moral consequence either because the very nature of the action is such as to have no moral consequence or because it is done involuntarily and unintentionally. For example, sleeping, walking, breathing, eating, handicraft and so forth in themselves have no moral consequence. Similarly, unintentional action is ineffective karma. In other words, if one accidentally steps on an insect, being unconscious of its existence, this also constitutes neutral karma because there is no intention - the intentional element is not there.

THE THEORY OF KARMA

Karma is the law of moral causation. The theory of Karma is a fundamental doctrine in Buddhism. This belief was prevalent in India before the advent of the Buddha. Nevertheless, it was the Buddha who explained and formulated this doctrine in the complete form in which we have it today.

What is the cause of the inequality that exists among mankind?

Why should one person be brought up in the lap of luxury, endowed with fine mental, moral and physical qualities, and another in absolute poverty, steeped in misery?

Why should one person be a mental prodigy, and another an idiot?

Why should one person be born with saintly characteristics and another with criminal tendencies?

Why should some be linguistic, artistic, mathematically inclined, or musical from the very cradle?

Why should others be congenitally blind, deaf, or deformed?

Why should some be blessed, and others cursed from their births?

Either this inequality of mankind has a cause, or it is purely accidental. No sensible person would think of attributing this unevenness, this inequality, and this diversity to blind chance or pure accident.

In this world nothing happens to a person that he does not for some reason or other deserve. Usually, men of ordinary intellect cannot comprehend the actual reason or reasons. The definite invisible cause or causes of the visible effect is not necessarily confined to the present life, they may be traced to a proximate or remote past birth.

According to Buddhism, this inequality is due not only to heredity, environment, "nature and nurture", but also to Karma. In other words, it is the result of our own past actions and our own present doings. We ourselves are responsible for our own happiness and misery. We create our own Heaven. We create our own Hell. We are the architects of our own fate.

Perplexed by the seemingly inexplicable, apparent disparity that existed among humanity, a young truth-seeker approached the Buddha and questioned him regarding this intricate problem of inequality:

"What is the cause, what is the reason, O Lord," questioned he, "that we find amongst mankind the short-lived and long-lived, the healthy and the diseased, the ugly and beautiful, those lacking influence and the powerful, the poor and the rich, the low-born and the high-born, and the ignorant and the wise?"

The Buddha's reply was:

"All living beings have actions (Karma) as their own, their inheritance, their congenital cause, their kinsman, their refuge. It is Karma that differentiates beings into low and high states."

He then explained the cause of such differences in accordance with the law of cause and effect.

Certainly we are born with hereditary characteristics. At the same time we possess certain innate abilities that science cannot adequately account for. To our parents we are indebted for the gross sperm and ovum that form the nucleus of this so-called being. They remain dormant within each parent until this potential germinal compound is vitalised by the karmic energy needed for the production of the foetus. Karma is therefore the indispensable conceptive cause of this being.

The accumulated karmic tendencies, inherited in the course of previous lives, at times play a far greater role than the hereditary parental cells and genes in the formation of both physical and mental characteristics.

The Buddha, for instance, inherited, like every other person, the reproductive cells and genes from his parents. But physically, morally and intellectually there was none comparable to him in his long line of Royal ancestors. In the Buddha's own words, he belonged not to the Royal lineage, but to that of the Aryan Buddhas. He was certainly a superman, an extraordinary creation of his own Karma.

According to the Lakkhana Sutta of Digha Nikaya, the Buddha inherited exceptional features, such as the 32 major marks, as the result of his past meritorious deeds. The ethical reason for acquiring each physical feature is clearly explained in the Sutta.

It is obvious from this unique case that karmic tendencies could not only influence our physical organism, but also nullify the potentiality of the parental cells and genes – hence the significance of the Buddha's enigmatic statement, - "We are the heirs of our own actions."

Dealing with this problem of variation, the Atthasalini, being a commentary on the Abhidharma, states:

"Depending on this difference in Karma appears the differences in the birth of beings, high and low, base and exalted, happy and miserable. Depending on the difference in Karma appears the difference in the individual features of beings as beautiful and ugly, high-born or low born, well-built or deformed. Depending on the difference in Karma appears the difference in worldly conditions of beings, such as gain and loss, and disgrace, blame and praise, happiness and misery."

Thus, from a Buddhist point of view, our present mental, moral intellectual and temperamental differences are, for the most part, due to our own actions and tendencies, both past and present.

Although Buddhism attributes this variation to Karma, as being the chief cause among a variety, it does not, however, assert that everything is due to Karma. The law of Karma, important as it is, is only one of the twenty-four conditions described in Buddhist Philosophy.

Refuting the erroneous view that "whatsoever fortune or misfortune experienced is all due to some previous action", the Buddha said:

"So, then, according to this view, owing to previous action men will become murderers, thieves, unchaste, liars, slanderers, covetous, malicious and perverts. Thus, for those who fall back on the former deeds as the essential reason, there is neither the desire to do, nor effort to do, nor necessity to do this deed, or abstain from this deed."

It was this important text, which states the belief that all physical circumstances and mental attitudes spring solely from past Karma that Buddha contradicted. If the present life is totally conditioned or wholly controlled by our past actions, then certainly Karma is tantamount to fatalism or determinism or predestination. If this were true, free will would be an absurdity. Life would be purely mechanistic, not much different from a machine. Being created by an Almighty God who controls our destinies and predetermines our future, or being produced by an irresistible Karma that completely determines our fate and controls our life's course, independent of any free action on our part, is essentially the same. The only difference lies in the two words God and Karma. One could easily be substituted for the other, because the ultimate operation of both forces would be identical.

Such a fatalistic doctrine is not the Buddhist law of Karma.

According to Buddhism, there are five orders or processes *(niyama)* which operate in the physical and mental realms.

They are:

1. Utu Niyama - physical inorganic order, e.g. seasonal phenomena of winds and rains. The unerring order of

seasons, characteristic seasonal changes and events, causes of winds and rains, nature of heat, etc., all belong to this group.

2. Bija Niyama - order of germs and seeds (physical organic order), e.g. rice produced from rice-seed, sugary taste from sugar-cane or honey, peculiar characteristics of certain fruits, etc. The scientific theory of cells and genes and the physical similarity of twins may be ascribed to this order.
3. Karma Niyama - order of act and result, e.g., desirable and undesirable acts produce corresponding good and bad results. As surely as water seeks its own level so does Karma, given opportunity, produce its inevitable result, not in the form of a reward or punishment but as an innate sequence. This sequence of deed and effect is as natural and necessary as the way of the sun and the moon.
4. Dhamma Niyama - order of the norm, e.g., the natural phenomena occurring at the advent of a Bodhisattva in his last birth. Gravitation and other similar laws of nature. The natural reason for being good and so forth, may be included in this group.
5. Citta Niyama - order or mind or psychic law, e.g., processes of consciousness, arising and perishing of consciousness, constituents of consciousness, power of mind, etc., including telepathy, telaesthesia, retro-cognition, premonition, clairvoyance, clairaudience, thought-reading and such other psychic phenomena which are inexplicable to modern science.

Every mental or physical phenomenon could be explained by these all-embracing five orders or processes which are laws in themselves. Karma as such is only one of these five orders. Like all other natural laws they demand no lawgiver.

Of these five, the physical inorganic order and the order of the norm are more or less mechanistic, though they can be controlled to some extent by human ingenuity and the power of mind. For example, fire normally burns, and extreme cold freezes, but man has walked scatheless over fire and meditated naked on Himalayan snows; horticulturists have worked marvels with flowers and fruits; Yogis have performed levitation. Psychic law is equally mechanistic, but Buddhist training aims at control of mind, which is possible by right understanding and skilful volition. Karma law operates quite automatically and, when the Karma is powerful, man cannot interfere with its inexorable result though he may desire to do so; but here also right understanding and skilful volition can accomplish much and mould the future. Good Karma, persisted in, can thwart the reaping of bad Karma, or as some Western scholars prefer to say 'action influence', is certainly an intricate law whose working is fully comprehended only by a Buddha. The Buddhist aims at the final destruction of all Karma.

What is Karma?

The Pali term Karma literally means action or doing. Any kind of intentional action whether mental, verbal, or physical, is regarded as Karma. It covers all that is included in the phrase "thought, word and deed". Generally speaking, all good and bad action constitutes Karma. In its ultimate sense Karma means all moral and immoral volition. Involuntary, unintentional or unconscious actions, though technically deeds, do not constitute Karma, because volition, the most important factor in determining Karma, is absent.

The Buddha says:

"I declare, O Bhikkhus, that volition is Karma. Having willed one acts by body, speech, and thought." (..Anguttara Nikaya)

Every volitional action of individuals, save those of Buddhas and Arahants, is called Karma. The exception made in their case is because they are delivered from both good and evil; they have eradicated ignorance and craving, the roots of Karma.

"Destroyed are their germinal seeds *(Khina bija)*; selfish desires no longer grow," states the Ratana Sutta of Sutta nipata.

This does not mean that the Buddha and Arahantas are passive. They are tirelessly active in working for the real well being and happiness of all. Their deeds ordinarily accepted as good or moral, lack creative power as regards themselves. Understanding things as they truly are, they have finally shattered their cosmic fetters – the chain of cause and effect.

Karma does not necessarily mean past actions. It embraces both past and present deeds. Hence in one sense, we are the result of what we were; we will be the result of what we are. In another sense, it should be added, we are not totally the result of what we were; we will not absolutely be the result of what we are. The present is no doubt the offspring of the past and is the present of the future, but the present is not always a true index of either the past or the future; so complex is the working of Karma.

It is this doctrine of Karma that the mother teaches her child when she says "Be good and you will be happy and we will love you; but if you are bad, you will be unhappy and we will not love you." In short, Karma is the law of cause and effect in the ethical realm.

Karma and Vipaka

Karma is action, and Vipaka, fruit or result, is its reaction.

Just as every object is accompanied by a shadow, even so every volitional activity is inevitably accompanied by its due effect. Karma is like potential seed: Vipaka could be likened to the fruit arising from the tree – the effect or result. Anisamsa and Adinaya are the leaves, flowers and so forth that correspond to external differences such as health, sickness and poverty – these are inevitable consequences, which happen at the same time. Strictly speaking, both Karma and Vipaka pertain to the mind.

As Karma may be good or bad, so may Vipaka, - the fruit – is good or bad. As Karma is mental so Vipaka is mental (of the mind). It is experienced as happiness, bliss, unhappiness or misery, according to the nature of the Karma seed. *Anisamsa* are the concomitant advantages – material things such as prosperity, health and longevity. When Vipaka's concomitant material things are disadvantageous, they are known as *Adinaya*, full of wretchedness, and appear as poverty, ugliness, disease, short life-span and so forth.

As we sow, we reap somewhere and sometime, in his life or in a future birth. What we reap today is what we have sown either in the present or in the past.

The Samyutta Nikaya states:

"According to the seed that's sown,
So is the fruit you reap there from,
Doer of good will gather good,
Doer of evil, evil reaps,
Down is the seed and thou shalt taste
The fruit thereof."

Karma is a law in itself, which operates in its own field without the intervention of any external, independent ruling agency.

Happiness and misery, which are the common lot of humanity, are the inevitable effects of causes. From a Buddhist point of view, they are not rewards and punishments, assigned by a supernatural, omniscient ruling power to a soul that has done good or evil. Theists, who attempt to explain everything in this and temporal life and in the eternal future life, ignoring a past, believe in a 'postmortem' justice, and may regard present happiness and misery as blessings and curses conferred on His creation by an omniscient and omnipotent Divine Ruler who sits in heaven above controlling the destinies of the human race. Buddhism, which emphatically denies such an Almighty, All merciful God-Creator and an arbitrarily created immortal soul, believes in natural law and justice which cannot be suspended by either an Almighty God or an All-compassionate Buddha. According to this natural law, acts bear their own rewards and punishments to the individual doer whether human justice finds out or not.

There are some who criticise thus: "So, you Buddhists, too, administer capitalistic opium to the people, saying: "You are born poor in this life on account of your past evil karma. He is born rich on account of his good Karma. So, be satisfied with your humble lot; but do good to be rich in your next life. You are being oppressed now because of your past evil Karma. There is your destiny. Be humble and bear your sufferings patiently. Do good now. You can be certain of a better and happier life after death."

The Buddhist doctrine of Karma does not expound such ridiculous fatalistic views. Nor does it vindicate a postmortem justice. The All-Merciful Buddha, who had no ulterior selfish motives, did not teach this law of Karma to protect the rich and comfort the poor by promising illusory happiness in an after-life.

While we are born to a state created by ourselves, yet by our own self-directed efforts there is every possibility for us to create new, favourable environments even here and now. Not only individually, but also, collectively, we are at liberty to create fresh Karma that leads either towards our progress or downfall in this very life.

According to the Buddhist doctrine of Karma, one is not always compelled by an 'iron necessity', for Karma is neither fate, nor predestination imposed upon us by some mysterious unknown power to which we must helplessly submit ourselves. It is one's own doing reacting on oneself, and so one has the possibility to divert the course of one's Karma to some extent. How far one diverts it depends on oneself.

Is one bound to reap all that one has sown in just proportion?

The Buddha provides an answer:

"If anyone says that a man or woman must reap in this life according to his present deeds, in that case there is no religious life, nor is an opportunity afforded for the entire extinction of sorrow. But if anyone says that what a man or woman reaps in this and future lives accords with his or her deeds present and past, in that case there is a religious life, and an opportunity is afforded for the entire extinction of a sorrow." (...Anguttara Nikaya)

Although it is stated in the Dhammapada that "not in the sky, nor in mid-ocean, or entering a mountain cave is found that place on earth where one may escape from (the consequences of) an evil deed", yet one is not bound to pay all the past arrears of one's Karma. If such were the case emancipation would be impossibility. Eternal recurrence would be the unfortunate result.

What is the cause of Karma?

Ignorance *(avijja)*, or not knowing things as they truly are, is the chief cause of Karma. Dependent on ignorance arise activities *(avijja paccaya samkhara)* states the Buddha in the *Paticca Samuppada* (Dependent Origination).

Associated with ignorance is the ally craving (*tanha*), the other root of Karma. Evil actions are conditioned by these two causes. All good deeds of a worldling *(putthujana)*, though associated with the three wholesome roots of generosity *(alobha)*, goodwill *(adosa)* and knowledge *(amoha)*, are nevertheless regarded as Karma because the two roots of ignorance and craving are dormant in him. The moral types of Supramundane Path Consciousness *(magga citta)* are not regarded as Karma because they tend to eradicate the two root causes.

Who is the doer of Karma?

Who reaps the fruit of Karma?

Does Karma mould a soul?

In answering these subtle questions, the Venerable Buddhaghosa writes in the Visuddhi Magga:

"No doer is there who does the deed;
Nor is there one who feels the fruit;
Constituent parts alone roll on;
This indeed! Is right discernment."

For instance, the table we see is apparent reality. In an ultimate sense the so-called table consists of forces and qualities.

For ordinary purposes a scientist would use the term water, but in the laboratory he would say H 2 0.

In this same way, for conventional purposes, such terms as man, woman, being, self, and so forth are used. The so-called fleeting forms consist of psychophysical phenomena, which are constantly changing not remaining the same for two consecutive moments.

Buddhists, therefore, do not believe in an unchanging entity, in an actor apart from action, in a perceiver apart from perception, in a conscious subject behind consciousness.

Who then, is the doer of Karma? Who experiences the effect?

Volition, or Will *(tetana)*, is itself the doer, Feeling *(vedana)* is itself the reaper of the fruits of actions. Apart from these pure mental states *(suddhadhamma)* there is no-one to sow and no-one to reap.

CLASSIFICATION OF KARMA

(A) With respect to different functions, Karma is classified into four kinds:

Reproductive Karma

Every birth is conditioned by a past good or bad karma, which predominated at the moment of death. Karma that conditions the future birth is called Reproductive Karma. The death of a person is merely 'a temporary end of a temporary phenomenon'. Though the present form perishes, another form which is neither the same nor absolutely different takes its place, according to the potential thought-vibration generated at the death moment, because the Karmic force which propels the life-flux still survives. It is this last thought, which is technically called Reproductive*(janaka)* Karma, that determines the state of a person in his subsequent birth. This may be either a good or bad Karma.

According to the Commentary, Reproductive Karma is that which produces mental aggregates and material aggregates at the moment of conception. The initial consciousness, which is termed the *patisandhi* rebirth consciousness, is conditioned by this Reproductive *(janaka)* Karma. Simultaneous with the arising of the rebirth-consciousness, there arise the 'body-decad', 'sex-decad' and 'base-decad' *(kaya-bhavavatthu dasakas).* (decad = 10 factors).

(a) The body-decad is composed of:

1. The element of extension *(pathavi).*
2. The element of cohesion *(apo).*

3. The element of heat *(tajo).*
4. The element of motion *(vayo).*

(b) The four derivatives *(upadana rupa):*

1. Colour *(vanna).*
2. Odour *(gandha).*
3. Taste *(rasa).*
4. Nutritive Essence *(oja)*

These eight (*mahabhuta* 4 + *upadana* 4 = 8) are collectively called *Avinibhoga Rupa* (indivisable form or indivisable matter).

(c) Vitality *(jivitindriya)* and Body *(kaya)*

These (*avinibhoga* 8 + *jivitindriya* 1 + Kaya 1 = 10) ten are collectively called "Body-decad" =(*Kaya dasaka).*

Sex-decad and Base-decad also consist of the first nine, sex *(bhava)* and seat of consciousness*(vathu)* respectively (i.e. eye, ear, nose, tongue, and body).

From this, it is evident that the sex of a person is determined at the very conception of a being. It is conditioned by Karma and is not a fortuitous combination of sperm and ovum cells. The Pain and Happiness one experiences in the course of one's lifetime are the inevitable consequence of Reproductive Kamma.

Supportive Karma

That which comes near the Reproductive *(janaka)* Kamma and supports it. It is neither good nor bad and it assists or maintains the action of the Reproductive (janaka) Karma in the course of one's lifetime. Immediately after conception till the death moment this Karma steps forward to support the Reproductive Karma. A moral supportive *(kusala upathambhaka)* Karma assists in giving health, wealth, happiness etc. to the being born with a moral Reproductive Karma. An immoral supportive Karma, on the other hand, assists in giving pain, sorrow, etc. to the being born with an immoral reproductive(*akusala janaka*) Karma, as for instance to a beast of burden.

Obstructive Karma Or Counteractive Karma

Which, unlike the former, tends to weaken, interrupt and

retard the fruition of the Reproductive Karma. For instance, a person born with a good Reproductive Karma may be subject to various ailments etc., thus preventing him from enjoying the blissful results of his good actions. An animal, on the other hand, who is born with a bad Reproductive Karma may lead a comfortable life by getting good food, lodging, etc., as a result of his good counteractive or obstructive *(upabidaka)* Karma preventing the fruition of the evil Reproductive Karma.

Destructive *(Upaghataka)* Karma

According to the law of Karma the potential energy of the Reproductive Karma could be nullified by a mere powerful opposing Karma of the past, which, seeking an opportunity, may quite unexpectedly operate, just as a powerful counteractive force can obstruct the path of a flying arrow and bring it down to the ground. Such an action is called Destructive *(upaghataka)* Karma, which is more effective than the previous two in that it is not only obstructive but also destroys the whole force. This Destructive Karma also may be either good or bad.

As an instance of operation of all the four, the case of Devadatta, who attempted to kill the Buddha and who caused a schism in the Sangha (disciples of the Buddha) may be cited. His good Reproductive Karma brought him birth in a royal family. His continued comfort and prosperity were due to the action of the Supportive Karma. The Counteractive or Obstructive Karma came into operation when he was subject to much humiliation as a result of his being excommunicated from the Sangha. Finally the Destructive Karma brought his life to a miserable end.

(B) There is another classification of Karma, according to the priority of effect:

Weighty *(Garuka)* Karma.

This is either weighty or serious – may be either good or bad. It produces its results in this life or in the next for certain. If good, it is purely mental as in the case of Jhana (ecstasy or absorption). Otherwise it is verbal or bodily. On the Immoral side, there are five immediate effective heinous crimes*(pancanantariya karma)*:

Matricide, Patricide, and the murder of an Arahant, the wounding of a Buddha and the creation of a schism in the Sangha. Permanent Scepticism *(Niyata Micchaditthi)* is also termed one of the Weighty *(garuka)* Karmas.

If, for instance, any person were to develop the *jhana* (ecstasy or absorption) and later were to commit one of these heinous crimes, his good Karma would be obliterated by the powerful evil Karma. His subsequent birth would be conditioned by the evil Karma in spite of his having gained the *jhana* earlier. Devadatta lost his psychic power and was born in an evil state, because he wounded the Buddha and caused a schism in the Sangha.

King Ajatasattu would have attained the first stage of Sainthood *(Sotapanna)* if he had not committed patricide. In this case the powerful evil Karma acted as an obstacle to his gaining Sainthood.

Proximate *(Asanna)* Karma Or Death-proximate Karma

This is that which one does or remembers immediately before the moment of dying. Owing to the great part it plays in determining the future birth, much importance is attained to this deathbed (*asanna*) Karma in almost all Buddhist countries. The customs of reminding the dying man of good deeds and making him do good acts on his deathbed still prevails in Buddhist countries.

Sometimes a bad person may die happily and receive a good birth if he remembers or does a good act at the last moment. A story runs that a certain executioner who casually happened to give some alms to the Venerable Sariputta remembered this good act at the dying moment and was born in a state of bliss. This does not mean that although he enjoys a good birth he will be exempt from the effects of the evil deeds which he accumulated during his lifetime. They will have there due effect as occasions arise.

At times a good person may die unhappy by suddenly remembering an evil act of his or by harbouring some unpleasant thought, perchance compelled by unfavourable circumstances. In the scriptures, Queen Mallika, the consort of King Kosala, remembering a lie she had uttered, suffered for about seven days in a state of misery when she lied to her husband to cover some misbehaviour.

These are exceptional cases. Such reverse changes of birth account for the birth of virtuous children to vicious parents and of vicious children to virtuous parents. As a result of the last thought moment being conditioned by the general conduct of the person.

Habitual *(Accina)* Karma

It is that which on habitually performs and recollects and for which one has a great liking. Habits whether good or bad becomes ones second nature, tending to form the character of a person. At unguarded moments one often lapses into one's habitual mental mindset. In the same way, at the death-moment, unless influenced by other circumstances, one usually recalls to mind one's habitual deeds.

Cunda, a butcher, who was living in the vicinity of the Buddha's monastery, died yelling like an animal because he was earning his living by slaughtering pigs.

King Dutthagamini of Ceylon (Sri Lanka) was in the habit of giving alms to the Bhikkhus (monks) before he took his own meals. It was his habitual Karma that gladdened him at the dying moment and gave him birth in the Tusita heaven.

Reserve Or Cumulative *(Katatta)* Karma

This literally means 'because done'. All actions that are not included in the aforementioned and those actions soon forgotten belong to this category. This is, as it were the reserve fund of a particular being.

(C) There is another classification of Karma according to the time in which effects are worked out:

1. Immediately Effective *(ditthadhammavedaniya*) Karma.
2. Subsequently Effective *(uppapajjavedaniya)* Karma.
3. Indefinitely Effective *(aparapariyavedaniya)* Karma.
4. Defunct or Ineffective *(ahosi)* Karma.

Immediately Effective Karma is that which is experienced in this present life. According to the Abhidhamma one does both good and evil during the javana process (thought-impulsion), which usually lasts for seven thought-moments. The effect of the first thought-moment, being the weakest, one may reap in this life itself. This is called the Immediately Effective Karma.

If it does not operate in this life, it is called 'Defunct or Ineffective' Karma.

The next weakest is the seventh thought-moment. Its effect one may reap in the subsequence birth. This is called 'Subsequently Effective' Karma.

This, too, is called Defunct or Ineffective Karma if it does not operate in the second birth. The effect of the intermediate thought-moments may take place at any time until one attains Nibbana. This type of Karma is known as 'Indefinitely Effective' Karma.

No one, not even the Buddhas and Arahantas, is exempt from this class of Karma which one may experience in the course of one's wandering in *Samsara*. There is no special class of Karma known as Defunct or Ineffective, but when such actions that should produce their effects in this life or in a subsequent life do not operate, they are termed Defunct or Ineffective Karma.

(D) The last classification of Karma is according to the plane in which the effect takes place, namely:

1. Evil Actions *(akusala kamma)* which may ripen in the sentient planes *(kammaloka)*. (Six celestial planes plus one human plane plus four woeful planes = eleven *kamaloka* planes.) Here are only four woeful *kamalokas.*
2. Good Actions (*kusala kamma*) which may ripen in the sentient planes except for the four woeful planes.
3. Good Actions *(kusala kamma)* which may ripen in the Realm of Form *(rupa brahamalokas)*. There are four *Arupa Brahma Lokas*.

QUESTIONS ON THE THEORY OF KARMA

Question: Do the Karmas of parents determine or affect the Karmas of their children?

Answer: Physically, the Karma of children is generally

determined by the Karma of their parents. Thus, healthy parents usually have healthy offspring, and unhealthy parents have unhealthy children. On the effect or how the Karma of their children is determined: the child's Karma is a thing apart of itself – it forms the child's individuality, the sum-total of its merits and demerits accumulated in innumerable past existences. For example, the Karma of the Buddha-to-be, Prince Siddhartha was certainly not influenced by the joint Karma of his parents, King Suddhodana and Queen Maya. The glorious and powerful Karma of our Buddha-to-be transcended the Karma of his parents which jointly were more potent than his own.

Question: If the Karma of parents do not influence those of their children, how would the fact be explained that parents who suffer from certain virulent diseases are apt to transmit these evils to their offsprings?

Answer: Where a child inherit such a disease it is due to the force of the parents' characteristics because of the force of the latter's Utu (conditions favourable to germination). Take, for example, two seeds from a sapling; plant one in inferior, dry soil; and the other in rich, moist soil. The result is that the first seed will sprout into a sickly sapling and soon show symptoms of disease and decay; while the other seed will thrive and flourish and grow up to be a tall and healthy tree.

It will be observed that the pair of seeds taken from the same stock grows up differently according to the soil into which they are put. A child's past Karma may be compared to the seed: the physical disposition of the mother to the soil; and that of the father to the moisture, which fertilised the soil. Roughly speaking, to illustrate our subject, we will say that, representing the sapling's germination, growth, and existence as a unit, the seed is responsible for one-tenth of them, the soil for six-tenths, and the moisture for the remainder, three-tenths. Thus, although the power of germination exists potentially in the seed (the child), its growth is powerfully determined and quickened by the soil (the mother) and the moisture (the father).

Therefore, even as the conditions of the soil and moisture

must be taken as largely responsible factors in the growth and condition of the tree. So must the influences of the parents (or progenitors, as in the case of the animal world) be taken into account in respect to the conception and growth of their offspring.

The parents' share in the Karma determining the physical factors of their issue is as follows: If they are human beings, then their offspring will be a human being. If they are cattle then their issue must be of their species. If the human being is Chinese, then their offspring must be of their race. Thus, the offspring are invariably of the same genera and species, etc., as those of the progenitors. It will be seen from the above that, although a child's Karma is very powerful in itself, if cannot remain wholly uninfluenced by those of it parents. It is apt to inherit the physical characteristic of its parents. Yet, it may occur that the child's Karma, being superlatively powerful, the influence of the parent's joint Karma cannot overshadow it. Of course, it need hardly be pointed out that the evil influences of parents can also be counteracted by the application of medical science.

All beings born of sexual cohabitation are the resultant effects of three forces:

1. The old Karma of past existence;
2. The seminal fluid of the mother, and
3. The seminal fluid of the father.

The physical dispositions of the parents may, or may not, be equal in force. One may counteract the other to a lesser or greater extent. The child's Karma and physical characteristics, such as race, colour, etc., will be the produce of the three forces.

Question: On the death of a sentient being, is there a 'soul' that wanders about at will?

Answer: When a sentient being leaves one existence, it is reborn either as a human being, a celestial being, (Deva or Brahama), and inferior animal, or a denizen of one of the regions of hell. The sceptics and the ignorant people held that there are intermediate stages – *antrabhava* – between these; and that there are being who are neither of the human, the celestial, the Deva or the Brahma worlds nor of any one of the stages of exist recognised in the scriptures – but are in an intermediate stage. Some assert that these transitional stages are possessed of the Five Khandhas (Five Aggregates: they are Matter *(rupa)*; Feeling *(vedana)*; Perception*(sanna)*; 4. Mental-activities *(sankhara)*; and Consciousness *(vinnana)*.

Some assert that these beings are detached 'souls' or spirits with no material encasement, and some again, that they are possessed of the faculty of seeing like Devas, and further, that they have power of changing at will, at short intervals, from one to any of the existence mentioned above. Others again hold the fantastic and erroneous theory that these beings can, and so, fancy themselves to be in other than the existence they are actually in. Thus, to take for example one such of these suppositious beings. He is a poor person – and yet he fancies himself to be rich. He may be in hell – and yet he fancies himself to be in the land of the Devas, and so on. This belief in intermediate stages between existences is false, and is condemned in the Buddhist teachings. A human being in this life who, by his Karma is destined to be a human being in the next, will be reborn as such; one who by his Karma is destined to be a Deva in the next will be appear in the land of the Devas; and one whose future life is to be in Hell, will be found in one of the regions of hell in the next existence.

The idea of an entity or soul or spirit 'going', 'coming', 'changing' or 'transmigrating' from one existence to another is an idea entertained by the ignorance and materialistic, and is certainly not justified by the Dhammas that there is no such thing as 'going', 'coming', 'changing', etc., as between existences. The conception, which is in accordance with the Dhamma, may perhaps be illustrated by the picture thrown out by a cinema projector, or the sound of emitted by the gramophone, and their relation to the film or the sound-box and records respectively. For example, a human being dies and is reborn in the land of Devas. Though these two existences are different, yet the link or continuity between the two at death is unbroken in point of time. The same is true in the case of a man whose further existence is to be in hell. The distance between Hell and the abode of man appears to be great. Yet, in point of time, the continuity of 'passage' from the one existence to the other is unbroken, and no intervening matter or space can interrupt the trend of a man's Karma from the world of human beings to the regions of Hell. The 'passage' from one existence to another is instantaneous, and the transition is infinitely quicker than the blink of an eyelid or a lightening-flash.

Karma determines the realm of rebirth and the state of existence in that realm of all transient being (in the cycle of existences, which have to be traversed till the attainment, at last, of Nibbana).

The results of Karma are manifold, and may be effected in many ways. Religious offerings *(dana)* may obtain for a man the privilege of rebirth as a human being, or as a deva, in one of the six deva worlds according to the degree of the merit of the deeds performed, and so with the observance of religious duties *(sila)*. The jhanas or states of absorption, are found in the Brahma world or Brahmalokas up to the summit, the twentieth Brahma world: And so with bad deeds, the perpetrators of which are to be found, grade by grade, down to the lowest depths of Hell. Thus are Karma, past, present and future were, are, and will ever be the sum total of our deeds, good, indifferent or bad. As was seen from the foregoing, our Karma determines the changes of our existences.

"Evil spirits" are, therefore, not beings in an intermediate or transitional stages of existence, but are really very inferior beings, and they belong to one of the following five realms of existence:

1. World of Men: 2. The Lowest plane of deva-world; 3. The region of hell; 4. Animals below men, and 5. Petas (ghosts).

Number 2 and 5 are very near the world of human beings. As their condition is unhappy, and they are popularly considered evil spirits. It is not true that all who die in this world are reborn as evil spirits; nor is it true that beings who die sudden or violent deaths are apt to be reborn in the lowest plane of the world of devas.

Question: Is there such a thing as a human being who is

reborn and who is able to speak accurately of his or her past existence?

Answer: Certainly, this is not an uncommon occurrence, and is in accordance with the tenets of Buddhism in respect to Karma.

The following (who form, an overwhelming majority of human beings) are generally unable to remember there past existences when reborn as human beings: Children who die young. Those who die old and senile. Those who are addicted to the drug or drink habit. Those whose mothers, during their conception, have been sickly or have had to toil laboriously, or have been reckless or imprudent during pregnancy. The children in the womb, being stunned and started, lose all knowledge of their past existence.

The following are possessed of a knowledge of their past existences, viz: Those who are not reborn (in the human world) but proceed to the world of the devas, of Brahmas, or to the regions of Hell, remember their past existences.

Those who die suddenly deaths from accidents, while in sound health, may also be possessed of this faculty in the next existence, provided that their mothers, in whose womb they are conceived, are healthy. Again, those who live steady, meritorious lives and who in their past existences have striven to attain, often attain it.

Lastly the Buddha, the Arahantas and Ariyas attain this gift which is known as *pubbenivasa abhnna*(Supernatural Power remembering previous existences).

Question: Which are the five Abhinna? Are they attainable only by the Buddha?

Answer: The five Abhinna (Supernatural Powers): Pali - *abhi*, excellent, *nana*, wisdom) are:

Iddhividha = Creative power;

Dibbasola = Divine Ear;

Cetopariya nana = Knowledge of others' thoughts;

Pubbenivasanussati = Knowledge of one's past existence;

Dibbacakkhu = The Divine eye.

The Abhinna are attainable not only by the Buddha, but also by Arantas and Ariyas, by ordinary mortals who practise according to the Scriptures (as was the case with hermits etc, who flourished before the time of the Buddha and who were able to fly through the air and traverse different worlds).

In the Buddhist Scriptures, we find, clearly shown, the means of attaining the five Abhinna. And even nowadays, if these means are carefully and perseveringly pursued, it would be possible to attain these. That we do not see any person endowed with the five Abhinna today is due to the lack of strenuous physical and mental exertion towards their attainment.

NATURE OF KARMA

In the working of Karma there are maleficent and beneficent forces and conditions to counteract and support this self-operating law. Birth *(gati)* time or condition *(kala)* substratum of rebirth or showing attachment to rebirth *(upadhi)* and effort *(payoga)* act as such powerful aids and hindrances to the fruition of Karma.

Though we are neither the absolutely the servants nor the masters of our Karma, it is evident from these counteractive and supportive factors that the fruition of Karma is influenced to some extent by external circumstances, surroundings, personality, individual striving, and so forth.

It is this doctrine of Karma that gives consolation, hope, reliance and moral courage to a Buddhist. When the unexpected happens, and he meets with difficulties, failures, and misfortune, the Buddhist realises that he is reaping what he has sown, and he is wiping off a past debt. Instead of resigning himself, leaving everything to Karma, he makes a strenuous effort to pull the weeds and sow useful seeds in their place, for the future is in his own hands.

He who believes in Karma does not condemn even the most corrupt, for they, too, have their chance to reform themselves at any moment. Though bound to suffer in woeful states, they have hope of attaining eternal Peace. By their own doings they have created their own Hells, and by their own doings they can create their own Heavens, too.

A Buddhist who is fully convinced of the law of Karma does not pray to another to be saved but confidently relies on him for his own emancipation. Instead of making any self-surrender, or calling on any supernatural agency, he relies on his own will power, and works incessantly for the well-being and happiness of all. This belief in Karma validates his effort and kindles his enthusiasm, because it teaches individual responsibility.

To the ordinary Buddhist, Karma serves as a deterrent, while to an intellectual, it serves as in incentive to do good. He or she becomes kind, tolerant, and considerate. This law of Karma explains the problem of suffering, the mastery of so-called fate and predestination of other religions and about all the inequality of mankind.

9

The Minor Disciplinary Proceedings

I. THE TAGGANIYA KAMMA (ACT OF REBUKE)

1.

1. At that time the Blessed One was staying at Getavana, in the grove of Anatha-pindika.

Now at that time the Bhikkhus who were followers of Panduka and of Lohitaka ,—who themselves were makers of strife, quarrelsome, makers of disputes, given to idle talk, and raisers of legal questions in the Samgha,—used to go up to such other Bhikkhus as were the same, and say, 'Do not allow such a one, venerable Sirs, to turn you back. Discuss loud and long. You are indeed cleverer, more wise, more well informed, more able at that (than your adversaries are) and do not you be afraid of them. We too will be on your side.' Thereby both disputes arose which had not arisen before; and disputes which had arisen grew hotter.

2. Those Bhikkhus who were modest were annoyed, murmured, and became indignant, saying, How can the Bhikkhus who are followers of Panduka and of Lohitaka act thus.' And those Bhikkhus told the matter to the Blessed One.

Then the Blessed One on that occasion, and in that connection, convened an assembly of the Order of Bhikkhus, and inquired of the Bhikkhus: 'Is it true, as they say, Bhikkhus, that those Bhikkhus who are followers of Panduka and Lohitaka,—who themselves (&c., as in § 1, down to the end)?'

'It is true, Lord!'

The Blessed Buddha rebuked them, saying, 'This is improper, O Bhikkhus, for those foolish persons, not according to rule, unsuitable, unworthy of a Samana, unbecoming, and ought not to be done. How can these foolish persons, O Bhikkhus, who themselves (&c., as in § 1, down to the end). This will not conduct, O Bhikkhus, either to the conversion of the unconverted, or to the increase of the converted; but rather to those who have not been converted being not converted, and to the turning back of those who have been converted.'

3. And when the Blessed One had rebuked those Bhikkhus in various ways,—speaking of the evils of being hard to satisfy in the matter of support or nourishment, of wishing for much, of discontent, of love of society, and of sloth; and speaking in praise of being easy to satisfy in the matter of support and nourishment, of wishing for little, of the contented man who has eradicated (evils from his mind), has quelled his passions , and is full of faith, of reverence, and of the exercise of zeal,—when he had thus held a religious discourse to the Bhikkhus as to what was fit and suitable in that respect, he addressed the Bhikkhus, and said: 'Let the Samgha, therefore, O Bhikkhus, carry out the Tagganiya-kamma (Act of Rebuke) against those Bhikkhus.

4. 'Now thus, O Bhikkhus, should it be carried out. In the first place the Bhikkhus who are followers of Panduka and Lohitaka ought to be warned; when they have been warned, they ought to be reminded (of the Rule in the Patimokkha against which they have offended); when they have been reminded, they ought to be charged with the (particular) offence; when they have been charged with the offence, some discreet and able Bhikkhu ought to lay the matter before the Samgha, saying,

Let the venerable Samgha hear me. These Bhikkhus who are followers of Panduka and Lohitaka, who themselves (&c., as in § 1, down to the end). If the time is fit for the Samgha (to do so) let the Samgha carry out the Tagganiya-kamma against the Bhikkhus who are followers of Panduka and Lohitaka.

"Such is the motion (natti).

Let the venerable Samgha hear me. The Bhikkhus who are followers of Panduka and Lohitaka, who themselves (&c., as in § 1, down to the end). The Samgha hereby carries out the Tagganiya-kamma against them. Whosoever of the venerable ones approves of the carrying out of the Tagganiya-kamma against the Bhikkhus who are followers of Panduka and Lohitaka, let him remain silent. Whosoever approves not thereof, let him speak.

A second time I say the same thing. Let the venerable Samgha (&c., as before 1). A third time I say the same thing. Let the venerable Samgha (&c., as before r).

The Tagganiya-kamma against the Bhikkhus who are followers of Panduka and Lohitaka has been carried by the Samgha. The Samgha approves (the motion). Therefore is it silent. Thus do I understand.

2.

1. 'There are three things, O Bhikkhus, by which, when a Tagganiya-kamma is characterised, it is against the Dhamma, and against the Vinaya, and difficult to be settled; (that is to say), when it has not been carried out in a full assembly of properly qualified persons, 'according to law and justice, and in the presence of the litigant parties —when it has been carried out without the accused person having been heard—when it has been carried out without the accused person having confessed himself guilty. A Tagganiya-kamma, O Bhikkhus, characterised by these three things is against the Dhamma, and against the Vinaya, and difficult to be settled.

'There are other three things, O Bhikkhus, by which, when a Tagganiya-kamma has been characterised, it is against the Dhamma, and against the Vinaya, and difficult to be settled; (that is to say), when it has been carried out though no fault has been committed—when it has been carried out for a Paragika or a Samghadisesa offence —when it has been carried out though the fault has been confessed. A Tagganiya-kamma, O Bhikkhus, characterised (&c., as before, down to) settled.

There are other three things, O Bhikkhus, by which, when

a Tagganiya-kamma has been characterised, it is against the Dhamma, and against the Vinaya, and difficult to be settled; (that is to say), when it has been carried out without the accused person having been warned—when it has been carried out without the accused person having been called upon to remember (whether he has or has not committed the offence)—when it has been carried out without the accused person having been convicted. A Tagganiya-kamma, O Bhikkhus, characterised (&c., as before, down to) settled.

'There are other three things, O Bhikkhus, by which, when a Tagganiya-kamma has been characterised, it is against the Dhamma, and against the Vinaya, and difficult to be settled; (that is to say), when it has not been carried out in a properly constituted meeting properly conducted —when it has been carried out without justice —when it has been carried out without the presence and approval of all the Bhikkhus belonging to the particular circuit. A Tagganiya-kamma, O Bhikkhus, characterised by these three things is (&c., as before, down to) settled.

There are other three things, O Bhikkhus, by which, when a Tagganiya-kamma has been characterised, it is against the Dhamma, and against the Vinaya, and difficult to be settled; (that is to say), when it has been carried out without the accused person having been heard—when it has been carried out without justice—when it has been carried out without the presence and approval of all the Bhikkhus belonging to the circuit. A Tagganiya-kamma, O Bhikkhus, characterised by these three things is (&c., as before, down to) settled.

'There are other three things (&c., as before, down to) that is to say, when it has been carried out without the accused person having been convicted—when it has been carried out without justice—when it has been carried out without the presence and approval of all the Bhikkhus belonging to the circuit.'

[And in a similar way each of the three things in paragraphs 2 and 3 of this section are united with the two things just repeated in each of paragraphs 4, 5, and 6, to make six further cases in which a Tagganiya-kamma is declared to be against the Dhamma, and against the Vinaya, and difficult to be revoked.]

3.

1. 'There are three things, O Bhikkhus, by which, when a Tagganiya-kamma is characterised, it is a proceeding in accordance with the Dhamma, a proceeding in accordance with the Vinaya, and is easy to be settled; (that is to say), when it has been carried out in a full assembly of qualified persons, according to law, and in the presence of the litigant parties—when it has been carried out after the accused person has been heard—when it has been carried out after the accused person has confessed himself guilty. A Tagganiya-kamma, O Bhikkhus, characterised by these three things is in accordance with the Dhamma, and in accordance with the Vinaya, and is easy to be settled.'

[And in a similar way the opposite of each of the twelve propositions in the last section is here laid down.]

4.

1. 'There are three things, O Bhikkhus, which, when they characterise a Bhikkhu, the Samgha, if it likes, should carry out the Tagganiya-kamma against him; (that is to say), when he is a maker of strife, quarrelsome, a maker of disputes, given to idle talk, and a raiser of legal questions in the Samgha — when he is dull, stupid, full of faults, and devoid of merit—when he is living in lay society, in unlawful association with the world. There are three things, O Bhikkhus, which, when the Samgha suspects (&c., as before, down to) against him.

There are other three things, O Bhikkhus, (&c., as before, down to) against him; (that is to say), when he has failed in morality as regards moral things—when he has failed in conduct as regards transgression—when he has failed in opinion as regards the principal matters of opinion . There are three things, O Bhikkhus, (&c., as before, down to) against him.

There are other three things, O Bhikkhus, (&c., as before, down to) against him; (that is to say), when he speaks in dispraise of the Buddha—when he speaks in dispraise of the

Dhamma—when he speaks in dispraise of the Samgha. These are three things, O Bhikkhus, (&c., as before, down to) against him.

2. 'There are three kinds of Bhikkhus, O Bhikkhus, against whom, if the Samgha likes, it should carry out the Tagganiya-kamma; (that is to say), one who is a maker of strife (&c., as in § 1, down to) a raiser of legal questions in the Samgha—one who is dull, stupid, full of faults, and devoid of merit—and one who is living in lay society, in unlawful association with the world. These are three kinds of Bhikkhus, O Bhikkhus, (&c., as before, down to) the Tagganiya-kamma.

'There are other three kinds of Bhikkhus, O Bhikkhus, against whom, if the Samgha likes, it should carry out the Tagganiya-kamma; (that is to say), one who has failed in morality in regard to moral matters—one who has failed in conduct as regards transgression—one who has failed in opinion as regards the principal matters of opinion. These are three kinds of Bhikkhus, O Bhikkhus (&c., as before, down to) the Tagganiya-kamma.

'There are other three kinds of Bhikkhus, O Bhikkhus, against whom, if the Samgha likes, it should carry out the Tagganiya-kamma; (that is to say), one who speaks in dispraise of the Buddha—one who speaks in dispraise of the Dhamma—one who speaks in dispraise of the Samgha. These are three kinds of Bhikkhus, O Bhikkhus (&c., as before, down to) the Tagganiya-kamma.'

5.

1. 'A Bhikkhu against whom the Tagganiya-kamma has been carried out ought to conduct himself aright. And herein this is the right conduct : he ought not to confer the Upasampada—he ought not to give a nissaya —he ought not to provide himself with a Samanera —he ought not to accept the office of giving exhortation to the nuns —and if he has accepted the office, he ought not to exhort the nuns —he ought not to commit the offence for which the Tagganiya-kamma has been carried out by the Samgha against him—nor any offence of a similar kind—nor any worse offence—he ought not to find fault with the proceeding (that has been carried out against

him)—nor with (the Bhikkhus) who have carried it out—he ought not to raise objection against a regular Bhikkhu's taking part in the Uposatha ceremony —or in the Pavarana ceremony —he ought not to issue commands (to a junior inhibiting him from going beyond the bounds, or summoning him to come before the elders)—he ought not to set on foot a censure against any other Bhikkhu —he ought not to ask another Bhikkhu to give him leave (to rebuke that Bhikkhu)—he ought not to warn (another Bhikkhu whom he supposes to be offending)—he ought not to call upon another Bhikkhu to remember (whether he has or has not committed an offence)—and he ought not to associate with the Bhikkhus.'

6.

1. So the Samgha carried out the Tagganiya-kamma against the Bhikkhus who were followers of Panduka and Lohitaka. And when they had been subjected by the Samgha to the Tagganiya-kamma and were conducting themselves aright in accordance thereto, they became subdued, and they sought for release ; and going up to the Bhikkhus they spake as follows: 'We, Sirs, have been subjected by the Samgha to the Tagganiya-kamma (&c., down to) release. What now should. we do?'

They told this thing to the Blessed One.

'Then, O Bhikkhus, let the Samgha revoke the Tagganiya-kamma carried out against the followers of Panduka and Lohitaka.

2. 'There are five things, O Bhikkhus, by which, when a Bhikkhu is characterised, a Tagganiya-kamma ought not to be revoked for him; (that is to say), when he confers the Upasampada—when he gives a nissaya—when he provides himself with a Samanera—when he accepts the office of giving exhortation to the nuns—and when, having accepted that office, he exhorts the nuns. These are the five things, O Bhikkhus (&c., as before, down to) revoked for him.

'There are other five things, O Bhikkhus, by which, when a Bhikkhu is characterised, a Tagganiya-kamma ought not to be revoked for him; (that is to say), when he commits the offence for which the Tagganiya-kamma has been carried out by the Samgha against him—or any other offence of a similar kind—or any worse offence—when he finds fault with the proceeding that has been carried out against him—or with the Bhikkhus who have carried it out. These are five things, O Bhikkhus (&c., as before, down to) revoked for him.

There are eight things, O Bhikkhus, by which, when a Bhikkhu is characterised, a Tagganiya-kamma ought not to be revoked for him; (that is to say), when he raises objections against a regular Bhikkhu's taking part in the Uposatha ceremony—or in the Pavarana ceremony—when he inhibits a junior from going beyond the bounds—when he sets on foot a censure against any other Bhikkhu—when he asks another Bhikkhu to give him leave to rebuke that Bhikkhu—when he warns another Bhikkhu whom he supposes to be offending—when he reminds another Bhikkhu of a rule against which he supposes that Bhikkhu to be offending—when he associates with the Bhikkhus. These are the eight things, O Bhikkhus (&c., as before, down to) revoked for him.'

7.

[This chapter is exactly the converse of the last.]

Here end the eighteen cases in which there ought to be a revocation (of the Tagganiya-kamma).

8.

1. 'Now, thus, O Bhikkhus, should the revocation be carried out. Those Bhikkhus who are followers of Panduka and Lohitaka should go before the Samgha, with their upper robe arranged over one shoulder, and should bow down at the feet of the elder Bhikkhus, and squatting down, and raising their hands with the palms joined together, should speak as follows: "We, Sirs, have been subjected by the Samgha to the Tagganiya-kamma, and are conducting ourselves aright in accordance thereto; and we have become subdued, and we seek for release, and beg for a revocation of the Tagganiya-kamma." And a second time they should beg [in the same words]. And a third time they should beg [in the same words]. Then a discreet and able Bhikkhu should lay the matter before the Samgha:

2. Let the venerable Samgha hear me. These Bhikkhus who are followers of Panduka and Lohitaka have been subjected (&c., as before), and they are conducting themselves (&c., as before), and they beg (&c., as before).

This is the motion (natti).

Let the venerable Samgha hear me. These Bhikkhus (&c., as before, down to) and they beg for a revocation of the Tagganiya-kamma. The Samgha revokes the Tagganiya-kamma for the Bhikkhus who are followers of Panduka and Lohitaka. Whosoever of the venerable ones approves of the revocation of the Tagganiya-kamma for the Bhikkhus who are followers of Panduka and Lohitaka, let him hold his peace. Whosoever approves not thereof, let him speak.

And a second time I say the same thing. Let the venerable Samgha (&c., as before, down to) let him speak.

And a third time I say the same thing. Let the venerable Samgha (&c., as before, down to) let him speak.

"The revocation of the Tagganiya-kamma for the Bhikkhus who are followers of Panduka and Lohitaka has been carried by the Samgha. The Samgha approves; therefore is it silent. Thus do I understand."

II. The Nissaya-kamma (Act of Subordination)

9.

1. Now at that time the venerable Seyyasaka was stupid, and indiscreet, and full of faults, and devoid of merit, and was living in lay society in unlawful association with the world . So much so that the Bhikkhus were worn out with placing him on probation, and with throwing him back to the beginning (of his probationary term), and with subjecting him to the manatta discipline, and with rehabilitating him. The moderate Bhikkhus were annoyed, and murmured, and became indignant (saying), 'How can the venerable Seyyasaka be so stupid (&c., as before), that the Bhikkhus are worn out (&c., as before)?'

Then those Bhikkhus told that matter to the Blessed One.

And the Blessed One on that occasion, and in that connection, convened a meeting of the Bhikkhusamgha, and asked the Bhikkhus, 'Is it true, O Bhikkhus, as they say, that the venerable Seyyasaka is stupid (&c., as before, down to) with rehabilitating him?'

'It is true, Lord!'

The Blessed Buddha rebuked him (saying), 'This is improper' (&c., as usual, compare I, 2, 3, down to), and addressed the Bhikkhus, and said, 'Let the Samgha therefore, O Bhikkhus, carry out the Nissaya-kamma (Act of Subordination) against the venerable Seyyasaka: "Thou must remain under the superintendence of others ."

2. 'Now thus, O Bhikkhus, should it be carried out. In the first place the Bhikkhu Seyyasaka ought to be warned; when he has been warned, he ought to be reminded ; when he has been reminded, he ought to be charged with the offence ; when he has been charged with the offence, some discreet and able Bhikkhu ought to lay the matter before the Samgha (saying),

"Let the venerable Samgha hear me (&c., as usual; see above, chapters 1. 4. and 8. 2).'"

10.

Chapters 2-5 are here repeated at length, Nissaya-kamma being substituted throughout for Tagganiya-kamma.

11.

1. So the Samgha carried out the Nissaya-kamma against the Bhikkhu Seyyasaka (saying), 'Thou must remain under the superintendence of others.'

And he, when subjected by the Samgha to the Nissaya-kamma, by resorting to and cultivating the acquaintance of good companions, associating with them, getting them to declare to him (the Dhamma), and asking them questions, became wise in the traditions; a man to whom the Nikayas had been handed down; a reciter of the Dhamma, of the Vinaya, and of the Matikas; clever, discreet, wise, modest, full of remorse, and docile; he conducted himself aright, he became subdued, he sought for release, and going up to the Bhikkhus, he spake as follows:

'I, Sirs, after having been subjected by the Samgha to the Nissaya-

kamma, am conducting myself aright, and have become subdued, and I seek for release. What now should I do?'

They told this thing to the Blessed One.

'Then, O Bhikkhus, let the Samgha revoke the Nissaya-kamma for the Bhikkhu Seyyasaka.

2. 'There are five things, O Bhikkhus (&c., as in chap. 6. 2, down to the end of chap. 7, reading throughout Nissaya-kamma for Tagganiya-kamma).'

12.

This chapter sets out the mode of revocation by a kamma-vaka precisely as above in chapter 8.

III. The Pabbaganiya-kamma (Act of Banishment)

13.

1. Now at that time the Bhikkhus who were followers of Assagi and Punabbasu were dwelling on the Kita Hill, wicked Bhikkhus, and shameless. Such as these were the evil practices they followed: they used to plant cuttings of flowers, and have them planted; they used to water flowers, and have them watered; they used to gather them, and have them gathered; they used to make them up into nosegays, and have them so made up; they used to make them up, and to have them made up, into wreaths, of the kind with the stalks together, and of the kind with the stalks separate, of the kind called mangarika, of the kind called vidhutika, of the kind called vatamsaka, of the kind called Avela , of the kind called urakkhada ;—and they then used to take or send wreaths of each of these various kinds to the wives and daughters and young women and sisters-in-law and female slaves in respectable families;—and they used to eat out of one dish, to drink out of one vessel, to sit on one seat, to lie on one bed, one mat, one coverlet, with the wives and daughters and young women and sisters-in-law and female slaves in respectable families;—and they used to eat food at the wrong time, and to drink strong drink, and to make use of garlands, and scents, and unguents;—and they used to dance, and sing, and play music, and wanton, and all these together in every combination.

2. And they used to amuse themselves at games with eight pieces and ten pieces, and with tossing up, hopping over diagrams formed on the ground, and removing substances from a heap without shaking the remainder; and with games at dice, and trap-ball; and with sketching rude figures, tossing balls, blowing trumpets, having matches at ploughing with mimic ploughs, tumbling, forming mimic wind-mills, guessing at measures, having chariot races, and archery matches, shooting marbles with the fingers, guessing other people's thoughts, and mimicking other people's acts;—and they used to practise elephant riding, and horse riding, and carriage driving, and archery, and swordsmanship;—and they used to run to and fro in front of elephants, and in front of horses, and in front of carriages and they used to exhibit signs of anger , and to wring their hands, and to wrestle, and to box with their fists;—and spreading their robes out as a stage they used to invite dancing girls, saying, 'Here you may dance, sister!' and greet her with applause. Thus manifold were the evil lives which they practised.

3. Now at that time a certain Bhikkhu who had spent the rainy season in the country of Kasi, and was on his way to visit the Blessed One, arrived at the Kita Hill. And that Bhikkhu in the early morning put on his under garment, and went, duly bowled and robed, to the Kita Hill for alms. And he was perfect in dignity, with his eyes cast down, and pleasing in appearance, whether in going in or in coming out, in looking or in watching, in bending in his arm or in stretching it forth .

Then the people on beholding that Bhikkhu, said, 'Who is this fellow like a fool of fools, or like an idiot of idiots, or like a simpleton of simpletons ? Who would give an alms when this fellow comes near! Now our own masters, the followers of Assagi and Punabbasu, are gentle, friendly, pleasant in speech, radiant with smiles, by no means fools, but open in countenance, and the first to speak. To such now it is fit to give an alms!'

And a certain lay-disciple saw that Bhikkhu as he was going along the Kita Hill for alms. And on seeing him, he went up to the place where he was; and on coming there he said to that Bhikkhu:

'Has your reverence received an alms?'

'No, my friend, I have received no alms!'

'Come, your reverence! Let us go to my house!'. So the lay-disciple took the Bhikkhu to his house, and gave him to eat, and asked him: 'Whither then is your reverence going?'

'I am on my way to Savatthi, my friend, to visit the Blessed One.'

'Then let your reverence bow down at the feet of the Blessed One in my name, and say, "The residence on the Kita Hill, Lord, has been spoiled. The Bhikkhus who are followers of Assagi and Punabbasu are dwelling on the Kita Hill, wicked Bhikkhus, and shameless. Such as these are the evil practices they follow (&c., as in §§ 1, 2, down to the end). And people, Lord, who were formerly believers and full of faith, are now become non-believers and void of faith; the opportunities of alms that were formerly open to the Samgha are now destroyed; worthy Bhikkhus forsake, and wicked Bhikkhus dwell in the place. Let, Lord, the Blessed One be pleased to send (other) Bhikkhus to the Kita Hill in order that the residence there may be re-established."'

5. 'Very well, my friend,' said the Bhikkhu, in assent, to that lay-disciple. And rising from his seat, he set out for Savatthi, and went straight on to Anatha-pindika's grove, to the Getavana in Savatthi, to the place where the Blessed One was staying. And on arriving there he saluted the Blessed One, and took his seat on one side.

Now it is the custom for the Blessed Buddhas to exchange words of greeting with incoming Bhikkhus. And the Blessed One said to that Bhikkhu, 'Do things go well with you, O Bhikkhu? Have you enough for your support? Have you accomplished your journey without too much fatigue? And whence, O Bhikkhu, have you come?'

'Things go well with me, Lord. I have enough for my support. And I have accomplished my journey without too much fatigue. I have spent the rainy season, Lord, in the land of Kasi; and on my way to Savatthi to visit the Blessed One I arrived at the Kita Hill. And after having dressed early in the morning, I went, Lord, duly bowled and robed, on to the Kita Hill for alms. And a certain lay-disciple saw me (&c., as above, down to the end of § 4, with the alterations necessary to the narrative form of speech). Thence, Lord, am I come.'

6. Then the Blessed One on that occasion, and in that connection, convened a meeting of the Bhikkhu-Samgha, and asked the Bhikkhus:

> *'Is it true, O Bhikkhus, as they say, that those Bhikkhus who are followers of Assagi and Punabbasu, and are dwelling on the Kita Hill, are wicked Bhikkhus, and shameless; and that such are the evil practices they follow (&c., as in § 4, down to the end)?'*

'It is true, Lord.'

The Blessed Buddha rebuked them, saying, 'How can they, O Bhikkhus, foolish persons that they are, follow such practices as these (&c., as in §§ 1, 2, down to the end)? This will not conduct, O Bhikkhus, to the conversion of the unconverted (&c., as usual. Compare chap. 1, § 2, down to the end).'

And when the Blessed Buddha had rebuked them, and had delivered a religious discourse, he addressed the venerable Sariputta and Moggallana, and said, 'Go now, Sariputta and Moggallana , to the Kita Hill. And on arriving there carry out the Pabbaganiya-kamma (Act of Banishment) against those Bhikkhus who are followers of Assagi and Punabbasu, to the effect that they may become your Saddhi-viharikas.'

'How, Lord, can we carry out the Pabbaganiyakamma against those Bhikkhus who are followers of Assagi and Punabbasu; for they are passionate men and violent?'

'Then do you go, Sariputta and Moggallana, together with a number of Bhikkhus.'

'So be it, Lord!' said Sariputta and Moggallana, in assent, to the Blessed One.

7. 'Now thus, O Bhikkhus, should it be carried out. In the first place the Bhikkhus who are followers of Assagi and Punabbasu ought to be warned: when they have been warned, they ought to be reminded (of the Rule in the Patimokkha against which they

have offended); when they have been reminded they ought to be charged with the offence; when they have been charged some discreet and able Bhikkhu ought to lay the matter before the Samgha, saying,

"Let the venerable Samgha hear me. These Bhikkhus who are followers of Assagi and Punabbasu are wicked Bhikkhus and shameless. Their evil practices are both seen and heard, and also that respectable families have been led astray by them is seen, too, and heard. If the time is fit for the Samgha to do so, let the Samgha carry out the Pabbaganiyakamma against those Bhikkhus who are followers of Assagi and Punabbasu, to the effect that the Bhikkhus who are followers of Assagi and Punabbasu are not to dwell on the Kita Hill'.

This is the motion (natti).

Let the venerable Samgha hear me. These Bhikkhus who are followers of Assagi and Punabbasu are wicked Bhikkhus and shameless. Their evil practices (&c., as before, down to) is seen, too, and heard. The Samgha hereby carries out the Pabbaganiya-kamma against them, to the effect that the Bhikkhus who are followers of Assagi and Punabbasu are not to dwell on the Kita Hill . Whosoever of the venerable ones approves of the carrying out of the Pabbaganiya-kamma against the followers (&c., as before) to the effect (&c., as before) let him remain silent. Whosoever approves not thereof, let him speak.

A second time I say the same thing. Let the venerable Samgha (&c., as before). A third time I say the same thing. Let the venerable Samgha (&c., as before).

The Pabbaganiya-kamma has been carried out by the Samgha against those Bhikkhus who are followers of Assagi and Punabbasu to the effect that those Bhikkhus who are followers of Assagi and Punabbasu are not to dwell on the Kita Hill'. The Samgha approves of it. Therefore is it silent. Thus do I understand.

14.

Here follow the twelve cases in which a Pabbaganiya-kamma is declared to be against the law, and according to law respectively, in the precise wording of chapters 2 and 3, reading

Pabbaganiya for Tagganiya. Then follow the six cases of permissive suspension in the precise wording of chapter 4, but in addition to the cases there given for the Tagganiya-kamma, §§ 1 and 2 of this chapter are respectively added at the end of §§ 1 and 2 of that chapter.

1. 'There are three things, O Bhikkhus, which when they characterise a Bhikkhu, the Samgha, if it likes, should carry out the Pabbaganiyakamma against him; (that is to say), when he is characterised by frivolity of action—when he is characterised by frivolity of speech—when he is characterised by frivolity both of action and of speech. These are the three things, O Bhikkhus (&c., as before, down to) against him.

'There are other three things, O Bhikkhus, which when they characterise a Bhikkhu, the Samgha, if it likes, should carry out the Pabbaganiyakamma against him; (that is to say), when he is characterised by absence of right-doing in action—when he is characterised by absence of right-doing in speech—when he is characterised by absence of right-doing both in action and in speech. These are the other three things, O Bhikkhus (&c., as before, down to) against him.'

'There are other three things (&c., as in each of the last paragraphs; the three things here being injury done by him to others in action, in speech, and both in action and in speech, owing to his own want of training in the precepts and practices of the order).'

'There are other three things (&c., as in each of the last paragraphs, the three things here being evilness of life in action, in speech, and both in action and in speech).

2. 'There are three kinds of Bhikkhus, O Bhikkhus, against whom, when the Samgha likes (to do so), it should carry out the Pabbaganiyakamma; (that is to say), one who is frivolous in action—one who is frivolous in speech—one who is frivolous both in action and in speech. These are the three kinds of Bhikkhus (&c., as above, down to) the Pabbaganiya-kamma.

There are other three kinds of Bhikkhus (&c., as in the last paragraph, substituting first, absence of right-doing—secondly, injury to others—and thirdly, evilness of life respectively in action, in speech, and both in action and in speech).'

15.

This chapter is identical with chapter 5, reading Pabbaganiya for Tagganiya.

16.

1. So the Bhikkhu-Samgha, with Sariputta and Moggallana at their head, proceeded to the Kita Hill, and there carried out the Pabbaganiyakamma against those Bhikkhus who were followers of Assagi and Punabbasu, to the intent that those Bhikkhus should no longer dwell on the Kita Hill. And they, when subjected by the Samgha to the Pabbaganiya-kamma, did not conduct themselves aright, they did not become subdued, they did not seek for release, they did not ask the Bhikkhus for forgiveness, they reviled them, they found fault with them , saying that they were offending by acting in partiality, in ill-feeling, in folly, and in fear; and they not only departed from the place, but also left the Order.

Those Bhikkhus who were moderate were offended, murmured, and became indignant, saying, 'How can those Bhikkhus who are followers of Assagi and Punabbasu, after having been subjected by the Samgha to the Pabbaganiya-kamma, refuse to conduct themselves aright (&c., as before, down to) leave the Order?' And those Bhikkhus told the matter to the Blessed One.

Then the Blessed One on that occasion, and in that connection, convened a meeting of the Bhikkhusamgha, and asked the Bhikkhus:

> *'Is it true, O Bhikkhus, as they say, that those Bhikkhus who are followers of Assagi and Punabbasu, after having been subjected by the Samgha to the Pabbaganiya-kamma, refuse (&c., as before, down to) leave the Order.?'*

'It is true, Lord!'

'How can those Bhikkhus who (&c., as before, down to) leave the Order? This will not conduct, O Bhikkhus, either to the conversion of the un-converted, or to the increase of the converted;

but rather to the unconverted being not converted, and to the turning back of those which have been converted.' And when the Blessed One had rebuked those Bhikkhus in various ways, and had delivered a religious discourse, he addressed the Bhikkhus, and said:

'Then, O Bhikkhus, let not the Samgha revoke the Pabbaganiya-kamma. There are five things, O Bhikkhus (&c., as before, from chapter 6, § 2, down to the end of chapter 7, reading Pabbaganiya for Tagganiya).

17.

1. 'Now thus, O Bhikkhus, should the revocation be carried out. The Bhikkhu, who has been subjected to the Pabbaganiya-kamma, should go before the Samgha.'

IV. The Patisaraniya-kamma (Act of Reconciliation)

18.

1. Now at that time the venerable Sudhamma was residing at Makkhikasanda in dependence upon Kitta the householder, superintending the new buildings he erected, and being constantly supplied by him with food. And whenever Kitta the householder wished to give an invitation to the Samgha, or to four or five Bhikkhus, or to a single one, he used not to invite them without making special mention of the venerable Sudhamma.

Now at that time a number of the Thera Bhikkhus, including the venerable Sariputta, and the venerable Maha Moggallana, and the venerable Maha Kakkana, and the venerable Maha Kotthita, and the venerable Maha Kappina, and the venerable Maha Kunda, and the venerable Anuruddha, and the venerable Revata, and the venerable Upali, and the venerable Ananda, and the venerable Rahula, as they were journeying through the country of Kasi, arrived at MakkhikAsanda. And Kitta the householder heard the news that the Thera Bhikkhus had arrived at MakkhikAsanda.

Then Kitta the householder went up to the place where the Thera Bhikkhus were, and on arriving there, he saluted the Thera Bhikkhus, and took his seat on one side. And when he was so seated the venerable Sariputta taught Kitta the householder, and incited him, and roused him, and gladdened him with religious discourse. And Kitta the householder, having been thus taught, and incited, and roused, and gladdened with religious discourse, said to the Thera Bhikkhus, 'May the venerable Theras consent to take their tomorrows meal, as incoming Bhikkhus, at my house.' And the Thera Bhikkhus signified, by silence, their consent.

2. Then perceiving that the Thera Bhikkhus had given their consent, Kitta the householder rose from his seat, and bowed down before the Thera Bhikkhus, and keeping them on his right hand as he passed them, went on to the place where the venerable Sudhamma was. And on arriving there, he saluted the venerable Sudhamma, and stood by on one side. And so standing, Kitta the householder said to the venerable Sudhamma: 'May the venerable Sudhamma consent to take his tomorrows meal at my house with the Theras.'

But the venerable Sudhamma, thinking, 'Formerly indeed this Kitta the householder, whenever he wished to give an invitation to the Samgha, or to four or five Bhikkhus, or to a single one, used not to invite them without making special mention of me; but now he has invited the Thera Bhikkhus without regarding me. This Kitta the householder is now incensed against me, unfavourable to me, takes pleasure in me no longer.' And so thinking he refused, saying, 'It is enough, O householder.'

And a second time Kitta the householder said to the venerable Sudhamma (&c., as before, with the same result). And a third time (&c., as before, with the same result).

Then Kitta the householder, thinking, 'What can the venerable Sudhamma do against me, whether he consents, or whether he does not consent,' saluted the venerable Sudhamma, and keeping him on his right hand as he passed him, departed thence.

3. And at the end of the night Kitta the householder made ready sweet food, both hard and soft, for the Thera Bhikkhus. And the venerable Sudhamma, thinking, 'I may as well go and see what Kitta the householder has made ready for the Thera Bhikkhus,' robed himself early in the morning, and went, duly bowled and robed, to the place where Kitta the householder

dwelt; and, on arriving there, he took his seat on a mat spread out for him.

Then Kitta the householder went up to the place where the venerable Sudhamma was; and after he had come there, he saluted the venerable Sudhamma, and took his seat on one side. And when he was so seated the venerable Sudhamma addressed Kitta the householder, and said: 'Though this great store of sweet food, both hard and soft, has been made ready by you, O householder, there is one thing yet wanting, that is to say, tila seed cake.

Though then, Sir, there is so much treasure in the ward of the Buddhas, yet there is but one thing of which the venerable Sudhamma makes mention, and that is tila seed cake. Long ago, Sir, certain merchants of Dakkhinapatha went, for the sake of their traffic, to the country of the East, and thence they brought back a hen. Now, Sir, that hen made acquaintance with a crow, and gave birth to a chicken. And, Sir, whenever that chicken tried to utter the cry of a cock it gave vent to a "caw," and whenever it tried to utter the cry of a crow, it gave vent to a "cock-a-doodle-do ." Just even so, Sir, though there is much treasure in the ward of the Buddhas, whenever the venerable Sudhamma speaks, the sound is "tila seed cake."'

4. 'You are abusing me, householder. You are finding fault with me, householder. This place, householder, is yours. I must go away from it,' said the venerable Sudhamma.

'I do not intend, Sir, to abuse the venerable Sudhamma, nor to find fault with him. Let, Sir, the venerable Sudhamma still dwell at MakkhikAsanda. Pleasant is this grove of plum trees, and I shall take good care to, provide the venerable Sudhamma with those things a recluse requires—to wit, with robes and food and lodging and medicine when he is sick.'

And a second time the venerable Sudhamma said: You are abusing me (&c., as before, with the same reply). And a third time the venerable Sudhamma said: 'You are abusing me (&c., as before, down to) I must go away from it.'

'Whither then, Sir, will the venerable Sudhamma go?'

'I shall go to Savatthi, O householder, to visit the Blessed One.'

'Then, Sir, let the Blessed One know all, both what you yourself have said, and what I have said. And I should not, Sir, be surprised if the venerable Sudhamma were to return again even to MakkhikAsanda.'

5. So the venerable Sudhamma gathered together his sleeping mat, and set out, with his bowl and his robe, for Savatthi. And he journeyed straight on to Savatthi, to the Getavana, Anathapindika's Grove, to the place where the Blessed One was; and on arriving there he bowed down before the Blessed One, and took his seat on one side. And when he was thus seated the venerable Sudhamma informed the Blessed One of all, both that he himself had said, and that Kitta the householder had said.

The Blessed Buddha rebuked him, saying, 'This was improper, O foolish one, not according to rule, unsuitable, unworthy of a Samana, and ought not to have been done. How is it that you, O foolish one, could put down and could lower by your censure Kitta the householder, he being a man of faith, a believing disciple, and a donor, a provider, and a supporter of the Samgha?' This will not conduct, O foolish one, either to the conversion of the unconverted, or to the increase of the converted; but rather to the unconverted not being converted, and to the turning back of those who have been converted.' And after he had rebuked him, and had delivered a religious discourse, he addressed the Bhikkhus, and said: 'Let therefore the Samgha, O Bhikkhus, carry out the Patisaraniya-kamma (Act of Reconciliation) against the Bhikkhu Sudhamma, saying, "You are to ask and obtain pardon of Kitta the householder."'

6. 'Now thus, O Bhikkhus, should it be carried out. In the first place the Bhikkhu Sudhamma ought to be warned: when he has been warned, he ought to be reminded (of the Rule in the Patimokkha against which he has offended); when he has been reminded, he ought to be charged with the offence; when he has been charged with the offence, some discreet and able Bhikkhu ought to lay the matter before the Samgha, saying,

Let the venerable Samgha hear me. This Bhikkhu Sudhamma has put down, and has lowered by censure Kitta the householder, a man of faith, a believing disciple, a donor, provider and supporter of the Samgha. If the time is fit for the Samgha to do so, let the Samgha carry out the Patisaraniya-kamma against the Bhikkhu Sudhamma.

This is the motion (natti).

Let the venerable Samgha hear me. This Bhikkhu (&c., as before, down to) supporter of the Samgha. The Samgha hereby carries out the Patisaraniya-kamma against the Bhikkhu Sudhamma with the words, 'You are to ask and obtain pardon of Kitta the householder.' Whosoever of the venerable ones approves of the carrying out of the Patisaraniya-kamma against Sudhamma the Bhikkhu, let him remain silent. Whosoever approves not thereof, let him speak.

A second time I say the same thing. Let the venerable. Samgha (&c., as before). A third time I say the same thing. Let the venerable Samgha (&c:, as before).

The Patisaraniya-kamma has been carried out against the Bhikkhu Sudhamma with the words, 'You are to ask and obtain pardon of Kitta the householder.' The Samgha approves the motion. Therefore is it silent. Thus do I understand

19.

Here the twelve cases of a proceeding against, and the twelve cases of a proceeding according to law are repeated of the Patisaraniya-kamma in the words of chapters 2 and 3 of the Tagganiya-kamma.

20.

1. 'There are five things, O Bhikkhus, which when they characterise a Bhikkhu, the Samgha, if it likes, should carry out the Patisaraniya-kamma against him; (that is to say), when he goes about to bring loss on the laity—when he goes about to do harm to the laity—when he goes about to deprive the laity of their dwellings—when he reviles and finds fault with the laity—when he brings about division between the laity. These are the five things, O Bhikkhus, which (&c., as above, down to) against him.'

'There are other five things, O Bhikkhus, which when they characterise a Bhikkhu, the Samgha, if it likes, should carry out the Patisaraniya-kamma against him; (that is to say), when he speaks to the laity in dispraise of the Buddha—when he speaks to the laity in dispraise of the Dhamma—when he speaks to the laity in dispraise of the Samgha—when he puts laymen down, and lowers them by censure—when he does not fulfil a promise made in accordance with the Rules to the laity. These are the other five things, O Bhikkhus, which (&c., as before, down to) against him.'

'There are five kinds of Bhikkhus, O Bhikkhus, against whom the Samgha, if it likes, should carry out the Patisaraniya-kamma; (that is to say), one who goes about to bring loss on the laity (&c., as in the last paragraph, down to the end).'

21.

Chapter 5, as to the right conduct of a Bhikkhu subjected to the Tagganiya-kamma, is repeated, reading Patisaraniya for Tagganiya.

22.

1. So the Samgha carried out the Patisaraniyakamma against Sudhamma the Bhikkhu, saying, 'You are to ask and obtain pardon of Kitta the householder. And after he had been subjected by the Samgha to the Patisaraniya-kamma, though he went to MakkkikAsanda, he was unable, being greatly troubled in his mind, to ask and obtain pardon of Kitta the householder, but returned again even to Savatthi.

Then the Bhikkhus asked him, 'Has Kitta the householder been induced by you to give you his pardon?'

'Indeed, though I went to MakkkikAsanda, I was unable, being greatly troubled in my mind, to ask and obtain pardon of Kitta the householder.'

'They told this thing to the Blessed One.'

2. 'Let, then, the Samgha, O Bhikkhus, appoint a companion messenger to Sudhamma the Bhikkhu, to ask and obtain pardon of Kitta the householder.

Now thus, O Bhikkhu, should the companion messenger be appointed. In the first place the Bhikkhu (who is to be sent) is to be asked (whether he is willing to go). After he has been asked, let some discreet and able Bhikkhu lay the matter before the Samgha, as follows:

> *Let the venerable Samgha hear me. If the time seems meet to the venerable Samgha, let the Samgha appoint such and such a Bhikkhu as a companion messenger to Sudhamma the Bhikkhu, to ask and obtain pardon of Kitta the householder.*

This is the motion (natti).

Let the venerable Samgha hear me. The Samgha hereby appoints such and such a Bhikkhu as a companion messenger to Sudhamma the Bhikkhu, to ask and obtain pardon of Kitta the householder. Whosoever of the venerable ones approves of such and such a Bhikkhu being appointed as a companion messenger to Sudhamma the Bhikkhu, let him remain silent. Whosoever approves not thereof, let him speak.

"Such and such a Bhikkhu has been appointed by the Samgha. (&c., as before). The Samgha approves thereof. Therefore is it silent. Thus do I understand."

3. 'Then, O Bhikkhus, let Sudhamma the Bhikkhu go, together with the Bhikkhu who is the companion messenger, to MakkhikAsanda, and ask pardon of Kitta the householder, saying, Pardon me, O householder; I desire to gain once more thy good pleasure." If, when he thus speaks, he pardons him, it is well. If he pardon him not, the Bhikkhu who is the companion messenger should say, "Pardon him, O householder; he desires to gain once more thy good pleasure." If, when he thus speaks, he pardon him, it is well. If he pardon him not, the Bhikkhu who is the companion messenger should say, "Pardon him, O householder; I desire to gain thy good pleasure." If, when he thus speaks, he pardon him, it is well. If he pardon him not, the Bhikkhu who is the companion messenger should say, "Grant pardon, O householder, to this Bhikkhu, in the name of the Samgha (I ask it)." If (&c., as before, down to). If he pardon him not, 'the Bhikkhu who is the companion

messenger—without going out of sight, and without going out of hearing, of Kitta the householder—should make Sudhamma the Bhikkhu arrange his robe on one shoulder, and squat down on his heels, and stretch forth his two hands with the palms together, and so confess his fault.'

23.

1. So the venerable Sudhamma went, with another Bhikkhu as companion messenger, to MakkhikAsanda, and obtained pardon of Kitta the householder. And he conducted himself aright, and he became subdued, and he sought for release (&c., as above, in chapters 6, 7, down to the end).

24.

In this chapter the Kammavaka of the revocation of the Patisaraniya-kamma is given in words precisely similar to those of chapters 8 and 12.

V. The Ukkhepaniya-kammas (Acts of Suspension)

for not acknowledging, and for not atoning for, an offence

25.

1. Now at that time the Blessed Buddha was dwelling at Kosambi, in the Ghosita Arama. And at that time the venerable Khanna, when he had committed a fault, was not willing to acknowledge the fault. Those Bhikkhus who were moderate were annoyed, murmured, and became indignant, saying, 'How can the venerable Khanna act so?' And those Bhikkhus told the matter to the Blessed One.

Then the Blessed One on that occasion, and in that connection, after he had convened a meeting of the Bhikkhu-samgha, asked the Bhikkhus:

'Is it true, O Bhikkhus, as they say, that Khanna *when he has committed a fault, is not willing to acknowledge the fault?'*

'It is true, Lord!'

The Blessed Buddha rebuked him, saying, 'How, O

Bhikkhus, can that foolish one act so? This will not conduct either to the conversion of the unconverted, or to the increase of the converted; but rather to those who have not been converted being not converted, and to the turning back of those who have been converted.'

And when the Blessed One had so rebuked him, and had delivered a religious discourse, he addressed the Bhikkhus and said: 'Let therefore the Samgha, O Bhikkhus, carry out against Khanna the Bhikkhu the Apattiya adassane Ukkhepaniya-kamma (the Act of Suspension which follows on not acknowledging a fault) to the intent that he shall not eat or dwell together with the Samgha .

'Now thus, O Bhikkhus, should it be carried out.' [Here follow the formal words of' the Kammavaka as in chapter 1, 4, with the necessary alterations owing to the difference of the fault and of the Kamma following on it. And at the end of the Kammavaka (after the words 'Thus I understand') the following sentence is added.

'And send a proclamation, O Bhikkhus, from residence to residence ; saying, "Khanna the Bhikkhu has been subjected by the Samgha to the Ukkhepaniya-kamma for not acknowledging a fault."'

26.

Here follow the twelve cases in which a Kamma is against the law, and the twelve in which it is according to law; and also the six permissive cases in which it may be carried out, if the Samgha likes, precisely as in chapters 2, 3, and 4.

27 1.

1. 'A Bhikkhu against whom the Ukkhepaniyakamma that follows on not acknowledging a fault has been carried out ought to conduct himself aright. And herein this is the right conduct: he ought not to confer the Upasampada—he ought not to give a nissaya —he ought not to provide himself with a Samanera —he ought not to accept the office of giving exhortation to the nuns —if he have accepted that office, he ought not to exhort the nuns —he ought not to commit the offence for which the

Ukkhepaniya-kamma that follows on not acknowledging a fault has been carried out against him—nor any offence of a similar kind—nor any worse offence—he ought not to find fault with the proceeding (that has been carried out against him)—nor with (the Bhikkhus) who have carried it out— he ought not to accept from a regular Bhikkhu reverence, or service, or salutation, or respect, nor allow him to provide a seat, or a sleeping-place, or water for the feet, or a footstool, or a foot-towel for him, nor to carry his bowl or his robe, nor to shampoo him —he ought not to harass a regular Bhikkhu with a complaint that he has failed in morality, or in conduct, or in doctrine, or in the mode of obtaining a livelihood—he ought not to cause division between a Bhikkhu and the Bhikkhus—he ought not to wear the outward signs of being a layman, or of being a follower of some other doctrine —he ought not to follow the professors of other doctrines—he ought to follow the Bhikkhus—he ought to train himself in the training of the Bhikkhus—he ought not to dwell under one and the same roof with a regular Bhikkhu, whether in a place formally declared to be a residence, or to be not a residence, or in a place which is neither the one nor the other—on seeing a regular Bhikkhu he ought to rise from his seat—he ought not to touch a regular Bhikkhu, either inside or outside (of the residence)—he ought not to raise objections against a regular Bhikkhu's taking part in the Uposatha ceremony —or in the Pavarana ceremony—he ought not to issue command (to a junior, inhibiting him from going beyond the bounds, or summoning him to appear before the elders)—he ought not to set on foot a censure against any other Bhikkhu—he ought not to ask another Bhikkhu to give him leave (to rebuke that Bhikkhu)—he ought not to warn (another Bhikkhu whom he supposes to be offending)—he ought not to remind (another Bhikkhu of a law against which he supposes that Bhikkhu to be offending)—and he ought not to associate with the Bhikkhus.'

28.

1. So the Samgha carried out against Khanna the Bhikkhu the Ukkhepaniya-kamma for not acknowledging a fault to the effect that he should not at or dwell together with the Samgha. And after

he had been subjected by the Samgha to the Ukkhepaniya-kamma for not acknowledging his fault he went from that residence to another residence.

And the Bhikkhus there did no reverence to him, rose not from their seats to welcome him, rendered him not service, offered him not salutation, paid not respect to him, offered him not hospitality, nor esteemed him, nor honoured him, nor supported him. And when he received from the Bhikkhus neither hospitality, nor welcome, nor esteem, nor honour, nor support, he went from that residence to another residence. And the Bhikkhus there did no reverence to him, rose not from their seats to welcome him, rendered him not service (&c., as before, down to:) he went from that residence to another residence. And when he received no hospitality he returned back again even to Kosambi. Then he conducted himself aright, and he became subdued, and he sought for release, and going up to the Bhikkhus he spake as follows: 'I, Sirs, having been subjected by the Samgha to the Ukkhepaniyakamma am conducting myself aright in accordance thereto, and I am become subdued, and I seek for release. What now should I do?'

They told this thing to the Blessed One.

'Then, O Bhikkhus, let the Samgha revoke the Ukkhepaniya-kamma for not acknowledging his fault carried out against Khanna the Bhikkhu.

2. 'There are five things, O Bhikkhus'

29.

'There are five things, O Bhikkhus

30.

'And thus, O Bhikkhus, should the revocation be carried out

31.

Now at that time the Blessed Buddha was dwelling at Kosambi, in the Ghosita Arama. And at that time the venerable Khanna, when he had committed a fault, was not willing to atone for that fault.

VI. The Ukkhepaniya-kamma

(for not renouncing a sinful doctrine)

32.

1. Now at that time the Blessed Buddha was staying at Savatthi, in the Getavana, the grove of Anathapindika. And at that time a certain Bhikkhu by name Arittha, who had formerly been a vulture tormentor , had fallen into a sinful belief of this kind; (that is to say), 'In this wise do I understand the Dhamma preached by the Blessed One, that to him who practises those things which have been declared by the Blessed One to be impediments, there will arise no impediment sufficient (to prevent his acquiring spiritual gifts) .'

Now many Bhikkhus heard that Arittha, who had formerly (&c., as before, down to:) to be impediments. And those Bhikkhus went up to the place where Arittha the Bhikkhu, who had formerly been a vulture tormentor, was; and on arriving there they asked Arittha the Bhikkhu, who had formerly been a vulture tormentor, 'Is it true, friend Arittha, as they say, that you have fallen into a sinful belief (&c., as above, down to) spiritual gifts?'

'Certainly! I do so understand the Dhamma preached by the Blessed One (&c., as before):

2. 'Say not so, friend Arittha. Bear not false-witness against the Blessed One. For neither is it seemly to bring a false accusation against the Blessed One, nor could the Blessed One have spoken so. By many a figure, friend Arittha, have the things which are impediments been declared to be impediments by the Blessed One, and also to be sufficient to prevent him who cultivates them (from attaining to spiritual gifts). Lusts have been declared by the Blessed One to be of short taste, full of pain, and full of despair, things wherein the danger is great. Lusts have been declared by the Blessed One to be like the bones of a skeleton, full of pain, and full of despair, things wherein the danger is great. Lusts have been declared by the Blessed One to be like lumps of raw meat, full (&c., as before, down to:) is great. Lusts have been declared by the Blessed One

to be like torches made of a wisp of hay...., like a pit full of live coals...., like the visions of a dream...., like a beggar's portion...., like the fruits of trees...., like the sword and the slaughterhouse...., like darts and clubs...., like snakes and creeping things, full of pain, and full of despair, things wherein the danger is great.'

Yet notwithstanding that Bhikkhu Arittha, who had formerly been a vulture tormentor, when thus being addressed by the Bhikkhus, remained steadfastly adhering, in the very same way, and with violence, to that sinful doctrine, declaring, 'Verily I do so understand the Dhamma preached by the Blessed One (&c., as before, in § 1).'

3. Then since those Bhikkhus were unable to move Arittha the Bhikkhu, who had formerly been a vulture tormentor, from that sinful doctrine, they went up to the place where the Blessed One was; and when they had come there, they told this thing to the Blessed One.

And the Blessed One on that occasion, and in that connection, convened a meeting of the Bhikkhusamgha, and asked Arittha the Bhikkhu, who had formerly been a vulture tormentor, 'Is it true, as they say, Arittha, that you have fallen into a sinful doctrine of such a kind (&c., as before, in § 1)?'

'Certainly, Lord! I do so understand (&c., as before, in § 1).'

'How can you, O foolish one, so understand the Dhamma preached by me? Have I not, by many a figure, O foolish one, declared the things which are impediments to be impediments, and sufficient to prevent him who cultivates them (from attaining to spiritual gifts)? Have not lusts been by me declared to be of short taste (&c., as above, down to:) like snakes and creeping things, full of danger, full of despair, things wherein the danger is great? Yet now you, O foolish one, by your having grasped that doctrine wrongly , are not only bearing false-witness against us, but you are also rooting yourself up, and are giving rise to much demerit, the which will be to you for a long time for an evil and a woe. This will not conduct, O foolish one, either to the conversion of the unconverted, or to the increase of the converted; but rather to those who are unconverted not being converted, and to the turning back of those who have been converted.'

When he had thus rebuked him, and had delivered a religious discourse, he addressed the Bhikkhus, and said: Let therefore the Samgha, O Bhikkhus, carry out against Arittha the Bhikkhu, who was formerly a vulture tormentor, the Ukkhepaniyakamma, for not renouncing a sinful doctrine, to the intent that he shall not eat or dwell together with the Samgha.'

4. 'Now thus, O Bhikkhus, should it be carried out. In the first place the Bhikkhu Arittha ought to be warned.'

33.

Here follow the twelve cases in which the Kamma is against the law, the twelve cases in which it is according to law, the six permissive cases in which it can be carried out if the Samgha likes, and the eighteen divisions of the right conduct for the convicted Bhikkhu to pursue 'Ukkhepaniya-kamma for not renouncing a sinful doctrine,' instead of 'Tagganiya-kamma.

34.

1. So the Samgha carried out against Arittha the Bhikkhu, who had formerly been a vulture tormentor, the Ukkhepaniya-kamma for not renouncing a sinful doctrine, to the intent that he should not eat nor dwell with the Samgha. And when he had been thus subjected by the Samgha to the Ukkhepaniya-kamma for not renouncing a sinful doctrine, he left the Order.

Those Bhikkhus who were moderate were annoyed, murmured, and became indignant, saying, 'How can Arittha the Bhikkhu, having been subjected by the Samgha to the Ukkhepaniya-kamma for not renouncing a sinful doctrine, leave the Order?' And those Bhikkhus told the matter to the Blessed One.

Then the Blessed One on that occasion, and in that connection, convened a meeting of the Bhikkhu-samgha, and asked the Bhikkhus, 'Is it true, O Bhikkhus, as they say, that Arittha the Bhikkhu, having been subjected (&c., as before, down to) left the Order?'

'It is true, Lord.'

The Blessed Buddha rebuked him, saying, 'How can Arittha the Bhikkhu (&c., as before, down to) leave the Order? This will not conduct either to the conversion of the unconverted, nor to the increase of the converted; but rather to those who have not been converted not being converted, and to the turning back of those who have been converted.'

And when he had rebuked him, and delivered a religious discourse, the Blessed One addressed the Bhikkhus, and said: 'Let then the Samgha, O Bhikkhus, revoke the Ukkhepaniya-kamma for not renouncing a sinful doctrine, which has been carried out against Arittha the Bhikkhu.

'There are five things, O Bhikkhus, '

35.

'Now thus, O Bhikkhus, should it be carried out.

10

The Natural Laws

The Buddhist texts recognize five laws holding sway over the natural order.

a. Physical inorganic law (*utuniyama*). This law governs inorganic processes, working through variations in heat to bring about changes in the body and the outer world. In the body it governs decay and illness, in the outer world wind and rain, the regular sequence of seasons, differences of climate, etc.

b. Physical organic law (*biijaniyama*). This law operates in both the animal and vegetable kingdoms to account for heredity, genetics, and the tendency of like to beget like.

c. Law of kamma (*kammaniyama*). Kamma is volitional action, bodily, verbal, or mental. Such action produces a result appropriate to itself. The result is not a reward or punishment meted out by some overseer but an inherent consequence of the action itself. Good actions bring happiness, bad actions bring suffering.

d. Law of the mind (*cittaniyama*) governs the order of consciousness and mental processes and also makes possible such feats as telepathy, telekinesis, clairvoyance, clairaudience, and recollection of past lives.

e. Law of the dhamma (*dhammaniyama*) accounts for the phenomena that occur at the last birth of a bodhisatta and also the happenings during the life and at the death of the Buddhas.

Dependent Origination

The doctrine of dependent origination shows that the sentient being is nothing but a flow of mental and physical phenomena which arises and continues in dependence on conditions. The layout of these conditions brings to light the cause of suffering and shows how suffering can be ended.

The doctrine is based on the following principle:

When *THIS* is present, there is *THAT*,

With the arising of *THIS, THAT* arises.

When *THIS* is not present, there isn't *THAT*,

With the cessation of *THIS, THAT* ceases.

Dependent origination is set forth in a series of relations:

1. Dependent on ignorance there are activities (*avijjapaccaya samkhara*);
2. Dependent on activities there is consciousness (*samkharapaccaya vinnanam*);
3. Dependent on consciousness there is mentality-materiality (*vinnanapaccaya nama-ruupam*);
4. Dependent on mentality-materiality there are the six bases (*namaruupapaccaya salayatanam*);
5. Dependent on the six bases there is contact (*salayatanapaccaya phasso*);
6. Dependent on contact there is feeling (*phassapaccaya vedana*);
7. Dependent on feeling there is craving (*vedanapaccaya tanha*);
8. Dependent on craving there is clinging (*tanhapaccaya upadanam*);
9. Dependent on clinging there is becoming (*upadanapaccaya bhavo*);
10. Dependent on becoming there is birth (*bhavapaccaya jati*);
11. Dependent on birth there is old age and death (*jatipaccaya jara maranam*).

The sequence of events covered by the doctrine falls into

three existences — the immediately past, the present, and the future one. The first two factors in the sequence refer to the past life, the last two to the future life, and the rest to this present existence. However, these events intersect, so the factors assigned to the past and future existences also can be found in the present. The doctrine indicates how and why we came into this present existence and where we came from, confuting two erroneous interpretations of our nature and destiny:

a. that there is a soul, either uncreated or of divine origin, lasting eternally into the future; and
b. that we came into existence from nowhere and face nothing but annihilation at death.

Dependent on Ignorance there are Activities: From an inconceivable beginning we have performed activities of body, speech, and mind dominated by ignorance. Ignorance is lack of insight into the Four Noble Truths. Any volitional action performed through ignorance becomes kamma with a potential to react, to bring about rebirth, and other consequences in accordance with the kammic law. Only the arahant, who has ended ignorance, can perform volitional acts without forming kamma.

Dependent on Activities there is Consciousness: After death the five aggregates disintegrate but kamma remains with its potential intact. This residual kamma helps form the embryo in the new existence. It is responsible for the rebirth consciousness, the first citta of the new life. The ovum and the sperm constitute the body of the embryo, kamma contributes the mind and mental functions. A kamma formation of the previous existence manifests itself as the passive consciousness which, from the very first moment of conception, receives all the potentialities resulting from past volitional actions. No consciousness passes over from one existence to the next but the stream of consciousness goes on, a flux, constantly becoming.

Dependent on Consciousness there is Mentality-materiality: The union of the ovum, sperm and rebirth consciousness brings the mental-material compound into being. Mentality (*nama*) signifies the mental factors conascent with passive consciousness—feeling (*vedana*), perception (*sanna*), volition (*cetana*), contact (*phassa*), and attention (*manasikara*). Materiality (*ruupa*) comprises the four primary elements of matter and their derivatives, described earlier. It must be noted that kamma plays a role in the arising of materiality too. At the moment of conception kamma generates three units of matter: the decads of sex, body, and the mind basis. In the course of life kamma causes and sustains the functioning of the senses and vitality. Rebirth consciousness is a conascent condition for the arising of materiality. Thereafter, consciousness conditions materiality via a number of relationships, to be given in the section on conditioning relationships below. Thus mentality and materiality are mutually dependent.

Dependent on Mentality-materiality there are the Six Bases: Once generated and nourished by the mother, the embryo starts to grow. As it grows it acquires four other physical sense bases—the eye, ear, nose, and tongue. The body base appeared at conception as did the sixth sense organ, the mind-base (a collective term for all forms of consciousness).

Dependent on the Six Sense bases there is Contact: Each physical sense base can be stimulated only by its appropriate sense object, i.e., eye-base by forms, ear-base by sounds, nose-base by smells, tongue base by tastes, and the tactile-base by touch. The mind-base can be stimulated by any thought or idea whether past, present, future, or timeless, whether real or imaginary, sensuous or abstract. When the sense base is stimulated, conditions are present for the appropriate consciousness to arise. The combination of the three—base, object, and consciousness — is called "contact."

Dependent on Contact there is Feeling: When contact is made with an object through the senses, feeling must also arise. Contact is a conascent condition feeling. The feeling may be agreeable, disagreeable, or neither. It is through feeling that we reap the results of previous kamma. Since kamma resultants differ from one person to another we each experience different feelings.

Dependent on Feeling there is Craving: Craving is of three kinds—craving for sense pleasures (*kamatanha*), craving for existence (*bhavatanha*), and craving for non-existence (*vibhavatanha*). We crave pleasant sensations experienced through the senses. When one pleasant object passes, as it must, we seek another, thirsting for a new pleasant sensation to replace the old. So the search goes on as craving knows no satiation. Besides pleasures, we also crave existence. In our ignorance we believe there is an abiding self within. Thence we strive and struggle to preserve this self and to provide it with the best conditions. But, at times, we also crave non-existence, as when in a mood of dejection we wish for annihilation, thinking death to be the end. Even if this craving does not become so drastic, it still springs up as the desire to destroy the causes of our distress.

Dependent on Craving there is Clinging. Clinging is an intensified form of craving. It has the nature of grasping and takes on four forms:

a. clinging to sense pleasures (*kamuadana*);
b. clinging to wrong views, principally eternalism and nihilism (*ditthuadana*);
c. clinging to rites and rituals (*siilabbatupadana*); and
d. clinging to a doctrine of self (*attavadupadana*). This is the most tenacious form of clinging, abandoned only when the stage of stream-entry is attained.

Dependent on Clinging there is Becoming: Clinging conditions volitional activities, unwholesome and wholesome, which set the stage for a new existence where they can ripen.

Dependent on Becoming there is Birth: The unexhausted kammic activities of this life bring about birth into a new existence, finding appropriate conditions to manifest themselves.

Dependent on Birth there is Old Age and Death: Once a person is born, decay and death inevitably follow, bringing in their trail sorrow, lamentation, pain, grief, and despair.

In order to cure any disease its cause must be known and removed. All other treatments are symptomatic. The Buddha taught dependent origination to point out the cause of suffering and to show how it can be uprooted.

To end suffering the cycle of causal origination must be broken at the right link. We cannot end suffering by destroying the psychophysical organism we inherited as a result of past kamma; this is not the answer to the problem. We cannot prevent the contact of the senses with their objects, nor the arising of feeling from contact. But our reactions to the feelings we experience, that is different, that is something we can control. We can control them through wisdom. If we understand the feelings that arise to be momentary and without a self, we will not react to them with craving. Thus the right link in the sequence that can be broken is the link between feeling and craving. Suffering ends with the destruction of craving.

The complete destruction of craving is a formidable task. But, though difficult, it can be approached by degrees. Craving can be gradually weakened and this will start us on the path towards the ideal. The less we crave, the fewer the disappointments; the less the suffering, the greater the peace. In the Four Noble Truths the Buddha teaches us all we need to know: the cause of suffering is craving; the way to achieve this is to follow the Noble Eightfold Path.

Modes of Conditioning

Buddhism teaches that all phenomena, mental and physical, arise through conditions. In the Abhidhamma the modes of conditionality are analysed into twenty-four types of relationship, each representing a tie between a condition and the phenomena it conditions. A brief account of these is as follows:

1. *Root condition* (*hetu paccaya*): The three unwholesome roots—greed, hate, and delusion—are root conditions for their associated unwholesome mental states and the material form they originate. Likewise, for the wholesome and indeterminate states—greedlessness, hatelessness, and undeludedness.
2. *Object condition* (*arammana paccaya*): Any state that is an object for consciousness and its factors is an object condition. Consciousness is of six kinds by way of eye,

ear, nose, tongue, body, and mind; each can arise only with its appropriate object.

3. *Predominance condition* (*adhipati paccaya*): This assists in the manner of being foremost, thereby exercising a dominating rose over the other mental states. It may be a conascent mental state or it may be an object which is given special importance by the mind.
4. & 5. *Proximity and Contiguity conditions* (*anantara paccaya, samanantara paccaya*): In our analysis of a thought process we saw that seventeen thought moments follow each other in rapid succession. Each thought moment, with its factors, stands to the next thought moment and its factors in the relation of proximity condition and contiguity condition. These two modes of conditioning are different only in name but not in essence.
6. *Conascence condition* (*sahajata paccaya*): When a number of phenomena arise simultaneously, each will function as a conascent condition for the others. For example, feeling arises as a conascent condition for its concomitants—perception, mental formations and consciousness—and each of these for the other three. The four primary elements are conascent conditions for each other and secondary matter. So too are mind and matter at conception.
7. *Mutuality condition* (*annamanna paccaya*): Just as each leg of a tripod helps support the other two, mentality and materiality help each other at the moment of birth. At all times the concomitant mental states are mutuality conditions for each other, as are the co-existent primary material elements.
8. *Support condition* (*nissaya paccaya*): This serves as a base or foundation for the arising of some other state. All conascent conditions are also support conditions but, further, any sense organ is a support condition for the appropriate consciousness and its mental factors.
9. *Decisive support condition* (*upanissaya paccaya*). This gives stronger support than the previous type of condition, one that acts as a decisive inducement.

10. *Pre-nascence condition* (*pure jata paccaya*): This refers to a state that has already arisen and, while still present, serves as a condition for something else that arises later. A particular sense consciousness arises because the pre-arisen sense organ and object are already present. Thus the organ and object are prenascent conditions for consciousness.
11. *Post-nascence condition* (*pacchajata paccaya*): This signifies a subsequently arisen state that sustains something already in existence. Hunger, for example, is a post-nascence condition for the preservation of the body as it results in food intake.
12. *Repetition condition* (*asevana paccaya*): Each javana thought moment—wholesome, unwholesome, or indeterminate—conditions and strengthens the subsequent ones. Thus each is a repetition condition for its successor. By analogy, the recitation of a verse becomes easier the more frequently it is repeated.
13. *Kamma condition* (*kamma paccaya*): This refers to a volition that conditions other states. It is of two kinds. One is wholesome or unwholesome volition that conditions the resultant mental states and material form produced by kamma. The other is conascent volition that conditions its concomitant mental states and material form originated by that volition. Thus kamma condition may be prior to or simultaneous with the states it conditions.
14. *Kamma result condition* (*vipaka paccaya*): Any mental phenomenon, citta or cetasika, that results from kamma is a kamma result condition for its associated mental phenomena and the kinds of material form it originates.
15. *Nutriment condition* (*ahara paccaya*): Four kinds of phenomena are called nutriments in the sense that they are strong conditions for other phenomena:
    a. material food sustains the physical body;
    b. contact conditions feeling;

c. volition conditions rebirth consciousness; and
d. rebirth consciousness serves as a nutriment for mind and materiality.

16. *Faculty condition* (*indriya paccaya*): There are twenty-two faculties: six sense bases, two sexes, the life faculty, five feelings, five feelings, five spiritual faculties, and three supra-mundane faculties. Except for the two sexes, the other twenty can exercise control in their respective spheres on the co-existent mental states and the material phenomena they originate. For example, mindfulness—one of the five spiritual faculties—has a controlling influence on the other four co-adjuncts during meditation.
17. *Jhana condition* (*jhana paccaya*): This refers to the seven jhana factors—initial thinking, discursive thinking, rapture, happiness, sadness, equanimity, and concentration—that condition their associated mental phenomena and the material phenomena they originate.
18. *Path condition* (*magga paccaya*): This comprises twelve factors. Four that lead to woeful states—the wrong path—are: wrong views, wrong aspiration, wrong effort and wrong concentration. Eight that lead to blissful states—the right path—are: right understanding, right aspiration, right speech, right action, right livelihood, right effort, right mindfulness, and right concentration. These eight make up the Noble Eightfold Path.
19. *Associated condition* (*sampayutta paccaya*): The four mental groups—feeling, perception, mental formations and consciousness—that aid each other because they arise and perish together and have an identical object and base, are association conditions for each other.
20. *Dissociation condition* (*vippayutta paccaya*): This refers to one phenomenon that aids another by not mixing with it, by being separate from it. Thus mental and material phenomena are dissociation conditions for one another as they aid each other's genesis by remaining distinct.

21. *Presence condition (atthi paccaya):* This refers to phenomena that condition other phenomena only in their presence either as conascent, prenascent, or postnascent conditions. To give an analogy, objects can be seen only if there is light.
22. *Absence condition* (*natthi paccaya*): This refers to one phenomenon which can condition the arising of another only when it has ceased. Specifically it refers to the cittas and mental factors which have to cease for their successors to arise. By analogy, light must disappear for darkness to prevail.
23. *Disappearance condition* (*vigata paccaya*): This is identical with 22.
24. *Non-disappearance condition* (*avigata paccaya*): This is identical with 21.

The doctrine of dependent origination (*paticca samuppada*) teaches us that our mental and physical components are effects resulting from causes. The conditions (*paccayas*) show that a variety of specific relationships obtain between these effects and their causes. A few examples will be given to illustrate how this knowledge helps us to understand the Buddha's teaching and to put it into practice.

A. *In relation to the teaching:*

a. *First Cause*: Buddhism does not postulate a first cause. The world is beginningless, a continuous arising and passing away of phenomena dependent on conditions. The assumption that the world must have had a beginning is due to our limited understanding. Buddhism teaches that the world consists of a countless number of world-systems arising, evolving, and disintegrating in accordance with natural laws. To this cosmic process there is no first point or outside cause. As the Buddha says: "Inconceivable, O monks, is this *samsara*. Not to be discovered is any first beginning of beings, who obstructed by ignorance and ensnared by craving, are hurrying and hastening through this round of rebirths." In fact, it is our ignorance, resulting in craving, that creates us over and over again.

b. *Ignorance*: Though in the doctrine of dependent origination ignorance was given as the first link, it must not be taken as a first cause. The commentator, Venerable Buddhaghosa, states in the *Visuddhi Magga* (translated by Bhikkhu Nanamoli):

'Nor from a single cause arise
One fruit or many, nor one fruit from many;
'Tis helpful, though, to utilize
One cause and one fruit as representative.'

The twenty-four conditions are so intricately related that nothing can stand by itself as a sufficient cause. Even ignorance arises and continues through conditions such as wrong companionship and wrong views. It is placed first, not because it is temporally first, but because it is the most fundamental condition for suffering.

c. *Selflessness*: In a doctrine that teaches all phenomena to be conditionally arisen there is no place for any form of abiding personality. Until, by insight meditation, one penetrates this truth, the delusion of a self will persist, obscuring the Four Noble Truths.

d. *Free Will*: Someone might say: "If all phenomena are conditionally arisen, then Buddhism is a form of fatalism, for we have no free will to control our destiny." Such a statement would not be correct. Will is volition (*cetana*), a mental state, determined ethically by its root condition (*hetu paccaya*). If the root is unwholesome, we can either restrain or indulge the volition; if the root is wholesome, we can encourage it or neglect it. In this exercise of will lies our freedom to guide our destiny.

B. *Application in practice:*

a. *Root condition*: Buddhist training is directed towards eliminating the defilements (*kilesa*). The foremost defilements are the three unwholesome roots—greed, hate, and delusion. From these spring others: conceit (*mana*), speculative views (*ditthi*), skeptical doubt (*vicikiccha*), mental torpor (*thiina*), restlessness (*uddhacca*), shamelessness (*ahirika*), lack of moral fear or conscience (*anottappa*). These defilements function at three levels:

1. Transgression (*viitikkama*) leading to evil bodily and verbal acts. This is checked by the practice of morality, observing the five precepts.
2. Obsession (*pariyu.t.thana*) when the defilements come to the conscious level and threaten to lead to transgression if not restrained by the practice of mindfulness.
3. Latency (*anusaya*) where they remain as tendencies ready to surface through the impact of sensory stimuli. Security from the defilements can be obtained only by destroying the three roots—greed, hate and delusion—at the level of latency. This requires insight-wisdom (*vipassana-panna*), the decisive liberating factor in Buddhism.

b. *Predominance condition*: This is of two kinds, a mental state or an object.

1. A mental state: Zeal (*chanda*), energy (*viriya*), purity of consciousness (*citta*), or investigating of phenomena (*viimamsa*) can, as a conascent mental state, dominate other mental states and the material phenomena they originate. Only one of these four can predominate at a time. We may illustrate how these four, in sequence, are applicable in practice. A meditator resolves to "achieve that which has not been achieved so far." At that time zeal becomes the predominant mental factor. Then energy dominates to bring forth right effort to suppress the mental hindrances. Free from the hindrances the purified mind is dominant. When the mind is pure and unified, the investigating factor takes over to gain insight into the three characteristics of existence—impermanence, unsatisfactoriness and selflessness.
2. An object: A Buddhist venerates an image of the Buddha, recollecting the supreme qualities of the

Enlightened One, and aspires to acquire similar virtues. At that time faith (*saddha*) in the Buddha, the Dhamma, and the Sangha becomes the predominant mental state. This faith, reasoned and rooted in understanding, inspires the mind with confidence and determination to pursue the practice. This is the principle behind the veneration of the Buddha image, which the uninformed call "idol worship."

c. *Decisive-support condition*: This acts by virtue of its cogency. It is of three kinds:

1. By way of an object (*arammana upanissaya paccaya*). The image of the Buddha, at the time of veneration, forms an object decisive support condition for the establishment of faith by way of conviction.
2. Proximate decisive support (*anantara upanissaya paccaya*). When one thought gives way to the next, the conviction in one stands as a decisive support for the thought that follows.
3. Natural decisive support (*pakati upanissaya paccaya*). Faith, virtue, generosity, and learning, by way of cogency, stand as natural decisive supports for the repeated arising of these wholesome factors. A good environment and companionship with the wise are natural decisive supports for wholesome mental states.

These three types of decisive support conditions have a bearing on our practice if we wish to fulfil the four preliminary conditions to stream entry (*sotapattiyanga*). These are:

(i) companionship with those of merit and good character (*sappurisa samseva*);
(ii) hearing the Dhamma (*saddhamma savanna*);
(iii) wise reflection (*yoniso manasikara*); and
(iv) living in conformity with the Dhamma (*dhammanudhammapatipatti*).

Nibbana

Nibbana is the fourth ultimate reality (*paramattha*

dhamma). Whereas the other three realities—consciousness (*citta*), mental formations (*cetasika*), and material phenomena (*ruupa*)—are conditioned, nibbana is not. It is neither created nor formed.

When the wanderer Jambukhadaka asked his uncle, the Venerable Sariputta, what the word "nibbana" means, the Venerable Sariputta replied that nibbana is the extinction of greed, hate, and delusion. But nibbana is not the mere extinction of these defilements. It is a state to be attained in this very existence by the extinction of greed, hate, and delusion.

Nibbana is the *summum bonum* of Buddhist practice, to be achieved only by following the Noble Eightfold Path. For most of us the journey along the Path will be long and arduous, but there are sign-posts on the way that will indicate we are going in the right direction. We will recognize these sign-posts when the fetters that bind us are broken in succession. When the first three fetters—personality view, doubt, and clinging to mere rules and rituals—are broken one becomes a "stream enterer" (*sotapanna*), one who has entered the stream to nibbana. The fetters, once broken, will never bind such a person again. This is the truth he knows without uncertainty. The stream-enterer will not be reborn in the four lower planes of existence. He will take rebirth seven times at the most, either in the human or heavenly planes.

When the next two fetters—sensuous craving and ill-will are attenuated, one becomes a "once-returner" (*sakadagamii*), due to return only once to the sense sphere world and then attain nibbana.

When all the lower five fetters are eradicated, the disciple becomes a "non-returner" (*anagami*), who will never return to the sense sphere world but, after death, will be reborn in a pure divine abode and attain nibbana there.

One who takes the next major step and eradicates the five higher fetters — desire for existence in fine material planes, desire for existence in the immaterial planes, conceit, restlessness, and ignorance — reaches the final goal. He is the *arahant*, free from all future becoming.

Each of these four supramundane stages involves two phases.

One is the "path" (*magga*) that eradicates the fetters, the other is the "fruit" (*phala*), moments of supramundane consciousness that result from the path, made possible by the path's work of eradication. The fruit is the enjoyment made available by the work of the path. The fruit can be entered and enjoyed many times after the appropriate path has been reached. The noble disciple determines to enter the fruit, then develops insight until he does so. The highest fruit is the fruit of arahantship. The arahant knows with certainty that his mind is devoid of defilements. He has penetrated the Four Noble Truths. He becomes neither despondent nor elated through contact with the eight worldly conditions—gain and loss, honour and dishonour, happiness and misery, praise and blame. He is free from sorrow, stainless, and safe. "Free from sorrow" because he no more weeps and laments; "stainless" because he has no more defilements; "safe" because there is no more birth for him.

Though the mind of the arahant is free from defilements, his body is still subject to decay, disease and injury, to pain and discomfort. He can overcome these by inducing supramundane consciousness, which is always at his disposal, but it would be impracticable for him to do so for any length of time. Therefore, during life, the arahant can enjoy only an intermittent release from suffering. This is called *sa-upadi-sesa-nibbana,* nibbana with the groups of existence still remaining, since he still exists as an individualized personality subject to the results of residual kamma. Thus, the Buddha met a foot injury when Devadatta hurled a rock at him, the Venerable Maha Moggallana was battered to death by professional criminals, and the Venerable Angulimala was hit by sticks and stones while on his alms round.

When the arahant dies he attains *an-upadi-sesa-nibbana,* nibbana without the aggregates remaining. He will not be reborn anywhere. Earlier he severed the chain of dependent origination at the link where feeling is followed by craving. Now he severs it at the link where becoming leads to new birth.

There has been much speculation as to what happens to the arahant after death — whether he exists, or does not exist, or both, or neither. This confusion arises from thinking in terms of an abiding entity that passes from life to life. The Buddha taught that such an abiding entity does not exist. It is an illusion. Life is a process of becoming, perishing at every moment, generated by kamma. Since there is no ego-entity, there is nothing to be annihilated and nothing to enter a state of eternal existence. When the arahant dies, the physio-mental process comes to an end for lack of the "fuel" needed to keep it going. This fuel is craving (*ta.nha*), which leads to grasping, which in turn leads to further becoming. If craving is totally extinguished, there can be no further becoming. When the body dies at the expiration of the life span, no new rebirth takes place. If there is no rebirth in any plane, then there is no decay, disease, and death; there is no sorrow, lamentation, pain, grief, or despair. This is the end of suffering.

11

The Path of Dhamma

THE PAIRS HEEDFULNESS

1. Mind precedes all mental states. Mind is their chief; they are all mind-wrought. If with an impure mind a person speaks or acts suffering follows him like the wheel that follows the foot of the ox.

2. Mind precedes all mental states. Mind is their chief; they are all mind-wrought. If with a pure mind a person speaks or acts happiness follows him like his never-departing shadow.

3. "He abused me, he struck me, he overpowered me, he robbed me." Those who harbor such thoughts do not still their hatred.

4. "He abused me, he struck me, he overpowered me, he robbed me." Those who do not harbor such thoughts still their hatred.

5. Hatred is never appeased by hatred in this world. By non-hatred alone is hatred appeased. This is a law eternal.

6. There are those who do not realize that one day we all must die. But those who do realize this settle their quarrels.

7. Just as a storm throws down a weak tree, so does Mara overpower the man who lives for the pursuit of pleasures, who is uncontrolled in his senses, immoderate in eating, indolent, and dissipated.

8. Just as a storm cannot prevail against a rocky mountain, so Mara can never overpower the man who lives meditating

on the impurities, who is controlled in his senses, moderate in eating, and filled with faith and earnest effort.

9. Whoever being depraved, devoid of self-control and truthfulness, should don the monk's yellow robe, he surely is not worthy of the robe.

10. But whoever is purged of depravity, well-established in virtues and filled with self-control and truthfulness, he indeed is worthy of the yellow robe.

11. Those who mistake the unessential to be essential and the essential to be unessential, dwelling in wrong thoughts, never arrive at the essential.

12. Those who know the essential to be essential and the unessential to be unessential, dwelling in right thoughts, do arrive at the essential.

13. Just as rain breaks through an ill-thatched house, so passion penetrates an undeveloped mind.

14. Just as rain does not break through a well-thatched house, so passion never penetrates a well-developed mind.

15. The evil-doer grieves here and hereafter; he grieves in both the worlds. He laments and is afflicted, recollecting his own impure deeds.

16. The doer of good rejoices here and hereafter; he rejoices in both the worlds. He rejoices and exults, recollecting his own pure deeds.

17. The evil-doer suffers here and hereafter; he suffers in both the worlds. The thought, "Evil have I done," torments him, and he suffers even more when gone to realms of woe.

18. The doer of good delights here and hereafter; he delights in both the worlds. The thought, "Good have I done," delights him, and he delights even more when gone to realms of bliss.

19. Much though he recites the sacred texts, but acts not accordingly, that heedless man is like a cowherd who only counts the cows of others-he does not partake of the blessings of the holy life.

20. Little though he recites the sacred texts, but puts the Teaching into practice, forsaking lust, hatred, and delusion,

with true wisdom and emancipated mind, clinging to nothing of this or any other world-he indeed partakes of the blessings of a holy life.

21. Heedfulness is the path to the Deathless. Heedlessness is the path to death. The heedful die not. The heedless are as if dead already.

22. Clearly understanding this excellence of heedfulness, the wise exult therein and enjoy the resort of the Noble Ones.

23. The wise ones, ever meditative and steadfastly persevering, alone experience Nibbana, the incomparable freedom from bondage.

24. Ever grows the glory of him who is energetic, mindful and pure in conduct, discerning and self-controlled, righteous and heedful.

25. By effort and heedfulness, discipline and self-mastery, let the wise one make for himself an island which no flood can overwhelm.

26. The foolish and ignorant indulge in heedlessness, but the wise one keeps his heedfulness as his best treasure.

27. Do not give way to heedlessness. Do not indulge in sensual pleasures. Only the heedful and meditative attain great happiness.

28. Just as one upon the summit of a mountain beholds the groundlings, even so when the wise man casts away heedlessness by heedfulness and ascends the high tower of wisdom, this sorrowless sage beholds the sorrowing and foolish multitude.

29. Heedful among the heedless, wide-awake among the sleepy, the wise man advances like a swift horse leaving behind a weak jade.

30. By Heedfulness did Indra become the overlord of the gods. Heedfulness is ever praised, and heedlessness ever despised.

31. The monk who delights in heedfulness and looks with fear at heedlessness advances like fire, burning all fetters, small and large.

32. The monk who delights in heedfulness and looks with fear at heedlessness will not fall. He is close to Nibbana.

33. Just as a fletcher straightens an arrow shaft, even so the discerning man straightens his mind-so fickle and unsteady, so difficult to guard.

34. As a fish when pulled out of water and cast on land throbs and quivers, even so is this mind agitated. Hence should one abandon the realm of Mara.

35. Wonderful, indeed, it is to subdue the mind, so difficult to subdue, ever swift, and seizing whatever it desires. A tamed mind brings happiness.

36. Let the discerning man guard the mind, so difficult to detect and extremely subtle, seizing whatever it desires. A guarded mind brings happiness.

37. Dwelling in the cave (of the heart), the mind, without form, wanders far and alone. Those who subdue this mind are liberated from the bonds of Mara.

38. Wisdom never becomes perfect in one whose mind is not steadfast, who knows not the Good Teaching and whose faith wavers.

39. There is no fear for an awakened one, whose mind is not sodden (by lust) nor afflicted (by hate), and who has gone beyond both merit and demerit.

40. Realizing that this body is as fragile as a clay pot, and fortifying this mind like a well-fortified city, fight out Mara with the sword of wisdom. Then, guarding the conquest, remain unattached.

41. Ere long, alas! this body will lie upon the earth, unheeded and lifeless, like a useless log.

42. Whatever harm an enemy may do to an enemy, or a hater to a hater, an ill-directed mind inflicts on oneself a greater harm.

43. Neither mother, father, nor any other relative can do one greater good than one's own well-directed mind.

44. Who shall overcome this earth, this realm of Yama and this sphere of men and gods? Who shall bring to perfection the well-taught path of wisdom as an expert garland-maker would his floral design?

45. A striver-on-the path shall overcome this earth, this realm of Yama and this sphere of men and gods. The striver-on-the-path shall bring to perfection the well-taught path of wisdom, as an expert garland-maker would his floral design.

46. Realizing that this body is like froth, penetrating its mirage-like nature, and plucking out Mara's flower-tipped arrows of sensuality, go beyond sight of the King of Death!

47. As a mighty flood sweeps away the sleeping village, so death carries away the person of distracted mind who only plucks the flowers (of pleasure).

48. The Destroyer brings under his sway the person of distracted mind who, insatiate in sense desires, only plucks the flowers (of pleasure).

49. As a bee gathers honey from the flower without injuring its colour or fragrance, even so the sage goes on his alms-round in the village.

50. Let none find fault with others; let none see the omissions and commissions of others. But let one see one's own acts, done and undone.

51. Like a beautiful flower full of colour but without fragrance, even so, fruitless are the fair words of one who does not practice them.

52. Like a beautiful flower full of colour and also fragrant, even so, fruitful are the fair words of one who practices them.

53. As from a great heap of flowers many garlands can be made, even so should many good deeds be done by one born a mortal.

54. Not the sweet smell of flowers, not even the fragrance of sandal, tagara, or jasmine blows against the wind. But the fragrance of the virtuous blows against the wind. Truly the virtuous man pervades all directions with the fragrance of his virtue.

55. Of all the fragrances-sandal, tagara, blue lotus and jasmine-the fragrance of virtue is the sweetest.

56. Faint is the fragrance of tagara and sandal, but excellent is the fragrance of the virtuous, wafting even amongst the gods.

57. Mara never finds the path of the truly virtuous, who abide in heedfulness and are freed by perfect knowledge.

58. Upon a heap of rubbish in the road-side ditch blooms a lotus, fragrant and pleasing.

59. Even so, on the rubbish heap of blinded mortals the disciple of the Supremely Enlightened One shines resplendent in wisdom.

60. Long is the night to the sleepless; long is the league to the weary. Long is worldly existence to fools who know not the Sublime Truth.

61. Should a seeker not find a companion who is better or equal, let him resolutely pursue a solitary course; there is no fellowship with the fool.

62. The fool worries, thinking, "I have sons, I have wealth." Indeed, when he himself is not his own, whence are sons, whence is wealth?

63. A fool who knows his foolishness is wise at least to that extent, but a fool who thinks himself wise is a fool indeed.

64. Though all his life a fool associates with a wise man, he no more comprehends the Truth than a spoon tastes the flavour of the soup.

65. Though only for a moment a discerning person associates with a wise man, quickly he comprehends the Truth, just as the tongue tastes the flavour of the soup.

66. Fools of little wit are enemies unto themselves as they move about doing evil deeds, the fruits of which are bitter.

67. Ill done is that action of doing which one repents later, and the fruit of which one, weeping, reaps with tears.

68. Well done is that action of doing which one repents not later, and the fruit of which one, reaps with delight and happiness.

69. So long as an evil deed has not ripened, the fool thinks it as sweet as honey. But when the evil deed ripens, the fool comes to grief.

70. Month after month a fool may eat his food with the tip of a blade of grass, but he still is not worth a sixteenth part of the those who have comprehended the Truth.

71. Truly, an evil deed committed does not immediately bear fruit, like milk that does not turn sour all at once. But smoldering, it follows the fool like fire covered by ashes.

72. To his own ruin the fool gains knowledge, for it cleaves his head and destroys his innate goodness.

73. The fool seeks undeserved reputation, precedence among monks, authority over monasteries, and honour among householders.

74. "Let both laymen and monks think that it was done by me. In every work, great and small, let them follow me"-such is the ambition of the fool; thus his desire and pride increase.

75. One is the quest for worldly gain, and quite another is the path to Nibbana. Clearly understanding this, let not the monk, the disciple of the Buddha, be carried away by worldly acclaim, but develop detachment instead.

76. Should one find a man who points out faults and who reproves, let him follow such a wise and sagacious person as one would a guide to hidden treasure. It is always better, and never worse, to cultivate such an association.

77. Let him admonish, instruct and shield one from wrong; he, indeed, is dear to the good and detestable to the evil.

78. Do not associate with evil companions; do not seek the fellowship of the vile. Associate with the good friends; seek the fellowship of noble men.

79. He who drinks deep the Dhamma lives happily with a tranquil mind. The wise man ever delights in the Dhamma made known by the Noble One (the Buddha).

80. Irrigators regulate the rivers; fletchers straighten the arrow shaft; carpenters shape the wood; the wise control themselves.

81. Just as a solid rock is not shaken by the storm, even so the wise are not affected by praise or blame.

82. On hearing the Teachings, the wise become perfectly purified, like a lake deep, clear and still.

83. The good renounce (attachment for) everything. The virtuous do not prattle with a yearning for pleasures. The wise

show no elation or depression when touched by happiness or sorrow.

84. He is indeed virtuous, wise, and righteous who neither for his own sake nor for the sake of another (does any wrong), who does not crave for sons, wealth, or kingdom, and does not desire success by unjust means.

85. Few among men are those who cross to the farther shore. The rest, the bulk of men, only run up and down the hither bank.

86. But those who act according to the perfectly taught Dhamma will cross the realm of Death, so difficult to cross.

87-88. Abandoning the dark way, let the wise man cultivate the bright path. Having gone from home to homelessness, let him yearn for that delight in detachment, so difficult to enjoy. Giving up sensual pleasures, with no attachment, let the wise man cleanse himself of defilements of the mind.

89. Those whose minds have reached full excellence in the factors of enlightenment, who, having renounced acquisitiveness, rejoice in not clinging to things-rid of cankers, glowing with wisdom, they have attained Nibbana in this very life.

90. The fever of passion exists not for him who has completed the journey, who is sorrowless and wholly set free, and has broken all ties.

91. The mindful ones exert themselves. They are not attached to any home; like swans that abandon the lake, they leave home after home behind.

92. Those who do not accumulate and are wise regarding food, whose object is the Void, the Unconditioned Freedom-their track cannot be traced, like that of birds in the air.

93. He whose cankers are destroyed and who is not attached to food, whose object is the Void, the Unconditioned Freedom-his path cannot be traced, like that of birds in the air.

94. Even the gods hold dear the wise one, whose senses are subdued like horses well trained by a charioteer, whose pride is destroyed and who is free from the cankers.

95. There is no more worldly existence for the wise one who,

like the earth, resents nothing, who is firm as a high pillar and as pure as a deep pool free from mud.

96. Calm is his thought, calm his speech, and calm his deed, who, truly knowing, is wholly freed, perfectly tranquil and wise.

97. The man who is without blind faith, who knows the Uncreated, who has severed all links, destroyed all causes (for karma, good and evil), and thrown out all desires-he, truly, is the most excellent of men. 11

98. Inspiring, indeed, is that place where Arahants dwell, be it a village, a forest, a vale, or a hill.

99. Inspiring are the forests in which worldlings find no pleasure. There the passionless will rejoice, for they seek no sensual pleasures.

100. Better than a thousand useless words is one useful word, hearing which one attains peace.

101. Better than a thousand useless verses is one useful verse, hearing which one attains peace.

102. Better than reciting a hundred meaningless verses is the reciting of one verse of Dhamma, hearing which one attains peace.

103. Though one may conquer a thousand times a thousand men in battle, yet he indeed is the noblest victor who conquers himself.

104-105. Self-conquest is far better then the conquest of others. Not even a god, an angel, Mara or Brahma can turn into defeat the victory of a person who is self-subdued and ever restrained in conduct.

106. Though month after month for a hundred years one should offer sacrifices by the thousands, yet if only for a moment one should worship those of perfected minds that honour is indeed better than a century of sacrifice.

107. Though for a hundred years one should tend the sacrificial fire in the forest, yet if only for a moment one should worship those of perfected minds, that worship is indeed better than a century of sacrifice.

108. Whatever gifts and oblations one seeking merit might offer in this world for a whole year, all that is not worth one fourth of the merit gained by revering the Upright Ones, which is truly excellent.

109. To one ever eager to revere and serve the elders, these four blessing accrue: long life and beauty, happiness and power.

110. Better it is to live one day virtuous and meditative than to live a hundred years immoral and uncontrolled.

111. Better it is to live one day wise and meditative than to live a hundred years foolish and uncontrolled.

112. Better it is to live one day strenuous and resolute than to live a hundred years sluggish and dissipated.

113. Better it is to live one day seeing the rise and fall of things than to live as hundred years without ever seeing the rise and fall of things.

114. Better it is to live one day seeing the Deathless than to live a hundred years without ever seeing the Deathless.

115. Better it is to live one day seeing the Supreme Truth than to live a hundred years without ever seeing the Supreme Truth.

116. Hasten to do good; restrain your mind from evil. He who is slow in doing good, his mind delights in evil.

117. Should a person commit evil, let him not do it again and again. Let him not find pleasure therein, for painful is the accumulation of evil.

118. Should a person do good, let him do it again and again. Let him find pleasure therein, for blissful is the accumulation of good.

119. It may be well with the evil-doer as long as the evil ripens not. But when it does ripen, then the evil-doer sees (the painful results of) his evil deeds.

120. It may be ill with the doer of good as long as the good ripens not. But when it does ripen, then the doer of good sees (the pleasant results of) his good deeds.

121. Think not lightly of evil, saying, "It will not come to

me." Drop by drop is the water pot filled. Likewise, the fool, gathering it little by little, fills himself with evil.

122. Think not lightly of good, saying, "It will not come to me." Drop by drop is the water pot filled. Likewise, the wise man, gathering it little by little, fills himself with good.

123. Just as a trader with a small escort and great wealth would avoid a perilous route, or just as one desiring to live avoids poison, even so should one shun evil.

124. If on the hand there is no wound, one may carry even poison in it. Poison does not affect one who is free from wounds. For him who does no evil, there is no ill.

125. Like fine dust thrown against the wind, evil falls back upon that fool who offends an inoffensive, pure and guiltless man.

126. Some are born in the womb; the wicked are born in hell; the devout go to heaven; the stainless pass into Nibbana.

127. Neither in the sky nor in mid-ocean, nor by entering into mountain clefts, nowhere in the world is there a place where one may escape from the results of evil deeds.

128. Neither in the sky nor in mid-ocean, nor by entering into mountain clefts, nowhere in the world is there a place where one will not be overcome by death.

129. All tremble at violence; all fear death. Putting oneself in the place of another, one should not kill nor cause another to kill.

130. All tremble at violence; life is dear to all. Putting oneself in the place of another, one should not kill nor cause another to kill.

131. One who, while himself seeking happiness, oppresses with violence other beings who also desire happiness, will not attain happiness hereafter.

132. One who, while himself seeking happiness, does not oppress with violence other beings who also desire happiness, will find happiness hereafter.

133. Speak not harshly to anyone, for those thus spoken to might retort. Indeed, angry speech hurts, and retaliation may overtake you.

134. If, like a broken gong, you silence yourself, you have approached Nibbana, for vindictiveness is no longer in you.

135. Just as a cowherd drives the cattle to pasture with a staff, so do old age and death drive the life force of beings (from existence to existence).

136. When the fool commits evil deeds, he does not realize (their evil nature). The witless man is tormented by his own deeds, like one burnt by fire.

137. He who inflicts violence on those who are unarmed, and offends those who are inoffensive, will soon come upon one of these ten states:

138-140 Sharp pain, or disaster, bodily injury, serious illness, or derangement of mind, trouble from the government, or grave charges, loss of relatives, or loss of wealth, or houses destroyed by ravaging fire; upon dissolution of the body that ignorant man is born in hell.

141. Neither going about naked, nor matted locks, nor filth, nor fasting, nor lying on the ground, nor smearing oneself with ashes and dust, nor sitting on the heels (in penance) can purify a mortal who has not overcome doubt.

142. Even though he be well-attired, yet if he is posed, calm, controlled and established in the holy life, having set aside violence towards all beings-he, truly, is a holy man, a renunciate, a monk.

143. Only rarely is there a man in this world who, restrained by modesty, avoids reproach, as a thoroughbred horse avoids the whip.

144. Like a thoroughbred horse touched by the whip, be strenuous, be filled with spiritual yearning. By faith and moral purity, by effort and meditation, by investigation of the truth, by being rich in knowledge and virtue, and by being mindful, destroy this unlimited suffering.

145. Irrigators regulate the waters, fletchers straighten arrow shafts, carpenters shape wood, and the good control themselves.

146. When this world is ever ablaze, why this laughter, why

this jubilation? Shrouded in darkness, will you not see the light?

147. Behold this body-a painted image, a mass of heaped up sores, infirm, full of hankering-of which nothing is lasting or stable!

148. Fully worn out is this body, a nest of disease, and fragile. This foul mass breaks up, for death is the end of life.

149. These dove-colored bones are like gourds that lie scattered about in autumn. Having seen them, how can one seek delight?

150. This city (body) is built of bones, plastered with flesh and blood; within are decay and death, pride and jealousy.

151. Even gorgeous royal chariots wear out, and indeed this body too wears out. But the Dhamma of the Good does not age; thus the Good make it known to the good.

152. The man of little learning grows old like a bull. He grows only in bulk, but, his wisdom does not grow.

153. Through many a birth in samsara have I wandered in vain, seeking in the builder of this house (of life). Repeated birth is indeed suffering!

154. O house-builder, you are seen! You will not build this house again. For your rafters are broken and your ridgepole shattered. My mind has reached the Unconditioned; I have attained the destruction of craving.

155. Those who in youth have not led the holy life, or have failed to acquire wealth, languish like old cranes in the pond without fish.

156. Those who in youth have not lead the holy life, or have failed to acquire wealth, lie sighing over the past, like worn out arrows (shot from) a bow.

157. If one holds oneself dear, one should diligently watch oneself. Let the wise man keep vigil during any of the three watches of the night.

158. One should first establish oneself in what is proper; then only should one instruct others. Thus the wise man will not be reproached.

159. One should do what one teaches others to do; if one would train others, one should be well controlled oneself. Difficult,

indeed, is self-control.

160. One truly is the protector of oneself; who else could the protector be? With oneself fully controlled, one gains a mastery that is hard to gain.

161. The evil a witless man does by himself, born of himself and produced by himself, grinds him as a diamond grinds a hard gem.

162. Just as a single creeper strangles the tree on which it grows, even so, a man who is exceedingly depraved harms himself as only an enemy might wish.

163. Easy to do are things that are bad and harmful to oneself. But exceedingly difficult to do are things that are good and beneficial.

164. Whoever, on account of perverted views, scorns the Teaching of the Perfected Ones, the Noble and Righteous Ones-that fool, like the bamboo, produces fruits only for self destruction.

165. By oneself is evil done; by oneself is one defiled. By oneself is evil left undone; by oneself is one made pure. Purity and impurity depended on oneself; no one can purify another.

166. Let one not neglect one's own welfare for the sake of another, however great. Clearly understanding one's own welfare, let one be intent upon the good.

167. Follow not the vulgar way; live not in heedlessness; hold not false views; linger not long in worldly existence.

168. Arise! Do not be heedless! Lead a righteous life. The righteous live happily both in this world and the next.

169. Lead a righteous life; lead not a base life. The righteous live happily both in this world and the next.

170. One who looks upon the world as a bubble and a mirage, him the King of Death sees not.

171. Come! Behold this world, which is like a decorated royal chariot. Here fools flounder, but the wise have no attachment to it.

172. He who having been heedless is heedless no more, illuminates this world like the moon freed from clouds.

173. He, who by good deeds covers the evil he has done, illuminates this world like the moon freed from clouds.

174. Blind is the world; here only a few possess insight. Only a few, like birds escaping from the net, go to realms of bliss.

175. Swans fly on the path of the sun; men pass through the air by psychic powers; the wise are led away from the world after vanquishing Mara and his host.

176. For a liar who has violated the one law (of truthfulness) who holds in scorn the hereafter, there is no evil that he cannot do.

177. Truly, misers fare not to heavenly realms; nor, indeed, do fools praise generosity. But the wise man rejoices in giving, and by that alone does he become happy hereafter.

178. Better than sole sovereignty over the earth, better than going to heaven, better even than lordship over all the worlds is the supramundane Fruition of Stream Entrance.

179. By what track can you trace that trackless Buddha of limitless range, whose victory nothing can undo, whom none of the vanquished defilements can ever pursue?

180. By what track can you trace that trackless Buddha of limitless range, in whom exists no longer, the entangling and embroiling craving that perpetuates becoming?

181. Those wise ones who are devoted to meditation and who delight in the calm of renunciation-such mindful ones, Supreme Buddhas, even the gods hold dear.

182. Hard is it to be born a man; hard is the life of mortals. Hard is it to gain the opportunity of hearing the Sublime Truth, and hard to encounter is the arising of the Buddhas.

183. To avoid all evil, to cultivate good, and to cleanse one's mind-this is the teaching of the Buddhas.

184. Enduring patience is the highest austerity. "Nibbana is supreme," say the Buddhas. He is not a true monk who harms another, nor a true renunciate who oppresses others.

185. Not despising, not harming, restraint according to the code of monastic discipline, moderation in food, dwelling in

solitude, devotion to meditation-this is the teaching of the Buddhas.

186-187. There is no satisfying sensual desires, even with the rain of gold coins. For sensual pleasures give little satisfaction and much pain. Having understood this, the wise man finds no delight even in heavenly pleasures. The disciple of the Supreme Buddha delights in the destruction of craving.

188. Driven only by fear, do men go for refuge to many places-to hills, woods, groves, trees and shrines.

189. Such, indeed, is no safe refuge; such is not the refuge supreme. Not by resorting to such a refuge is one released from all suffering.

190-191. He who has gone for refuge to the Buddha, the Teaching and his Order, penetrates with transcendental wisdom the Four Noble Truths-suffering, the cause of suffering, the cessation of suffering, and the Noble Eightfold Path leading to the cessation of suffering.

192. This indeed is the safe refuge, this the refuge supreme. Having gone to such a refuge, one is released from all suffering.

193. Hard to find is the thoroughbred man (the Buddha); he is not born everywhere. Where such a wise man is born, that clan thrives happily.

194. Blessed is the birth of the Buddhas; blessed is the enunciation of the sacred Teaching; blessed is the harmony in the Order, and blessed is the spiritual pursuit of the united truth-seeker.

195-196. He who reveres those worthy of reverence, the Buddhas and their disciples, who have transcended all obstacles and passed beyond the reach of sorrow and lamentation-he who reveres such peaceful and fearless ones, his merit none can compute by any measure.

197. Happy indeed we live, friendly amidst the hostile. Amidst hostile men we dwell free from hatred.

198. Happy indeed we live, friendly amidst the afflicted (by craving). Amidst afflicted men we dwell free from affliction.

199. Happy indeed we live, free from avarice amidst the

avaricious. Amidst the avaricious men we dwell free from avarice.

200. Happy indeed we live, we who possess nothing. Feeders on joy we shall be, like the Radiant Gods.

201. Victory begets enmity; the defeated dwell in pain. Happily the peaceful live, discarding both victory and defeat.

202. There is no fire like lust and no crime like hatred. There is no ill like the aggregates (of existence) and no bliss higher than the peace (of Nibbana).

203. Hunger is the worst disease, conditioned things the worst suffering. Knowing this as it really is, the wise realize Nibbana, the highest bliss.

204. Health is the most precious gain and contentment the greatest wealth. A trustworthy person is the best kinsman, Nibbana the highest bliss.

205. Having savored the taste of solitude and peace (of Nibbana), pain-free and stainless he becomes, drinking deep the taste of the bliss of the Truth.

206. Good is it to see the Noble Ones; to live with them is ever blissful. One will always be happy by not encountering fools.

207. Indeed, he who moves in the company of fools grieves for longing. Association with fools is ever painful, like partnership with an enemy. But association with the wise is happy, like meeting one's own kinsmen.

208. Therefore, follow the Noble One, who is steadfast, wise, learned, dutiful and devout. One should follow only such a man, who is truly good and discerning, even as the moon follows the path of the stars.

209. Giving himself to things to be shunned and not exerting where exertion is needed, a seeker after pleasures, having given up his true welfare, envies those intent upon theirs.

210. Seek no intimacy with the beloved and also not with the unloved, for not to see the beloved and to see the unloved, both are painful.

211. Therefore hold nothing dear, for separation from the dear is painful. There are no bonds for those who have nothing beloved

or unloved.

212. From endearment springs grief, from endearment springs fear. From him who is wholly free from endearment there is no grief, whence then fear?

213. From affection springs grief, from affection springs fear. From him who is wholly free from affection there is no grief, whence then fear?

214. From attachment springs grief, from attachment springs fear. From him who is wholly free from attachment there is no grief, whence then fear?

215. From lust springs grief, from lust springs fear. From him who is wholly free from craving there is no grief; whence then fear?

216. From craving springs grief, from craving springs fear. From him who is wholly free from craving there is no grief; whence then fear?

217. People hold dear him who embodies virtue and insight, who is principled, has realized the truth, and who himself does what he ought to be doing.

218. One who is intent upon the Ineffable (Nibbana), dwells with mind inspired (by supramundane wisdom), and is no more bound by sense pleasures-such a man is called "One Bound Upstream."

219. When, after a long absence, a man safely returns from afar, his relatives, friends and well-wishers welcome him home on arrival.

220. As kinsmen welcome a dear one on arrival, even so his own good deeds will welcome the doer of good who has gone from this world to the next.

221. One should give up anger, renounce pride, and overcome all fetters. Suffering never befalls him who clings not to mind and body and is detached.

222. He who checks rising anger as a charioteer checks a rolling chariot, him I call a true charioteer. Others only hold the reins.

223. Overcome the angry by non-anger; overcome the wicked

by goodness; overcome the miser by generosity; overcome the liar by truth.

224. Speak the truth; yield not to anger; when asked, give even if you only have a little. By these three means can one reach the presence of the gods.

225. Those sages who are inoffensive and ever restrained in body, go to the Deathless State, where, having gone, they grieve no more.

226. Those who are ever vigilant, who discipline themselves day and night, and are ever intent upon Nibbana-their defilements fade away.

227. O Atula! Indeed, this is an ancient practice, not one only of today: they blame those who remain silent, they blame those who speak much, they blame those who speak in moderation. There is none in the world who is not blamed.

228. There never was, there never will be, nor is there now, a person who is wholly blamed or wholly praised.

229. But the man whom the wise praise, after observing him day after day, is one of flawless character, wise, and endowed with knowledge and virtue.

230. Who can blame such a one, as worthy as a coin of refined gold? Even the gods praise him; by Brahma, too, is he praised.

231. Let a man guard himself against irritability in bodily action; let him be controlled in deed. Abandoning bodily misconduct, let him practice good conduct in deed.

232. Let a man guard himself against irritability in speech; let him be controlled in speech. Abandoning verbal misconduct, let him practice good conduct in speech.

233. Let a man guard himself against irritability in thought; let him be controlled in mind. Abandoning mental misconduct, let him practice good conduct in thought.

234. The wise are controlled in bodily action, controlled in speech and controlled in thought. They are truly well-controlled.

235. Like a withered leaf are you now; death's messengers await you. You stand on the eve of your departure, yet you have

made no provision for your journey!

236. Make an island for yourself! Strive hard and become wise! Rid of impurities and cleansed of stain, you shall enter the celestial abode of the Noble Ones.

237. Your life has come to an end now; You are setting forth into the presence of Yama, the king of death. No resting place is there for you on the way, yet you have made no provision for the journey!

238. Make an island unto yourself! Strive hard and become wise! Rid of impurities and cleansed of stain, you shall not come again to birth and decay.

239. One by one, little by little, moment by moment, a wise man should remove his own impurities, as a smith removes his dross from silver.

240. Just as rust arising from iron eats away the base from which it arises, even so, their own deeds lead transgressors to states of woe.

241. Non-repetition is the bane of scriptures; neglect is the bane of a home; slovenliness is the bane of personal appearance, and heedlessness is the bane of a guard.

242. Unchastity is the taint in a woman; niggardliness is the taint in a giver. Taints, indeed, are all evil things, both in this world and the next.

243. A worse taint than these is ignorance, the worst of all taints. Destroy this one taint and become taintless, O monks!

244. Easy is life for the shameless one who is impudent as a crow, is backbiting and forward, arrogant and corrupt.

245. Difficult is life for the modest one who always seeks purity, is detached and unassuming, clean in life, and discerning.

246-247. One who destroys life, utters lies, takes what is not given, goes to another man's wife, and is addicted to intoxicating drinks-such a man digs up his own root even in this world.

248. Know this, O good man: evil things are difficult to control. Let not greed and wickedness drag you to protracted misery.

249. People give according to their faith or regard. If one becomes discontented with the food and drink given by others, one does not attain meditative absorption, either by day or by night.

250. But he in who this (discontent) is fully destroyed, uprooted and extinct, he attains absorption, both by day and by night.

251. There is no fire like lust; there is no grip like hatred; there is no net like delusion; there is no river like craving.

252. Easily seen is the fault of others, but one's own fault is difficult to see. Like chaff one winnows another's faults, but hides one's own, even as a crafty fowler hides behind sham branches.

253. He who seeks another's faults, who is ever censorious-his cankers grow. He is far from destruction of the cankers.

254. There is no track in the sky, and no recluse outside (the Buddha's dispensation). Mankind delights in worldliness, but the Buddhas are free from worldliness.

255. There is not track in the sky, and no recluse outside (the Buddha's dispensation). There are no conditioned things that are eternal, and no instability in the Buddhas.

256. Not by passing arbitrary judgments does a man become just; a wise man is he who investigates both right and wrong.

257. He who does not judge others arbitrarily, but passes judgment impartially according to the truth, that sagacious man is a guardian of law and is called just.

258. One is not wise because one speaks much. He who is peaceable, friendly and fearless is called wise.

259. A man is not versed in Dhamma because he speaks much. He who, after hearing a little Dhamma, realizes its truth directly and is not heedless of it, is truly versed in the Dhamma.

260. A monk is not Elder because his head is gray. He is but ripe in age, and he is called one grown old in vain.

261. One in whom there is truthfulness, virtue, inoffensiveness, restraint and self-mastery, who is free from defilements and is wise-he is truly called an Elder.

262. Not by mere eloquence nor by beauty of form does a man become accomplished, if he is jealous, selfish and deceitful.

263. But he in whom these are wholly destroyed, uprooted and extinct, and who has cast out hatred-that wise man is truly accomplished.

264. Not by shaven head does a man who is indisciplined and untruthful become a monk. How can he who is full of desire and greed be a monk?

265. He who wholly subdues evil both small and great is called a monk, because he has overcome all evil.

266. He is not a monk just because he lives on others' alms. Not by adopting outward form does one become a true monk.

267. Whoever here (in the Dispensation) lives a holy life, transcending both merit and demerit, and walks with understanding in this world-he is truly called a monk.

268. Not by observing silence does one become a sage, if he be foolish and ignorant. But that man is wise who, as if holding a balance-scale accepts only the good.

269. The sage (thus) rejecting the evil, is truly a sage. Since he comprehends both (present and future) worlds, he is called a sage.

270. He is not noble who injures living beings. He is called noble because he is harmless towards all living beings.

271-272. Not by rules and observances, not even by much learning, nor by gain of absorption, nor by a life of seclusion, nor by thinking, "I enjoy the bliss of renunciation, which is not experienced by the worldling" should you, O monks, rest content, until the utter destruction of cankers (Arahantship) is reached.

273. Of all the paths the Eightfold Path is the best; of all the truths the Four Noble Truths are the best; of all things passionlessness is the best: of men the Seeing One (the Buddha) is the best.

274. This is the only path; there is none other for the purification of insight. Tread this path, and you will bewilder Mara.

275. Walking upon this path you will make an end of suffering.

Having discovered how to pull out the thorn of lust, I make known the path.

276. You yourselves must strive; the Buddhas only point the way. Those meditative ones who tread the path are released from the bonds of Mara.

277. "All conditioned things are impermanent"-when one sees this with wisdom, one turns away from suffering. This is the path to purification.

278. "All conditioned things are unsatisfactory"-when one sees this with wisdom, one turns away from suffering. This is the path to purification.

279. "All things are not-self"-when one sees this with wisdom, one turns away from suffering. This is the path to purification.

280. The idler who does not exert himself when he should, who though young and strong is full of sloth, with a mind full of vain thoughts-such an indolent man does not find the path to wisdom.

281. Let a man be watchful of speech, well controlled in mind, and not commit evil in bodily action. Let him purify these three courses of action, and win the path made known by the Great Sage.

282. Wisdom springs from meditation; without meditation wisdom wanes. Having known these two paths of progress and decline, let a man so conduct himself that his wisdom may increase.

283. Cut down the forest (lust), but not the tree; from the forest springs fear. Having cut down the forest and the underbrush (desire), be passionless, O monks!

284. For so long as the underbrush of desire, even the most subtle, of a man towards a woman is not cut down, his mind is in bondage, like the sucking calf to its mother.

285. Cut off your affection in the manner of a man plucks with his hand an autumn lotus. Cultivate only the path to peace, Nibbana, as made known by the Exalted One.

286. "Here shall I live during the rains, here in winter and summer"-thus thinks the fool. He does not realize the danger

(that death might intervene).

287. As a great flood carries away a sleeping village, so death seizes and carries away the man with a clinging mind, doting on his children and cattle.

288. For him who is assailed by death there is no protection by kinsmen. None there are to save him-no sons, nor father, nor relatives.

289. Realizing this fact, let the wise man, restrained by morality, hasten to clear the path leading to Nibbana.

290. If by renouncing a lesser happiness one may realize a greater happiness, let the wise man renounce the lesser, having regard for the greater.

291. Entangled by the bonds of hate, he who seeks his own happiness by inflicting pain on others, is never delivered from hatred.

292. The cankers only increase for those who are arrogant and heedless, who leave undone what should be done and do what should not be done.

293. The cankers cease for those mindful and clearly comprehending ones who always earnestly practice mindfulness of the body, who do not resort to what should not be done, and steadfastly pursue what should be done.

294. Having slain mother (craving), father (self-conceit), two warrior-kings (eternalism and nihilism), and destroyed a country (sense organs and sense objects) together with its treasurer (attachment and lust), ungrieving goes the holy man.

295. Having slain mother, father, two brahman kings (two extreme views), and a tiger as the fifth (the five mental hindrances), ungrieving goes the holy man.

296. Those disciples of Gotama ever awaken happily who day and night constantly practice the Recollection of the Qualities of the Buddha.

297. Those disciples of Gotama ever awaken happily who day and night constantly practice the Recollection of the Qualities of the Dhamma.

298. Those disciples of Gotama ever awaken happily who day

and night constantly practice the Recollection of the Qualities of the Sangha.

299. Those disciples of Gotama ever awaken happily who day and night constantly practice Mindfulness of the Body.

300. Those disciples of Gotama ever awaken happily whose minds by day and night delight in the practice of non-violence.

301. Those disciples of Gotama ever awaken happily whose minds by day and night delight in the practice of meditation.

302. Difficult is life as a monk; difficult is it to delight therein. Also difficult and sorrowful is the household life. Suffering comes from association with unequals; suffering comes from wandering in samsara. Therefore, be not an aimless wanderer, be not a pursuer of suffering.

303. He who is full of faith and virtue, and possesses good repute and wealth-he is respected everywhere, in whatever land he travels.

304. The good shine from afar, like the Himalaya mountains. But the wicked are unseen, like arrows shot in the night.

305. He who sits alone, sleeps alone, and walks alone, who is strenuous and subdues himself alone, will find delight in the solitude of the forest.

306. The liar goes to the state of woe; also he who, having done (wrong), says, "I did not do it." Men of base actions both, on departing they share the same destiny in the other world.

307. There are many evil characters and uncontrolled men wearing the saffron robe. These wicked men will be born in states of woe because of their evil deeds.

308. It would be better to swallow a red-hot iron ball, blazing like fire, than as an immoral and uncontrolled monk to eat the alms of the people.

309. Four misfortunes befall the reckless man who consorts with another's wife: acquisition of demerit, disturbed sleep, ill-repute, and (rebirth in) states of woe.

310. Such a man acquires demerit and an unhappy birth in the future. Brief is the pleasure of the frightened man and woman, and the king imposes heavy punishment. Hence, let no man consort

with another's wife.

311. Just as kusa grass wrongly handled cuts the hand, even so, a recluse's life wrongly lived drags one to states of woe.

312. Any loose act, any corrupt observance, any life of questionable celibacy-none of these bear much fruit.

313. If anything is to be done, let one do it with sustained vigour. A lax monastic life stirs up the dust of passions all the more.

314. An evil deed is better left undone, for such a deed torments one afterwards. But a good deed is better done, doing which one repents not later.

315. Just as a border city is closely guarded both within and without, even so, guard yourself. Do not let slip this opportunity (for spiritual growth). For those who let slip this opportunity grieve indeed when consigned to hell.

316. Those who are ashamed of what they should not be ashamed of, and are not ashamed of what they should be ashamed of-upholding false views, they go to states of woe.

317. Those who see something to fear where there is nothing to fear, and see nothing to fear where there is something to fear-upholding false views, they go to states of woe.

318. Those who imagine evil where there is none, and do not see evil where it is-upholding false views, they go to states of woe.

319. Those who discern the wrong as wrong and the right as right-upholding right views, they go to realms of bliss.

320. As an elephant in the battlefield withstands arrows shot from bows all around, even so shall I endure abuse. There are many, indeed, who lack virtue.

321. A tamed elephant is led into a crowd, and the king mounts a tamed elephant. Best among men is the subdued one who endures abuse.

322. Excellent are well-trained mules, thoroughbred Sindhu horses and noble tusker elephants. But better still is the man who has subdued himself.

323. Not by these mounts, however, would one go to the

Untrodden Land (Nibbana), as one who is self-tamed goes by his own tamed and well-controlled mind.

324. Musty during rut, the tusker named Dhanapalaka is uncontrollable. Held in captivity, the tusker does not touch a morsel, but only longingly calls to mind the elephant forest.

325. When a man is sluggish and gluttonous, sleeping and rolling around in bed like a fat domestic pig, that sluggard undergoes rebirth again and again.

326. Formerly this mind wandered about as it liked, where it wished and according to its pleasure, but now I shall thoroughly master it with wisdom as a mahout controls with his ankus an elephant in rut.

327. Delight in heedfulness! Guard well your thoughts! Draw yourself out of this bog of evil, even as an elephant draws himself out of the mud.

328. If for company you find a wise and prudent friend who leads a good life, you should, overcoming all impediments, keep his company joyously and mindfully.

329. If for company you cannot find a wise and prudent friend who leads a good life, then, like a king who leaves behind a conquered kingdom, or like a lone elephant in the elephant forest, you should go your way alone.

330. Better it is to live alone; there is no fellowship with a fool. Live alone and do no evil; be carefree like an elephant in the elephant forest.

331. Good are friends when need arises; good is contentment with just what one has; good is merit when life is at an end, and good is the abandoning of all suffering (through Arahantship).

332. In this world, good it is to serve one's mother, good it is to serve one's father, good it is to serve the monks, and good it is to serve the holy men.

333. Good is virtue until life's end, good is faith that is steadfast, good is the acquisition of wisdom, and good is the avoidance of evil.

334. The craving of one given to heedless living grows like

a creeper. Like the monkey seeking fruits in the forest, he leaps from life to life (tasting the fruit of his kamma).

335. Whoever is overcome by this wretched and sticky craving, his sorrows grow like grass after the rains.

336. But whoever overcomes this wretched craving, so difficult to overcome, from him sorrows fall away like water from a lotus leaf.

337. This I say to you: Good luck to all assembled here! Dig up the root of craving, like one in search of the fragrant root of the birana grass. Let not Mara crush you again and again, as a flood crushes a reed.

338. Just as a tree, though cut down, sprouts up again if its roots remain uncut and firm, even so, until the craving that lies dormant is rooted out, suffering springs up again and again.

339. The misguided man in whom the thirty-six currents of craving strongly rush toward pleasurable objects, is swept away by the flood of his passionate thoughts.

340. Everywhere these currents flow, and the creeper (of craving) sprouts and grows. Seeing that the creeper has sprung up, cut off its root with wisdom.

341. Flowing in (from all objects) and watered by craving, feelings of pleasure arise in beings. Bent on pleasures and seeking enjoyment, these men fall prey to birth and decay.

342. Beset by craving, people run about like an entrapped hare. Held fast by mental fetters, they come to suffering again and again for a long time.

343. Beset by craving, people run about like an entrapped hare. Therefore, one who yearns to be passion-free should destroy his own craving.

344. There is one who, turning away from desire (for household life) takes to the life of the forest (i.e., of a monk). But after being freed from the household, he runs back to it. Behold that man! Though freed, he runs back to that very bondage!

345-346. That is not a strong fetter, the wise say, which is made of iron, wood or hemp. But the infatuation and longing for jewels and ornaments, children and wives-that, they say, is a far stronger fetter, which pulls one downward and, though seemingly loose, is hard to remove. This, too, the wise cut off. Giving up sensual pleasure, and without any longing, they renounce the world.

347. Those who are lust-infatuated fall back into the swirling current (of samsara) like a spider on its self-spun web. This, too, the wise cut off. Without any longing, they abandon all suffering and renounce the world.

348. Let go of the past, let go of the future, let go of the present, and cross over to the farther shore of existence. With mind wholly liberated, you shall come no more to birth and death.

349. For a person tormented by evil thoughts, who is passion-dominated and given to the pursuit of pleasure, his craving steadily grows. He makes the fetter strong, indeed.

350. He who delights in subduing evil thoughts, who meditates on the impurities and is ever mindful-it is he who will make an end of craving and rend asunder Mara's fetter.

351. He who has reached the goal, is fearless, free from craving, passionless, and has plucked out the thorns of existence-for him this is the last body.

352. He who is free from craving and attachment, is perfect in uncovering the true meaning of the Teaching, and knows the arrangement of the sacred texts in correct sequence-he, indeed, is the bearer of his final body. He is truly called the profoundly wise one, the great man.

353. A victor am I over all, all have I known. Yet unattached am I to all that is conquered and known. Abandoning all, I am freed through the destruction of craving. Having thus directly comprehended all by myself, whom shall I call my teacher?

354. The gift of Dhamma excels all gifts; the taste of the Dhamma excels all tastes; the delight in Dhamma excels all delights. The Craving-Freed vanquishes all suffering.

355. Riches ruin only the foolish, not those in quest of the Beyond. By craving for riches the witless man ruins himself as well as others.

356. Weeds are the bane of fields, lust is the bane of mankind.

Therefore, what is offered to those free of lust yields abundant fruit.

357. Weeds are the bane of fields, hatred is the bane of mankind. Therefore, what is offered to those free of hatred yields abundant fruit.

358. Weeds are the bane of fields, delusion is the bane of mankind. Therefore, what is offered to those free of delusion yields abundant fruit.

359. Weeds are the bane of fields, desire is the bane of mankind. Therefore, what is offered to those free of desire yields abundant fruit.

360. Good is restraint over the eye; good is restraint over the ear; good is restraint over the nose; good is restraint over the tongue.

361. Good is restraint in the body; good is restraint in speech; good is restraint in thought. Restraint everywhere is good. The monk restrained in every way is freed from all suffering.

362. He who has control over his hands, feet and tongue; who is fully controlled, delights in inward development, is absorbed in meditation, keeps to himself and is contented-him do people call a monk.

363. That monk who has control over his tongue, is moderate in speech, unassuming and who explains the Teaching in both letter and spirit-whatever he says is pleasing.

364. The monk who abides in the Dhamma, delights in the Dhamma, meditates on the Dhamma, and bears the Dhamma well in mind-he does not fall away from the sublime Dhamma.

365. One should not despise what one has received, nor envy the gains of others. The monk who envies the gains of others does not attain to meditative absorption.

366. A monk who does not despise what he has received, even though it be little, who is pure in livelihood and unremitting in effort-him even the gods praise.

367. He who has no attachment whatsoever for the mind and body, who does not grieve for what he has not-he is truly called

a monk.

368. The monk who abides in universal love and is deeply devoted to the Teaching of the Buddha attains the peace of Nibbana, the bliss of the cessation of all conditioned things.

369. Empty this boat, O monk! Emptied, it will sail lightly. Rid of lust and hatred, you shall reach Nibbana.

370. Cut off the five, abandon the five, and cultivate the five. The monk who has overcome the five bonds is called one who has crossed the flood.

371. Meditate, O monk! Do not be heedless. Let not your mind whirl on sensual pleasures. Heedless, do not swallow a red-hot iron ball, lest you cry when burning, "O this is painful!"

372. There is no meditative concentration for him who lacks insight, and no insight for him who lacks meditative concentration. He in whom are found both meditative concentration and insight, indeed, is close to Nibbana.

373. The monk who has retired to a solitary abode and calmed his mind, who comprehends the Dhamma with insight, in him there arises a delight that transcends all human delights.

374. Whenever he sees with insight the rise and fall of the aggregates, he is full of joy and happiness. To the discerning one this reflects the Deathless.

375. Control of the senses, contentment, restraint according to the code of monastic discipline-these form the basis of holy life here for the wise monk.

376. Let him associate with friends who are noble, energetic, and pure in life, let him be cordial and refined in conduct. Thus, full of joy, he will make an end of suffering.

377. Just as the jasmine creeper sheds its withered flowers, even so, O monks, should you totally shed lust and hatred!

378. The monk who is calm in body, calm in speech, calm in thought, well-composed and who has spewn out worldliness-he, truly, is called serene.

379. By oneself one must censure oneself and scrutinize oneself. The self-guarded and mindful monk will always live in happiness.

380. One is one's own protector, one is one's own refuge. Therefore, one should control oneself, even as a trader controls a noble steed.

381. Full of joy, full of faith in the Teaching of the Buddha, the monk attains the Peaceful State, the bliss of cessation of conditioned things.

382. That monk who while young devotes himself to the Teaching of the Buddha illumines this world like the moon freed from clouds.

383. Exert yourself, O holy man! Cut off the stream (of craving), and discard sense desires. Knowing the destruction of all the conditioned things, become, O holy man, the knower of the Uncreated (Nibbana)!

384. When a holy man has reached the summit of two paths (meditative concentration and insight), he knows the truth and all his fetters fall away.

385. He for whom there is neither this shore nor the other shore, nor yet both, he who is free of cares and is unfettered-him do I call a holy man.

386. He who is meditative, stainless and settled, whose work is done and who is free from cankers, having reached the highest goal-him do I call a holy man.

387. The sun shines by day, the moon shines by night. The warrior shines in armor, the holy man shines in meditation. But the Buddha shines resplendent all day and all night.

388. Because he has discarded evil, he is called a holy man. Because he is serene in conduct, he is called a recluse. And because he has renounced his impurities, he is called a renunciate.

389. One should not strike a holy man, nor should a holy man, when struck, give way to anger. Shame on him who strikes a holy man, and more shame on him who gives way to anger.

390. Nothing is better for a holy man than when he holds his mind back from what is endearing. To the extent the intent to harm wears away, to that extent does suffering subside.

391. He who does no evil in deed, word and thought, who is restrained in these three ways-him do I call a holy man.

392. Just as a brahman priest reveres his sacrificial fire, even so should one devoutly revere the person from whom one has learned the Dhamma taught by the Buddha.

393. Not by matted hair, nor by lineage, nor by birth does one become a holy man. But he in whom truth and righteousness exist-he is pure, he is a holy man.

394. What is the use of your matted hair, O witless man? What of your garment of antelope's hide? Within you is the tangle (of passion); only outwardly do you cleanse yourself.

395. The person who wears a robe made of rags, who is lean, with veins showing all over the body, and who meditates alone in the forest-him do I call a holy man.

396. I do not call him a holy man because of his lineage or high-born mother. If he is full of impeding attachments, he is just a supercilious man. But who is free from impediments and clinging-him do I call a holy man.

397. He who, having cut off all fetters, trembles no more, who has overcome all attachments and is emancipated-him do I call a holy man.

398. He who has cut off the thong (of hatred), the band (of craving), and the rope (of false views), together with the appurtenances (latent evil tendencies), he who has removed the crossbar (of ignorance) and is enlightened-him do I call a holy man.

399. He who without resentment endures abuse, beating and punishment; whose power, real might, is patience-him do I call a holy man.

400. He who is free from anger, is devout, virtuous, without craving, self-subdued and bears his final body-him do I call a holy man.

401. Like water on a lotus leaf, or a mustard seed on the point of a needle, he who does not cling to sensual pleasures-him do I call a holy man.

402. He who in this very life realizes for himself the end of

suffering, who has laid aside the burden and become emancipated-him do I call a holy man.

403. He who has profound knowledge, who is wise, skilled in discerning the right or wrong path, and has reached the highest goal-him do I call a holy man.

404. He who holds aloof from householders and ascetics alike, and wanders about with no fixed abode and but few wants-him do I call a holy man.

405. He who has renounced violence towards all living beings, weak or strong, who neither kills nor causes others to kill-him do I call a holy man.

406. He who is friendly amidst the hostile, peaceful amidst the violent, and unattached amidst the attached-him do I call a holy man.

407. He whose lust and hatred, pride and hypocrisy have fallen off like a mustard seed from the point of a needle-him do I call a holy man.

408. He who utters gentle, instructive and truthful words, who imprecates none-him do I call a holy man.

409. He who in this world takes nothing that is not given to him, be it long or short, small or big, good or bad-him do I call a holy man.

410. He who wants nothing of either this world or the next, who is desire-free and emancipated-him do I call a holy man.

411. He who has no attachment, who through perfect knowledge is free from doubts and has plunged into the Deathless-him do I call a holy man.

412. He who in this world has transcended the ties of both merit and demerit, who is sorrowless, stainless and pure-him do I call a holy man.

413. He, who, like the moon, is spotless and pure, serene and clear, who has destroyed the delight in existence-him do I call a holy man.

414. He who, having traversed this miry, perilous and delusive round of existence, has crossed over and reached the other shore; who is meditative, calm, free from doubt, and, clinging to nothing,

has attained to Nibbana-him do I call a holy man.

415. He who, having abandoned sensual pleasures, has renounced the household life and become a homeless one; has destroyed both sensual desire and continued existence-him do I call a holy man.

416. He who, having abandoned craving, has renounced the household life and become a homeless one, has destroyed both craving and continued existence-him do I call a holy man.

417. He who, casting off human bonds and transcending heavenly ties, is wholly delivered of all bondages-him do I call a holy man.

418. He who, having cast off likes and dislikes, has become tranquil, is rid of the substrata of existence and like a hero has conquered all the worlds-him do I call a holy man.

419. He who in every way knows the death and rebirth of all beings, and is totally detached, blessed and enlightened-him do I call a holy man.

420. He whose track no gods, no angels, no humans trace, the arahant who has destroyed all cankers-him do I call a holy man.

421. He who clings to nothing of the past, present and future, who has no attachment and holds on to nothing-him do I call a holy man.

422. He, the Noble, the Excellent, the Heroic, the Great Sage, the Conqueror, the Passionless, the Pure, the Enlightened one-him do I call a holy man.

423. He who knows his former births, who sees heaven and hell, who has reached the end of births and attained to the perfection of insight, the sage who has reached the summit of spiritual excellence-him do I call a holy man.

12

Twelve Principles of Buddhism

1. Self salvation is for any man the immediate task. If a man lay wounded by a poisoned arrow he would not delay extraction by demanding details of the man who shot it or the length and make of the arrow. There will be time for ever-increasing understanding of the Teaching during the treading of the Way. Meanwhile, begin now by facing life as it is, learning always by direct and personal experience.

2. The first fact of existence is the law of change or impermanence. All that exists, from a mole to a mountain, from a thought to an empire, passes through the same cycle of existence; birth, growth, decay and death. Life alone is continuous, ever seeking self-expression in new forms. "Life is a bridge; therefore build no house on it." Life is a process of flow, and he who clings to any form, however splendid, will suffer by resisting the flow.

3. The law of change applies equally to the "soul". There is no principle in an individual which is immortal and unchanging. Only the "Namelessness", the Ultimate Reality, is beyond change, and all forms of life, including man, are manifestations of this Reality. No one owns the life which flows in him any more than the electric light bulb owns the current which gives it light.

4. The universe is the expression of law. All effects have causes, and man's soul or character is the sum total of his

previous thoughts and acts. Karma, meaning action-reaction, governs all existence, and man is the sole creator of his circumstances, and his reaction to them, his future condition and his final destiny. By right thought and action he can gradually purify his inner nature, and so by self-realization attain in time liberation from rebirth. The process covers great periods of time, involving life after life on earth, but ultimately every form of life will reach enlightenment.

5. Life is one and indivisible, though its ever-changing forms are innumerable and perishable. There is, in truth, no death, though every form must die. From an understanding of life's unity arises compassion, a sense of identity with the life in other forms. Compassion is described as the "Law of laws-eternal harmony", and he who breaks this harmony of life will suffer accordingly and delay his own enlightenment.

6. Life being One, the interests of the part should be those of the whole. In his ignorance man thinks he can successfully strive for his own interests, and his wrongly-directed energy of selfishness produces its cause. The Buddha taught four Noble Truths:

a) The omnipresence of suffering;
b) its cause, wrongly-directed desire;
c) its cure, the removal of the cause; and
d) the Noble Eightfold Path of self-development which leads to the end of suffering.

7. The Eightfold Path consists of: (1)Right Views or preliminary understanding, (2) Right Aims or Motives, (3) Right Speech, (4) Right Acts, (5) Right Livelihood, (6) Right Effort, (7) Right Concentration or mind-development, and, finally, (8) Right Samadhi, leading to full Enlightenment. As Buddhism is a way of living, not merely a theory of life, the treading of this Path is essential to self-deliverance. "Cease to do evil, learn to do good, cleanse your own heart: this is the Teaching of the Buddhas".

8. Reality is incomprehensible, and a God with attributes is not the final Reality. But the Buddha, a human being, became the All-Enlightened One, and the purpose of life is the

attainment of Enlightenment. This state of consciousness, Nirvana, the extinction of the limitations of selfhood, is attainable on earth. All men and all other forms of life contain the potentiality of Enlightenment, and the purpose therefore consists in becoming what you are: "Look within; thou art Buddha".

9. From potential to actual Enlightenment there lies the Middle Way, the Eightfold Path from desire to peace", a process of self-development between the "opposites", avoiding all extremes. The Buddha trod this Way to the end, and the only faith required in Buddhism is the reasonable belief that where a Guide has trodden its is worth our while to tread. The Way must be trodden by the whole man, nor merely the best of him, and heart and mind must be developed equally. The Buddha was the All-Compassionate as well as the All-Enlightened One.

10. Buddhism lays great stress on the need of inward concentration and meditation, which leads in time to the development of the inner spiritual faculties. The subjective life is as important as the daily round, and periods of quietude for inner activity are essential for a balanced life. The Buddhist should at all times be "mindful and self-possessed", refraining from mental and emotional attachment to "the passing show". This increasingly watchful attitude to circumstances, which he knows to be his own creation, helps him to keep his reaction to it always under control.

11. The Buddha said: "Work out your own salvation with diligence". Buddhism knows no authority for truth save the intuition of the individual, and that is authority for himself alone. Each man suffers the consequences of his own acts, and learns thereby, while helping his fellow man to the same deliverance; nor will prayer to the Buddha or to any God prevent an effect following its cause. Buddhist monks are teachers and examplars, and in no sense intermediaries between Reality and the individual. The utmost tolerance is practiced towards all other religions and philosophies, for no man has the right to interfere in his neighbour's journey to the Goal.

12. Buddhism is neither pessimistic or "escapist", nor does

it deny the existence of God or soul, though it places its own meaning on these terms. It is, on the contrary, a system of thought, a religion, a spiritual science and a way of life, which is reasonable, practical and all embracing. For over two thousand years it has satisfied the spiritual needs of nearly one-third of mankind. It appeals to the West because it has no dogmas, satisfies the reason and the heart alike, insists on self-reliance coupled with tolerance for other points of view, embraces science, religion, philosophy, psychology, ethics and art, and points to man alone as the creator of his present life and sole designer of his destiny.

13

Buddhism and the Practice of Law

With the world being rife with so many ills such as famine and epidemic disease, economic depression, political corruption at home and abroad, bottom-line globalization, warfare, and natural disasters due to global warming and run-of-the-mill hurricanes, tidal waves, and twisters, we all have reason to get a bit confused and down in the mouth.

Attorneys who deal with individuals during their times of greatest conflict, as I do, have extra reasons to wonder at the human soul – what with friends and family at each other's throats over money-focused lawsuits; con-artists defrauding innocent victims; lovers slinging mud at each other in child custody battles and filing restraining orders full of false allegations; corporate investors and CEO's outright lying on the witness stand; people robbing, beating, and just plain killing one another in fits of desperation and rage; and politicians, judges, and lawyers fanning the flames or just turning away from all the injustice.

People have asked me why I am an attorney fighting the good fight when the mountain of iniquity is so enormous, and looming larger everyday. I could quote Ozzy Osbourne and say, "I don't want to change the world, and I don't want the world to change me." But I won't. Rather, I do want to change the world, but I remain conservatively optimistic about such a lofty goal. More importantly, my work is my meditation – a meditation similar to that which I feel while working in my little garden, pulling out crabgrass and thistle to make room for the daffodils and paperwhites, belladonna, and meyer lemon tree.

I know that I can't help everybody who calls my me, and that at the end of the month, I too have to pay the rent, feed the dogs, and buy food at the market. Yet when I help couples find a peaceful path through divorce and custody disputes, businesses avoid costly litigation, a defendant in criminal court achieve a better alternative than jail or justly avoid a guilty verdict altogether, or a client find justice in the thick of a lawsuit in federal or state court, I not only accept the kind words, hugs, and high fives of people who are truly glad they met me, but I also feel a sacred sense of inner peace and a sense of having helped my community to be a better place to live.

I have been interested in Buddhism for a long time, and I find some inspiration for my law practice in the ethics laid out by the Buddha. I would not call myself a Buddhist, per se, yet I very much appreciate the Buddha's teachings (or "Dharma"). The Dharma is very ethics-focused. It accentuates ethical thinking, ethical speech, and ethical actions – even social justice activism. It prizes concentration and perseverence, and to attain these attributes, the Buddha recommends meditative focus and forming alliances with others working towards similar goals to inspire and teach you along the way. Here below is a little primer on the Buddha's teachings. As you read, you can see clearly where a social justice attorney might find such a philosophy meaningful and inspirational.

The Dharma is comprised of two main ideas – the Four Noble Truths and the Eight-Fold Path. The word "Buddha" means the one who is "awake" or "enlightened" in Sanskrit, an ancient language from India. Thus, "Buddha" is a title, as the Buddha's birth name was Siddhartha Gautama. He was born in Lumbini, Nepal around 500 BC, and he was a prince of the Shakya dynasty. You can read more about his life in various books and online articles. In Buddhism, while the Buddha is holy, he is not a deity or god, but rather the principle teacher of Buddhism, which does not focus on any particular divinity and thus is often called a philosophy rather than a religion.

Be that as it may, Buddha's "Four Noble Truths" (rendered in their most simple form) state that life is full of suffering because we often do wrong things which will hurt us (Karma) and others; but we don't have to go about life this way – rather, we can do right things and work hard to try to reach perfect enlightenment (Nirvana), which is seeing things as they really are and being released from suffering.

Needless to say, that's a hard goal to hit, but Buddhism is more about "process" than "product", as Jackson Pollock might say.

Basically, Buddha's "Eight-Fold Path" outlines these "right things" to do, which I summarize below in a very short-handed version (noting that the full version of the Eight-Fold Path has indeed 8 very long sections, full of verbose descriptions and examples):

(1) Think good – which means think in an ethical and logical manner. As explained by the Buddha in his teachings, "goodness" means kindness, empathy, compassion, helpfulness, and all that other stuff that makes up what we all know as right and good.

(2) Intend good – have a "good heart" and be resolved to do good.

(3) Speak good – don't lie, be abusive, slander, falsely flatter, gossip, cause disputes with your words, or waste words with idle chatter. And, as Bob Marley says, "the truth is an offence, children, but not a sin." The Buddha would simply likely clarify that by stating, it's ok to speak true but offensive words to somebody, but only when conservatively proper and absolutely necessary. I particularly appreciate this whole idea of "speaking good," along with the next one:

(4) Act good and Do Good Work – act legally and morally according to universally common understandings of both, e.g., don't break any laws, and don't lie, cheat, steal, kill, commit acts of sexual misconduct, etc; and work for social justice and the betterment of people's lives, rather than being greedy and self-centered. One of my favorite

sayings of the Buddha, relating to this idea of Acting Good, is: "He who hesitates is already lost."

(5) Persevere, Focus, and Concentrate:

(a) To do good, you have to try hard, keep your eyes on the prize, and focus. In other words, keep ever-vigilant, ethically awake, and spiritually conscious.

(b) Avoid the 5 worst interruptions of Concentration: empty lust, anger, laziness, worry, and doubt.

(c) Find inspiration through the "7 factors of Enlightenment" – The enlightened person is deeply mindful; is able to tell the difference between different spiritual states of being; and is full of energy, passion, tranquility, concentration, and grace.

(d) Take Refuge in the "Three Jewels" – Find inspiration in the example of the Buddha, the Dharma (Buddha's teachings), and a Community of persons seeking enlightenment. This last idea of forming a Community of like-minded social justice professionals, for example, motivated me to join the National Lawyers Guild and become a member of the San Francisco Chapter's Board of Directors a couple years ago.

As an attorney working in the public interest and as a longtime student of Buddhist and other noble philosophies, I find myself meditating on concepts or feelings of justice, truth, and peace while writing long, persuasive legal briefs, arguing a client's case before a judge, or even while examining a witness on the stand. Similar to the feeling I derive from my private practice of yoga or my long, meditative motorcycle rides through the back countryside of Northern and Central California, I find an intense and focused spiritual centeredness in my practice of the law – much like I imagine Charlie Chaplin's character must have felt while he was wrenching various nuts and bolts inside that great and metaphorical Machine in his classic film, *Modern Times*, except without all the accompanying hilarity, of course.

There are a few variations on Buddhist philosophy. Here is a summary of three major variations:

Tibetan Buddhists simplify the Dharma to 3 things by stating that it is essential to practice good thoughts, speech, and actions. They also emphasize the importance of having guidance in the process of doing these 3 good things by way of a guru (a spiritual guide) and by way of spiritual focus on a masculine deity and a feminine deity (god), as we are each comprised of both masculine and feminine aspects and must strive to enlighten our whole self. Tibetan Buddhists say, "Better to be a wild and silly monkey swinging from the vines in a jungle than a person who does not make another person who is greater than himself his teacher and guide."

Tantric Buddhism, also known as Tantra, additionally focuses on a loving and deeply passionate relationship between true lovers as a way of attaining Nirvana, as each lover becomes the guru (teacher) and counterpart god/ goddess for the other.

Zen Buddhism focuses more on wild humor, mischievous but enlightening trickery, abstract poetry, creative passion, and a strong student-teacher spiritual relationship to help the student achieve the goals of Buddhism – think Mr. Miyagi from *The Karate Kid,* but more focused on a sacred and spiritual goal, rather than simply kicking butt and getting the girl. A particularly famous book on Zen Buddhism is*Zen and the Art of Motorcycle Maintenance,* by Robert Pirsig, which focuses on a more earthly "get your hands dirty" approach to Buddhism, rather than lofty and monastic notions of enlightenment which can often be confused by naive practitioners with a holier-than-thou practice of Buddhism. To learn more about Zen Buddhism, I very strongly recommend listening to audio recordings of the insightful and entertaining lectures of Alan Watts on the subject.

Bibliography

Anesaki, Masaharu: *Nichiren, the Buddhist Prophet,* Cambridge, Harvard University Press, 1916.

Candragomin, S. : *Difficult Beginnings: Three Works on the Bodhisattva Path,* Boston, MA: Shambhala, 1985.

Cole, Alan : *Mothers and Sons in Chinese Buddhism,* Stanford, CA: Stanford University Press, 1998.

Dayal, Har: *The Bodhisattva Doctrine in Buddhist Sanskrit Literature,* London, Kegan Paul, 1932.

Gregory, Peter N. : *Buddhism in the Sung,* Honolulu, HI: University of Hawaii Press, 2002.

Gupta, K. : *Buddhism in Mathura : A Detailed Study of Buddhist Tradition, Archaeology and Art,* Bharatiya Kala Prakashan, Delhi, 2009.

James C. Jodo Shinshu : *Shin Buddhism in Medieval Japan,* Bloomington, IN: Indiana University Press, 1989.

Keown, Damien: *The Nature of Buddhist Ethics,* New York, St. Martin's Press, 1992.

Maillard, Monique : *Buddhism in Afghanistan and Central Asia,* Leiden: E.J. Brill, 1976.

Nanamoli, Bhikkhu: *The Life of the Buddha,* Kandy, Buddhist Publication Society, 1972.

Naudou, Jean: *Buddhists of Kashmir,* Delhi, Motilal Banarsidass, 1980.

Ramanan, K. V.: *Nagarjuna's Philosophy as Presented in Maha-Prajnaparamita-Sastra,* Delhi, Motilal Banarsidass, 1978.

Strachan, Paul: *Pagan: Art and Architecture of Old Burma,* Whiting Bay, Scotland: Kiscadale Publications, 1989.

Thaye, Jampa : *The Garland of Gold: The Early Kagyu Masters in India and Tibet,* Bristol: Ganesha Press, 1990.

Williams, Paul: *The Reflexive Nature of Awareness,* London, Curzon, 1997.

Index

❑❑❑